Best Seat in the House

A Father, a Daughter, a Journey Through Sports

Christine Brennan

A LISA DREW BOOK

SCRIBNER

New York London Toronto Sydney

A LISA DREW BOOK/SCRIBNER
1230 Avenue of the Americas
New York, NY 10020

Copyright © 2006 by Christine Brennan

All rights reserved, including the right of
reproduction in whole or in part in any form.

SCRIBNER *and design are trademarks of*
Macmillan Library Reference USA, Inc., used under license
by Simon & Schuster, the publisher of this work.

A LISA DREW BOOK *is a trademark of Simon & Schuster, Inc.*

For information about special discounts for bulk purchases,
please contact Simon & Schuster Special Sales:
1-800-456-6798 or business@simonandschuster.com

Text set in Sabon
DESIGNED BY LAUREN SIMONETTI
Manufactured in the United States of America

1   2   3   4   5   6   7   8   9   10

Library of Congress Cataloging-in-Publication Data
Brennan, Christine.
Best seat in the house: a father, a daughter, a journey through sports / Christine Brennan.
p. cm.
"A Lisa Drew book."
1. Brennan, Christine. 2. Women sportswriters—United States—Biography.
3. Women sportswriters—Family relationships—United States.
4. Fathers and daughters—United States. I. Brennan, James, 1926–2003. II. Title.

GV742.42.B72A3 2003
070.4'4979609—dc22
[B]
2005054197

ISBN-13: 978-0-7432-5436-6
ISBN-10: 0-7432-5436-8

*For Kate, Jim, and Amy, who shared
the best seat in the house with me*

BEST SEAT
IN THE
HOUSE

CONTENTS

A GIFT

I had written thousands of stories in my twenty years in sports journalism when I sat down to write my *USA Today* column for May 17, 2001.

I had covered six Super Bowls, a dozen college bowl games, and every Olympics since the 1984 Los Angeles Games. I had covered the Washington Redskins for the *Washington Post* and the Miami Hurricanes for the *Miami Herald*. I had been to Wimbledon, the Masters, the World Series, the occasional NASCAR race, the Kentucky Derby, and the NBA and NHL play-offs. I reported from the Soviet Union once, Cuba five times. I wrote columns about issues that enraged some people and heartened others. I broke front-page news and even wrote a few tearjerkers.

But with all the places I had been, the people I had talked to, the stories I had covered, I had never written about the person who had meant the most to me in sports and in my career.

And so, that day, I did.

* * *

Old Sportsman Saw Way Before Title IX
By Christine Brennan

We often hear these days about how it all began, this women's sports craze, or movement, or revolution, call it what you will. Conventional wisdom says it started with the passage of Title IX in 1972, followed by Billie Jean King's victory over Bobby Riggs in 1973.

But I knew things were stirring even earlier than that.

I knew it because the first women's sports advocate I met was a man. I don't remember how we were introduced, and I won't bother you with his name. But I quickly came to find out that he was not your typical women's libber. He voted for Nixon. And Reagan. And Goldwater and Eisenhower and probably even Dewey. You see, this women's rights advocate was, and still is, a rock-ribbed Republican, which tells you everything you need to know about party labels and stereotypes, although I'm fairly certain he has never thought of himself as a women's libber, at least not until recently.

I got my first inkling something was up with this man when his almost-eight-year-old daughter told him what she wanted for her birthday, and he went right out and bought it for her. It was a baseball mitt. Today, that would not make news. But this didn't happen today. It happened in 1966.

Immediately, this man became the only guy in town who was playing catch in the backyard with a girl. What were the neighbors to think?

He went back to the store and bought the girl a baseball bat.

Things escalated from there. His daughter soon wanted more from sports. It wasn't enough to simply play with the boys in the neighborhood. She asked her father if she could go to some games with him. It was like magic. As soon as she asked, it started happening. She and her younger siblings attended dozens of sporting events, from Toledo Mud Hens and

Detroit Tigers games in the summer to Toledo and Michigan football games in the fall. Neighborhood kids clamored to come, too. Boys, girls; it didn't matter to this man, this latter-day Pied Piper with the season tickets.

But one time, there was a problem. It was a cold November day and snow was on the ground for the crucial Michigan–Ohio State game. A decision had to be made. Stay home and watch on TV? Or go? To this man, it was an easy call. "We've got to be able to smell it," he declared. And so their mother bundled up the three oldest children, and off they went to Ann Arbor with their father.

When they got to massive Michigan Stadium, the children couldn't believe their eyes. They looked around and saw many other fathers, but no children. The other fathers all had brought their wives. But these lucky kids; their father had brought them.

The children's good fortune continued. On summer Sunday afternoons, when many fathers were hitting golf balls with their pals at the country club, this man brought his three daughters and one son to a public par-3 course to learn the game. And when he was invited by friends to play at restrictive clubs, he said no. He wasn't going to set foot anywhere his girls couldn't go.

In the years that followed, this man would attend almost every high school game his children ever played. It was one thing to go to a football game on a Friday night; he did that. It was another thing entirely to dash out of the office on a Tuesday afternoon in time for the tip-off of a girls' basketball game. He did that, too. Often, he was the only father in the stands.

I'm telling you these stories about this man because today is a milestone for him. Today, he turns 75. It's not a national holiday. It's not an important day in women's sports history. It's just a very significant day to a little girl who grew up knowing that there would always be a place for her in sports.

Happy Birthday, Dad.

in Detroit, the Indians in Cleveland, the Reds in Cincinnati. Unlike so many children in other parts of the country, I didn't have to pick one team to cheer for. I had a half dozen in my big Midwestern backyard. But those weren't the only teams I followed. When I tried to fall asleep at night, I didn't count sheep. I recited World Series teams, going backward from 1968, until I didn't know them anymore.

My father turned to look at me.

"You want to call in?" Dad asked.

I shook my head no. I pictured a sports fan, a man, already at his phone somewhere else in Toledo, dialing in, answering correctly, winning the tickets.

We listened for a few moments.

"We still don't have any callers," the radio announcer said.

Dad looked at me and smiled. I pushed my chair away from the table and walked to the phone. I still thought I would be too late. I picked up the phone and looked at my father, then my mother. They nodded approvingly without saying a word. I dialed the number.

A man answered at the radio station. I recognized his voice. It was the announcer. Everyone in the kitchen fell silent. Mom reached for the kitchen radio and twisted the knob to turn down the sound so I wouldn't get distracted, then ran to their bedroom to listen.

"So," the announcer asked, "you know the answer?"

"Yes," I said in the firmest eleven-year-old voice I could muster. "Fred Toney and James Vaughn."

"Oh, we've got a young fan here," the announcer chuckled. "And what teams did they play for?"

He was adding another question, right then, on the air. It wasn't a problem. I knew the answer.

"The Cincinnati Reds and the Chicago Cubs," I replied.

"You're right! You win the tickets! What's your name?"

"Christine Brennan," I said.

Silence.

"Oh," the announcer said. "You're a girl."

* * *

My first press box was in our family room, ten feet from the television. Every Saturday morning during baseball season, I pulled Mom's manual Olympia typewriter off a closet shelf, set it on a small table, and typed up a three- or four-paragraph preview of the NBC "Major League Game of the Week." My brother, Jim, who was four years younger than I was, would do research, looking up statistics in the *Toledo Blade* sports section. He was very thorough for a seven-year-old, giving me all the information I asked for. We wrote about the starting pitchers, about who was hitting well, about what to expect in the game. My stories had a circulation of six—five not counting me: my father, a former high school tackle and shot putter who once had a tryout with the Chicago Bears; my mother; and my siblings. There were four Brennan children; I was born in May of 1958, my sister Kate in November of 1959, Jim in June of 1962, and my sister Amy in August of 1967.

Those little stories flew off my fingertips. I had read hundreds of articles about baseball in the *Blade*, the *Toledo Times*, and the *Detroit Free Press*. I also had some previous writing experience. My parents gave me a diary for Christmas of 1968. It had a blue and green floral print on the cover and a lock that I never used. My first entry, on January 1, 1969, was typical of what I believed my diary should be: "Woke up late after staying up last night to wait for the New Year. After lunch, went to the Sports Arena to ice skate. After that, watched the Rose Bowl and Orange Bowl. In the Rose Bowl, Ohio State won over USC, 27–16. In the Orange Bowl, Penn State won over Kansas, 15–14."

I sounded like a stringer for the Associated Press.

Barely a day went by when I did not report in my diary the score of a University of Toledo Rockets basketball game, or an NFL play-off game, or, when spring came, the score of a Toledo Mud Hens or a Detroit Tigers game or the Saturday "Game of the Week." My entries also covered the daily activities of a girl turning eleven: memorizing spelling words, going to classes at the Toledo Museum of Art, skating on someone's frozen backyard.

My entry for February 28 was particularly memorable: "Today I begged my Dad to try to get tickets for the Rockets' game tomorrow against Miami (O.). It is Steve Mix's last game. Daddy will try to get tickets."

Steve Mix was the first big sports superstar I idolized. He was the University of Toledo basketball team's six-seven, 220-pound center. With his broad shoulders and tree-trunk arms, Mix lumbered through the key and under the basket like a giant, and we loved him for it.

Steve Mix in the Field House.
(Courtesy of the University of Toledo)

"The Mixmaster!" Dad would yell, his deep voice booming above the crowd, as Mix grabbed a rebound and threw his elbows side to side, churning like a blender to protect the ball. I would look up and smile at my father, a big block of a man at six feet and two hundred pounds, with a quarter-inch crew cut and black-rimmed glasses.

And when Mix laid in a basket, rolling it off his fingertips as he blew through the lane "like a freight train," as Dad said, we cheered mightily.

The Rockets won the Mid-American Conference championship in the 1966–67 season, going 23–2 and making the NCAA Tournament, which was quite a feat because only twenty-three teams qualified for the tournament that year. Mix and his teammates cut down the net after they clinched their spot in the tournament, and the next morning, I was stunned to see it hanging off a kitchen cabinet in the home of one of my friends whose father was a University of Toledo professor with connections to the team. We were living in the well-manicured middle-class enclave of Old Orchard in West Toledo, just across busy Bancroft Street from the university. The old Field House where the basketball team played—no one called it the men's team because there was no women's team that we knew of back then—was a five-minute walk from our home. Dad and I had gone to a few games that season, but not the one that clinched the title. Instead, I listened to every minute of that crucial game on the radio. Seeing that net the next day made it real to me.

We went to a few games the next year, Dad and I, and on occasion, Kate and Jim. We went to several more the next, which was the 1968–69 season. Mix was a senior that season, and the March 1 game was Toledo's last, our final chance to see him play. My father did find two tickets—he bought them from a student—and we joined the crush of spectators streaming into the Field House. The building held just four thousand fans. It was hard to say if the more remarkable quality about the old barn of a gym was the heat or the acoustics. Let's call it a tie. It was the hottest, loudest place I had ever been.

Dad and I found our seats in the last row, just under the ceiling at the top of the student section. We were a long way from the court. "But we're here!" Dad said, turning to me with a big smile. "That's the important thing. We can smell it."

We could smell, see, and hear every second of Mix's finale. I don't remember how many points he scored. I do remember breathing in every moment of the event as if it were pure oxygen. I kept looking around the gym, taking mental pictures of every significant moment. I could feel my heart racing. This was, I would later come to understand, the adrenaline rush of the big event: so many people gathered in one place, and us with them, for a grand, two-hour high-wire act. Nothing that happened within the confines of the usual routine of my young life could match this. Nothing even came close.

When the horn sounded near the end of the game, which Toledo lost, 70–65, Dad nudged me and motioned for me to look toward the Toledo bench.

"They're taking him out," Dad said.

Steve Mix was walking slowly toward the Rockets bench down on the floor many rows below us. Coach Bob Nichols shook his hand. His teammates patted him on the back. Someone handed him a towel. Mix sat down hard.

"And thus a great career comes to an end," Dad said.

I looked at Dad. I tried to blink back my tears. Dad smiled at me. I thought I saw a tear forming in his eye too.

Dad introduced me to sports when I was only four, during the 1962 World Series between the New York Yankees and the San Francisco Giants. While watching the first game of the series on our black-and-white television, I made a pronouncement that Mom recorded in my baby book: "Yogi Bear is going to catch. When he gets the ball, he'll steal it, as he does the picnic baskets."

The next summer, I used one of Dad's old gloves when we first played catch in our backyard. Dad immediately taught me how to throw the baseball properly, firing it from behind my right ear without the slightest hint of the motion that has come to be known as "throwing like a girl." I don't remember hearing anyone use those words until late in elementary school; certainly my father or mother never used them. Nor did the boys I played ball with every spring and summer day in our neighborhood. I was the only girl who regularly played with them—and I threw like they did.

Then something wonderful happened. As my eighth birthday approached, I asked for my own baseball mitt. Dad went to a sporting goods store and bought a light brown, perfectly smooth, pristine Rawlings glove. Written in script on the palm of the glove was the name Tony Cloninger, with a drawing of a man throwing a baseball. Imprinted nearby were these words: "The Finest in the Field!"

I didn't know who Tony Cloninger was, so I checked the sports section to find out. He was a right-handed pitcher for the Atlanta Braves who was to gain fame later that year, 1966, for hitting two grand slams in one game against the San Francisco Giants. Unfortunately, I never saw him play in person or on TV. Cloninger existed only in newspaper photos, on baseball cards, in the box scores, and in the palm of my glove.

When Dad gave me the glove, I held it to my face and inhaled deeply. All the boys did that with their gloves, so I did it too. My glove smelled new and fresh and natural. This was the scent of baseball. I used my new mitt every day that summer, playing with the boys in the neighborhood in the morning and afternoon, then with my father when he came home from work in the evening and it stayed light until after nine o'clock.

I took to sports naturally when I was a little girl because I never really was little. My mother said I was born size 6X and kept right on growing. I was the only Brownie Scout, Mom said, who outgrew her dress in the second grade, when at the age of seven, I was already four and a half feet tall and weighed more than seventy pounds. By the time I was nine, I was five feet tall and one hundred pounds. What was bad for Brownies, however, was good for sports. While the boys were ambivalent or downright inhospitable to most girls who wanted to play with them, they specifically asked me to join them, and sometimes picked me first when we chose up sides.

With my dark brown hair cut in the simplest of pageboys, I was the tomboy of the neighborhood. I broke my arm falling out of a tree when I was seven. That same year, I asked for G.I. Joe, not Barbie, for Christmas—and that's what Santa brought. While Kate was innately drawn to Mom's side at the stove, I obliviously walked by them—Mom, Kate, and the stove—as if they were invisible on my way outside to play catch.

Because I played with the boys all day, I wanted to look like they did, so I wore baggy T-shirts and grass-stained shorts and pedal pushers. When we went swimming in the pool that Mom and Dad had had built in our backyard, I often swam topless. Not that it mattered, not at that age. I was five or six at the time. If the boys could swim topless, I said to Mom and Dad, why couldn't I? They smiled and told me it was just fine. I was seven or eight when I switched to a girl's bathing suit. This required no family intervention; it just happened like most things do when parents don't push their children, by my mother buying me a girl's suit and my one day putting it on.

My swimming attire at the age of five.

In those days, I was clamoring for as much from sports as I could get. I kept asking for more trips to the backyard to play catch with Dad, kept hoping for more visits to the University of Toledo for a basketball or football game, kept wanting more time in front of the television or beside the radio with my father to understand the games better. I desperately wanted to learn to keep score of baseball games, to understand the sport's strange numbering system—the catcher was 2, the shortstop was 6, the center fielder, 8.

Dad wasn't pushing me to do this. I was asking, and Dad happily obliged. I wondered years later if Dad thought of me as his first son, and he laughed and shook his head. "No, you wanted to play sports and learn about sports, and you were a happy child, so your mother and I thought that was just fine. We wanted you to do what you wanted to do."

If Dad wasn't home, I turned to my best friend, David Hansen. David was my first running mate—a triplet with a brother, Douglas, and a sister, Laurie. We became such good friends that they labeled me "the Fourth Triplet," a title I believe I hold for life. They all called me Christy back then. I would later become Chris or Christine to everyone else, but not to the Hansens, and especially not to David. Nearly forty years later, when I talk to David, I'm still Christy Brennan, which is fine with me. David and I spent our summer days trading baseball cards, fiddling with his transistor radio dial trying to tune in the Chicago Cubs from two hundred miles away, and racing around the block on our new bikes. One day we got the great idea to attach a rope to the collar of the Hansens' large boxer, McDuff, so he could drag us around the block on our skateboards as if we were waterskiing. There were more skinned knees in the neighborhood that summer than any year before or since.

David Hansen and I had just about everything in common. Our mothers always wondered if we would eventually get married. (We did not.) David was ten months older, but we were the same height as kids, perfectly compatible for playing sports all day long. My first sleepover, when I was seven, was not at a girl's house, but at David's. We slept in sleeping bags in the Hansens' basement. It didn't take me long to get there: we lived two doors apart on Barrington Drive in Old Orchard. David and his siblings and I and mine played in our neighborhood Monday through Friday, then went to art classes together at the museum Saturday mornings and to church Sunday mornings. I sometimes missed a Sunday, but the triplets never did. They couldn't. Their father was our minister at Christ Presbyterian Church.

There was only one boy in the neighborhood taller than I was back then, Clifford Siegel. Clifford was the triplets' age, a year ahead of me in school, and he lived with his grandparents just a few doors down from our home. One day, he stood on the sidewalk, refusing to move as I barreled toward him on my bicycle.

"You better move!" I yelled.

"I dare you to hit me!" Clifford yelled back.

I did.

I flew off my bike one way, Clifford flew another way. But we both bounced up, dusted ourselves off, and within an hour were meeting up with the other kids at Goddard Field, a grassy expanse two blocks from our homes, playing baseball once again. If we weren't pretending we were Mickey Mantle when we were up to bat, we were Al Kaline, the great Detroit Tiger. Other days, we played kickball, or running bases, or tag, or someone brought a kite and we ran so fast we sometimes fell trying to coax it off the ground. Goddard Field was right across Bancroft Street from the University of Toledo's soaring, limestone Gothic clock tower. We told time by the black hands on that clock; when the hour hand reached six, we dashed those two blocks home for dinner, often to meet again in an hour or so to ride bikes or play another sport, assuming that Dad wasn't home yet and ready to play catch with me.

The University of Toledo clock tower.

—

Professional baseball turned one hundred in the spring of 1969; I turned eleven. We watched the weekly games on TV, but mostly, baseball came into our home through the radio. Dad already had taught me every last detail of how to keep score; then, just in time for the Toledo Mud Hens season, he bought me a ringed, blue baseball score book. I would plug in a radio on the end table beside the sofa in our living room, then close the doors to our family room and kitchen, where everyone else was doing chores, homework, or watching TV. There I'd sit, night after night, by myself, listening to the Mud Hens on WCWA 1230 AM. I had my pencil and the score book on my lap and my well-worn copy of the *Blade*'s special Mud Hens pullout section, with all the players' pictures and biographies, at my side. Occasionally I switched to the Detroit Tigers game on the radio, but even though they had won the World Series the year before, I preferred the Mud Hens, who were the Tigers' Triple-A, International League farm club. They were ours.

I listened to those games from places that felt far away, cities like Syracuse and Rochester and Richmond. I pictured what the stadiums might look like, heard the sounds coming from them through the radio—one day I was sure I heard a hot dog vendor's yell—and, for that night, I wished I could be there. Dad soon let me in on a little secret: many of the Hens' road games were re-creations. The crowd noise and crack of the bat were produced in a studio, he said, and the announcer simply was reading the play-by-play coming over a ticker. Alas, the hot dog vendor probably never existed. I was surprised by Dad's news, but hardly crushed. I began to listen more intently to see if I could tell the difference between a real away game and a re-created one. The big give-away was the sound of the crowd noise; after an inning in which it sounded the same no matter who was up to bat or what the batter did, junior sleuth that I was, I knew it was fake.

My mind wandered those evenings sitting on the sofa by myself. I never knew what the other team's players looked like. I didn't know what color their uniforms were. There was no way to know if the radio announcer didn't mention it; the local TV stations never went on the road with the Mud Hens, so there were no game highlights to be seen. It was still a full decade before the launch of ESPN, even longer before the arrival of local sports cable stations. I had to rely on the stories and black-and-white photos in the newspaper to tell me what the game must have looked like. That, and my imagination. Years later, a sportswriting colleague told me that he had the same problem. When his favorite major-leaguer was traded, he wrote to ask him a simple question: "What number are you wearing with your new team?"

The newspaper sports section then became my guide, and many days, I grew impatient waiting for it. We subscribed to the afternoon *Blade,* and it arrived around 4 P.M., sometimes 4:30. So eager was I to start in on the box scores and the wire reports of the previous night's major-league games that I sometimes stood quietly in our foyer, waiting for the *thunk* on the doorstep.

Even after listening to the entire Mud Hens game the previous night, I devoured the newspaper stories the next day. I realized I actually was more interested in reading about a game after I had spent the night listening to it. Even at this early age, I was intrigued to see how the writers described it, what they chose to emphasize. I pored over the box scores and analyzed the International League standings to see who had gained a game or who had fallen back. I did the same for the Tigers and the other major-league teams, but I spent the most time on the Mud Hens.

A few years later, the television show *M*A*S*H* and its nutty Corporal Klinger, played by Toledoan Jamie Farr, introduced the nation to the Mud Hens. People came to realize then what I was understanding in the 1960s, that our Mud Hens were the very essence of minor-league ball. They had been around forever and had a colorful history. Dad told me the great Casey Stengel even had been Toledo's manager in the late 1920s and early 1930s. Back in the late 1800s, the team had been alternately known as the Blue Stockings, the Toledos (the Toledo Toledos?), the Maumees (for the river that runs through town), and the Swamp Angels. For a while, their stadium was located in marshland inhabited by ducklike birds. Amused by these creatures that occasionally joined them in the outfield, opposing players began calling them "mud hens." In 1896, this became the team's permanent nickname. What a godsend this would become a century later when merchandisers inherited the earth and people wanted offbeat souvenirs like hats with a hen on them.

The man who brought the Mud Hens to life for me in our living room every night in 1969 was Frank Gilhooley, a local sportscaster with a rich, jolly voice. He was the Hens' radio play-by-play man. There was a language to sports, and I began to learn it from him. One night, Gilhooley mentioned "the hot corner." I didn't know what that was. I waited for him to use the term again, to see if I could figure it out, but before he did, Dad walked into the living room.

"What's the hot corner, Dad?"

If this question surprised him, coming out of the blue as it did, he didn't miss a beat. "That's another term for third base."

I thought about that for a moment.

"Because the ball can come off the bat of a hitter really fast down there at third?"

"Exactly," Dad replied.

Another time, Gilhooley talked about a double play going 6–4–3, and, because Dad had taught me how to keep score, I knew that meant the play went from the shortstop to the second baseman to the first baseman.

One night, Gilhooley announced a contest to name an all-time Mud Hens roster, position by position. A couple of weeks later, he took time away from calling the game to read one submission.

As he read the names, I listened very carefully: "Tom Timmermann. Ike Brown. Bob Christian. Don Pepper . . ."

Every name he read was a player who had been with the team that year or the year before, when the Hens won the International League pennant. Brown and Timmermann were playing in the game I was listening to that night.

As the list was being read over the air, my father walked into the room. He stopped and stood over me, listening intently with me as Gilhooley finished.

"Must be from a young fan," Gilhooley said to his listeners. I could hear a smile in his voice.

"But there's no name on it," he said, "so we'll never know who sent it in."

I don't remember what Gilhooley said next, although I do know he chuckled. I looked straight ahead. My father started to leave the room.

"Dad?"

My voice stopped him.

"That was me."

As I thought about it years later, I didn't put my name on that piece of paper because, at eleven, I thought voting for an all-star team was the same as voting in an election. I thought you were supposed to remain anonymous. I remember feeling embarrassed until Dad looked down at me and smiled.

"You know that was yours," he said softly. "That's all that matters."

From that moment on, I put my name on anything I ever wrote.

As for my all-time Hens, they didn't fare too badly.

Pitcher Tom Timmermann and infielder Ike Brown were called up by the Detroit Tigers on the same day later that season. They both played their first major-league game on the road, in Yankee Stadium. Timmermann, who was six-foot-four and wore thick, black-framed glasses, played for Detroit and Cleveland for parts of six seasons. In 1970, he had twenty-seven saves as a relief pitcher for Detroit and was named Tiger of the Year. Brown, who always seemed to be laughing on his way out of the dugout, played for the Tigers for portions of six seasons.

Outfielder Bob Christian led the Mud Hens in hitting in 1968 with a .317 average. He was in his early twenties, but every picture I saw of him made him look younger. He had a sweet smile. Christian played parts of three seasons in the majors with Detroit and the Chicago White Sox, and I followed him in the box scores. But in February 1974, I opened the paper and was shocked to read that he had died of leukemia. He was just twenty-eight.

I found out about Don Pepper many years later. While covering a golf tournament, I stopped LPGA star Dottie Pepper to ask if she was related to the Hens' old first baseman.

"Related?" she said. "I'm his daughter."

I soon asked Dad if I could see the Hens in person, if we could go to some games. Dad said yes, and he bought season tickets along the first-base line.

There was no better ballpark for a child to become introduced to baseball than the old Lucas County Recreation Center in Maumee, Ohio, a suburb just south of Toledo. That's where the Mud Hens played until they moved to a new downtown ball-park in 2002. The old stadium was a former horse-racing track, with one long grandstand that was parallel to the third-base line, augmented by a set of bleachers, put in for baseball, that hugged the first-base line.

This odd setup caused the players' clubhouse to be separated from the stadium. To get to the locker room, players from both teams had to walk through a public corridor. That meant they had to walk by us, so this became a gold mine for autographs. The first time we went to the park, we noticed other children gathering behind the first-base bleachers, so we asked Dad if we too could go to the area between the stadium and the club-house when the game ended. Dad thought it was a great idea. First came one player, then another, then it was a parade, a steady stream of ballplayers, their spikes clicking on the con-crete as they came toward us. With our Bic ballpoint pens poised and ready, we raced around like ants, asking the players to sign our programs, our mitts, even the free bats we received on Bat Day.

This was so exciting to me, to meet the players, even for just a few seconds. We not only got to see the Mud Hens up close, but also stars on other teams. I knew all of their names from the radio broadcasts; some of them, like Ralph Garr, Bobby Grich, and Al Bumbry, went on to become well-known major-leaguers. But we focused our efforts mostly on the Hens. It is for this rea-son that, almost every game we went to, it seemed, I ended up with big Tom Timmermann's autograph—on my glove, on a baseball, on the game program. I figured I had more Tom Tim-mermanns than anyone on the planet. When the last player had finally shaken loose to open the clubhouse door, we then came together—Kate, Jim, the Hansen triplets, and I—and compared notes, like children after a night of trick-or-treating.

In 1969, Dad also started taking us to a major-league game or two every year in Detroit, which was just an hour's drive away. The year before, 1968, had been a big year for the Tigers. They won the American League pennant, then the World Series in seven games over the St. Louis Cardinals. We didn't go to any games that year, but I listened to many on the radio, and all of us kids knew the words to "Go Get 'Em, Tigers" so well that we can sing them to this day.

We were not big Indians fans—Cleveland was twice as far away as Detroit—although Dad did try to take me to a game in the summer of 1969 with the tickets I won in the radio contest. We got halfway there when a hose broke in the engine of Dad's car and we had to pull over. By the time the car was fixed, the game was nearly over in Cleveland, so we turned around and headed home. I was so disappointed that day, but Dad grabbed me by the shoulders and looked me in the eye and promised me we would try again, and we did, later in the season. My free tickets were good only for the game we missed, so Dad bought us two more to watch the Indians play the Chicago White Sox. As we sat among rows and rows of empty seats in Cleveland's seventy-six-thousand-seat Municipal Stadium, a picture of which should have been placed next to the word *cavernous* in the dictionary, Dad smiled and put his arm around my shoulders. "You deserve to be here. You got that question right. We're here because of you." I beamed.

Usually, we went up to Detroit when the White Sox were in town. My father and mother were born on the South Side of Chicago and didn't move to Toledo until a few months before I was born. During one twi-night doubleheader in 1971, Dad bought each of us a White Sox batting helmet at the concession stand. For this one night, we cheered against the Tigers and for Dad's South Side Sox. The Tigers fans behind us in our upper-deck seats got a kick out of the gaggle of kids sitting in front of them— Kate, Jim, and me, as well as the three Hansens, whose mother was from Chicago—each wearing a hard, plastic Chicago helmet. Every time Detroit scored, a woman rapped each of us on the top of our helmets and teased us about being from Chicago.

"Should we tell her we're from Toledo, Dad?" I asked softly.

"No," Dad replied mischievously, in an exaggerated whisper. "Let's keep her guessing."

There was nothing wrong with making people think you were

from Chicago, Dad told me later. Dad liked the White Sox, but he actually lived and died with the Cubbies, as he called them. It wasn't easy to cheer for the Chicago Cubs, Dad told me in 1969. He said the same thing in 1979, 1989, and 1999. But the Cubs were his favorites, and had been since his childhood. Although he was a Southsider, he actually grew up cheering for the North Side Cubs because his father never forgave Shoeless Joe Jackson and the White Sox for throwing the 1919 World Series.

Dad's favorite player was the Cubs' Ernie Banks, whose career was winding down in 1969. Dad always said Banks was the greatest ballplayer never to make it to the World Series. He told me how smoothly and fluidly Banks played the game, and when I finally got the chance to see the Cubs on one of those Saturday TV games in 1969, I realized what Dad loved about Banks, how he held the bat so effortlessly, moving his fingers over it as if he were holding a flute. "Let's play two," Ernie loved to say, and Dad enjoyed quoting him, sometimes bellowing out the words as he drove a car full of children to another game. Dad loved the man's spirit. "Now, that," Dad would say, "is a ballplayer."

In hindsight, the 1969 season was probably the wrong one to pick to start rooting for the Cubs. Dad was ecstatic that they were in first place in June, but as a seasoned Cubs fan, he also was wary. And if he was, so was I. In late June, I had to take a week-long break from baseball and go to camp with Kate in the Irish Hills of southeastern Michigan. Most kids look forward to going to summer camp, but I was of two minds on this. I was excited to go, but I hated to miss a day, much less a whole week, of the baseball season. Dad knew how anxious I was, so he wrote to me three times (and to Kate three times as well), while Mom wrote two letters to each of us. With each letter to me, Dad sent the entire *Toledo Times* sports section, folded up.

On June 25, 1969, he wrote:

Christy, dear,
    Well, the Hens dropped another one and Ike Brown finally got shut out. At least our Cubs won another one but look out for those Mets, they are hot.

Did you know that General Custer made his famous "Last Stand" 93 years ago today?

It is bright and sunny today—I hope you and Katie are swimming.

Love and kisses, Daddy
xoxoxoxoxo

Dad was right. The Mets were hot. This was 1969, after all. They were so hot that they became known as the "Miracle Mets."

But the fact is, we were growing up as American League kids. Jim and I watched the Tigers every chance we had on their telecasts into the Toledo market, and we listened every night we could to the legendary Ernie Harwell call their games on "The Great Voice of the Great Lakes," Detroit's WJR radio, 760 AM. The Tigers' road games emanated from even farther-flung cities than the Mud Hens' did, places that intrigued me even more, ballparks in big cities I dreamed of visiting someday. But it wasn't just the Tigers. There were games going on all over the country, and I wanted to know the score of each one. I was the kind of child who always stayed busy, who didn't want to go to sleep because I didn't want to miss anything. And here was a world in which every day, many times a day, there was another first pitch. In baseball, there always was something going on.

The Tigers' road swings out west were by far the most enchanting. I had never heard of something important just starting when I was going to sleep. This was exciting to me, and comforting. I wasn't any more afraid of the dark than your average child, but I wasn't any less afraid of it either. The truck that trundled by at 2 A.M. on a busy street near our house always provided a reassuring message that people were still awake and doing something productive as I slept. I felt the same way when the Tigers were on a West Coast swing, which meant their games from Oakland–Alameda County Coliseum or the Big A in Anaheim began at 10:30 or 11 P.M.

In his bedroom across the hall, Jim usually fell asleep first while listening to Ernie Harwell; I sometimes would go into his room to turn off his clock radio, then walk into my room and turn mine on before nodding off myself. Mom or Dad came up later to turn off my radio. Harwell must have lulled to sleep countless children night after night in the Great Lakes states in those glorious baseball seasons in the late sixties and early seventies.

I went to sleep thinking of baseball, and I woke up thinking of baseball. I memorized the numbers that mattered: Babe Ruth's 714 home runs, Joe DiMaggio's fifty-six-game hitting streak. "That's the only record that won't fall in baseball," Dad said of DiMaggio's feat. "No one will ever do that again."

Dad maintained a reverence for the record, but not for the team for which DiMaggio played. When I told Dad that I felt sorry for the New York Yankees because they had had a few poor seasons in the late 1960s, Dad did not suppress the urge to give me another baseball history lesson, right then and there: "Don't ever feel sorry for the New York Yankees!"

I became absurdly superstitious watching games of the teams I liked, often refusing to get up from a chair for as long as an hour if things were going well. If I crossed my legs and the Tigers hit a home run, my legs stayed crossed. Kate and Jim and even Amy, who was just a little girl, were in on this too, helping in their own way, in their own seats. During the 1972 American League play-offs, the Tigers faced Oakland and things weren't going well as the A's were headed to the first of their three consecutive world championships. I told my siblings I was going to stand on the stone hearth of our fireplace to see if that helped.

The Tigers scored. So on the hearth I stayed. For the next two innings, I couldn't move, hoping more Detroit runs would come. They didn't, the Tigers lost, and I finally stepped down onto the carpet.

There was one other way we connected to baseball back then—by buying, collecting, and trading baseball cards. Topps baseball cards were stacked by the cash register at Ace Drug on Bancroft Street, packaged with a hard stick of pink bubble gum, and available for a nickel a pack. Trading these cards was a very serious matter. Our philosophy was to unload any doubles we accumulated; sometimes we even ended up with three of a kind and really had to wheel and deal with siblings and friends. Kate joined in and accumulated so many Larry Dierkers over the course of one summer—she must have had a half dozen cards featuring the Houston Astros pitcher—that she shrieked in delight when she one day opened a pack and found it Dierker-less. A prized possession became a misprinted Jim Bunning card that read "Im Bunning." For a few days, until I showed the card to Dad, we thought his name really might be Im.

Baseball cards were the currency of our sports passion, but after a few years, we were not content to simply covet, trade, and hoard them. We started to send them away to be autographed. I sent cards to two dozen players, including Brooks Robinson, Hank Aaron, Ferguson Jenkins, Johnny Bench, Harmon Killebrew, Bob Gibson, and even Ted Williams when he was managing the Washington Senators in 1969. Each one came back autographed, some in envelopes that I swore were addressed by the player himself.

I sent cards to Aaron twice; one was his 1969 Topps card, the other the All-Time Home Run Leaders card, which came

In 1973, before Hank Aaron broke
Babe Ruth's record, I sent this card to
Aaron and he autographed it.

out at the beginning of the 1973 season. Babe Ruth still was first on this card with his 714 homers. Aaron was second with 673 and Willie Mays third with 654. I had this card, which Aaron signed in blue ballpoint, stashed in my bedroom desk the night in 1974 that he broke Ruth's home-run record. His historic 715th home run in Atlanta was caught on the fly in the bullpen beyond the outfield fence by a Braves relief pitcher named Tom House. I also had House's autograph on several baseballs and programs in my room. Before he went up to the major leagues, he played for the minor-league Richmond Braves and came to Toledo to play the Mud Hens on several occasions.

I kept my baseball cards in a shoe box—except for the autographed ones, which I stored in that desk drawer. Much of the rest of the sports memorabilia I was collecting—pictures, programs, ticket stubs—went into scrapbooks. I spent rainy summer days cutting out articles and pictures from my *Sports Illustrated* magazines and glueing them in. I had asked Mom and Dad for a subscription to *SI* for my tenth birthday; the magazine started coming that spring. Years later, several sportswriter friends and I were discussing one of our rites of passage: What was on the cover of your first *SI*? For me, it was Don Drysdale and his consecutive scoreless innings streak. I still remember the line of 0's across the top of the magazine, nine innings' worth, a testament to Drysdale's perfection.

My first scrapbook was devoted almost entirely to those *SI* clippings and souvenirs, page after page of Cubs and White Sox and Tigers memorabilia. But in their midst, on one page by itself, I glued a colorful brochure for the forklift truck business Dad started, the Brennan Industrial Truck Company. The brochure featured a photo of Dad smiling at his desk and another of him and four coworkers posing at the wheel of forklift trucks, Dad in a business suit. Page after page of my sports heroes—and then there was my Dad.

2

"Dad, Do You Have the Tickets?"

On Saturday, October 11, 1969, I was in conflict. My sixth-grade Girl Scout troop was heading to Greenfield Village in Dearborn, Michigan, an hour north of Toledo, for a field trip. The University of Toledo Rockets football team was playing at rival Bowling Green twenty minutes south of Toledo the same afternoon. I already had signed up for the Girl Scout trip, so Mom and Dad said that was that, I was going. We never even discussed going to Bowling Green for the game.

My parents did make one allowance for the importance of the Toledo–Bowling Green game; troop leaders permitting, I could take my transistor radio with me to press to my ear now and then to check the score of the game.

I must have been quite a sight, a gigantic Girl Scout in my regulation green dress—which always seemed to be too short no matter how many times my mother lowered the hem—tagging along a few steps behind the rest of the troop, straining to keep the signal of Toledo's WSPD, 1370 AM, on my radio up in the suburbs of Detroit. The broadcast faded in and out most of the afternoon. At the very end of the game, it came back in.

The Rockets were behind, 26–24. There were just forty-nine seconds remaining. They were back at their 32-yard line. The silky-voiced play-by-play man, Jerry Keil, was growing anxious. So was I.

Toledo was moving the ball. "First down and ten . . . the ball on the Toledo forty-eight now . . ."

"Chuck Ealey back to pass . . . There's a flag on the play. . . . Pass interference on Bowling Green! First and ten, Toledo, at the Bowling Green twenty-eight."

"Ealey back, looking . . . complete to Don Fair to the twenty-one yard line!"

Now there were just two seconds remaining. Ken Crots, Toledo's senior kicker, was running onto the field to try a thirty-seven-yard field goal. Keil reported that a strong wind was blowing through the open-end stadium directly into Crots's face.

"Oh no," I said to myself. There was no one else to talk to. I was all alone on a sidewalk. The Girl Scouts were up ahead, having moved on without me.

With the radio pressed so hard to my ear that it was hurting and turning red, I hung on Keil's words.

"Here's the snap. . . .

"The kick is up. . . .

"It's . . .

"Good!"

I leaped for joy. We won, 27–26. The Rockets were 4–0 in the young season. Undefeated! I dashed ahead to join my friends. I couldn't wait to tell them Toledo had won in such an exciting fashion.

The other girls gave me a bemused look. "That's nice," one of them said. They didn't care about football, not one bit. But I didn't care that they didn't care. I was extraordinarily happy in this world of my own creation, a place where a football could slice through a gusting wind in an enemy stadium and bring joy to a Girl Scout listening on the radio seventy-five miles away.

* * *

I began going to University of Toledo football games in 1964, when I was six. Dad, the former lineman, was gloriously re-united with the game several years earlier, not long after we moved into Old Orchard. The Rockets played in the Glass Bowl, a quaint stadium built out of limestone in the 1930s that looked like a fortress with walls topped by battlements. It seated only 16,500 in the 1960s. The stadium was named for the city's pri-mary industry; Toledo was known as the Glass Capital of the World because Owens-Illinois, Libbey Owens Ford, and Owens-Corning Fiberglas all were headquartered there.

We lived so close that I could see the glow of the Glass Bowl lights from our front yard. The stadium was tucked in the back of the campus behind the clock tower, no more than a ten-minute walk from home. The lights beckoned me; what was going on inside that stadium was a mystery. I couldn't wait to find out what attracted my father to it.

The Rockets played most of their games on Saturday nights because Saturday afternoons in the Toledo area belonged to the University of Michigan, forty-five minutes to the north in Ann Arbor, or Ohio State, three hours to the south in Columbus. The University of Toledo couldn't compete with Michigan or Ohio State, so it didn't even try. In the early sixties, when I was too young to go with him, Dad would step out our front door, walk past two homes on Barrington to Bancroft, cross over to the campus, and buy himself a ticket to the game. It might be the Toledo–Bowling Green game, or Toledo–Miami of Ohio, or Toledo–Kent State. Sometimes he would find another young fa-ther in the neighborhood to join him. Often he would go alone, usually staying only for the first half before walking back home to help Mom with us.

When Dad started to take me to games, we would walk to-gether, hand in hand. We would wait at the light at Bancroft, then cross and walk toward the lights in the Glass Bowl. Some-times I wanted to run. I couldn't wait to get there. Pretty soon, we would be among hundreds of spectators, funneling through the entrances into the game. I held Dad's hand tightest then.

Once inside the Glass Bowl, I was in awe of the brightness of the field under the towers of light rising high into the night sky. The Rockets' colors were midnight blue and gold, and I loved how the light danced off those dark helmets as the players moved around the field. Often it grew cold by the second half, but I told Dad I didn't want to leave, so he bundled me inside his big jacket, and we stayed.

Within a year or two, Dad was not only bringing me along, and Kate, he was buying tickets for a half dozen neighborhood children who couldn't wait to get swallowed up in the group. Most fathers were taking their wives to these games. Dad took us. Our mother happily stayed home with Jim, and later Amy, until they were old enough to join us. Mom, who wasn't a big sports fan, always said she got more things accomplished with us out of the house anyway.

One day in 1967, Dad surprised me by bringing home the team's press guide, officially called the *Football Dope Book for Press, Radio, Television*. I leafed through it for hours that season, memorizing the names of our players, where they were from, and what their statistics were the previous season. That press guide was so important to me that when the season ended, I glued it into my scrapbook with the other sports memorabilia, then had to be careful as I turned the page because the book was so heavy. I looked at those Rockets as my own, as our neighborhood secret.

But then our fortunes started to change, and people began taking notice of the Rockets, just a little. TU—as we called the University of Toledo back then—became the Mid-American Conference co-champion in 1967 with a 9–1 record. Two of our seniors, quarterback John Schneider and linebacker Tom Beutler, were drafted into the National Football League, but the best player on that team was sophomore defensive back Curtis Johnson, who became a starter for the great Miami Dolphin No-Name defense of the early seventies. When Johnson went to Miami, the Dolphins instantly became my favorite NFL team. A few years later, I even sent their coach, Don Shula, a poem I wrote:

> The Miami Dolphins are the best
> In the east and in the west.
> And in the Super Bowl I know
> They will prove it through rain or snow.

It went on from there—three more verses, none better than the first.

By the fall of 1969, I was becoming more interested in football than I was in baseball. My fascination for this sport was growing by the day, growing almost as fast as I was. And with good reason. The Toledo Rockets kept winning week after week that season. We had season tickets on the 40-yard line, behind the visiting team's bench. They were great seats. The morning after every game, before getting ready for church, I dashed downstairs to find the huge slab of the Sunday *Blade* waiting for me on the kitchen table. I pulled out the Sports section and read every article on the Rockets. I hung on to the quotes, rereading them several times, even going back to a story in the afternoon to read it again. The Sunday after the Bowling Green game, Ken Crots said that he had been afraid even to look at the goalposts before he kicked the ball. I smiled. He was as scared as I had been.

By mid-November, the Rockets still were undefeated and had clinched the Mid-American Conference championship. They were heading to the Tangerine Bowl in Orlando to play David-son. I was ecstatic. This was a time in college football when there were only eleven bowl games, and my team was going to one of them.

With no more home games to go to at the Glass Bowl that season, we turned our attention to an entirely different football venue, one that was as grand as Toledo's was modest, one that was as famous as Toledo's was obscure, one that was as celebrated as Toledo's was unknown.

On November 22, 1969, Dad took Kate, Jim, and me to Ann Arbor for our first Michigan–Ohio State football game. It was our first Big Ten game as well. After it was over, some called it the greatest Big Ten game ever played. More than thirty-five years later, it's still believed to be one of the best of all time. Most people never get the chance to see such a game in all their life. We kids saw it on our first try.

Early in the week, Dad bought four end-zone tickets for the game from friends who were Michigan alums. At 10:30 A.M. on a cold Saturday morning, Mom began bundling up Kate, Jim, and me. She was a bit concerned that it was too cold for us that day.

"You could always stay home and watch the game on television," Mom said halfheartedly, already knowing how that idea would be received.

Dad replied with his usual refrain: "We've got to be able to smell it."

The day of the game felt like Christmas morning. All that week, I counted the days to Saturday. "Don't wish your life away," Dad told me. He was right, but I couldn't help it. I was ready to go early. I got antsy in the kitchen, and by the time we got to the car I had made a checklist in my head. Did we have everything? Binoculars? Blanket? Sandwiches?

As we pulled out of the driveway in our station wagon on this day of all days, the day of the great game, I wanted to make sure we had the most important thing.

"Dad, do you have the tickets?"

"No," Dad shot back.

"What?!"

Dad glanced at me out of the corner of his eye and smiled. He reached into his jacket pocket to produce an envelope. He held it up.

"Honey, I have the tickets."

Dad filled the early minutes of our ride with conversation about the assassination of President John F. Kennedy, which had happened six years ago that day. Dad loved history more than football, and he knew the date of every important event. As usual, he lit a cigar and cracked open the window, and class was in session. "Even when you're adults, you'll always talk about the day the president was shot," he said.

On our way, we passed numerous small towns on the tabletop farmland of southeastern Michigan. The drive would have been unremarkable, a bit dull even, if it hadn't been for our destination. We were headed to the Emerald City, as far as I was concerned, the Emerald City of college sports, Ann Arbor—and Michigan Stadium.

We soon came upon the first real traffic jam I had ever witnessed going to a sporting event. Cars with maize and blue *M* flags flapping in the breeze passed cars with scarlet and gray Buckeye bumper stickers. Horns honked. People waved and pumped their fists in their windows. The last few miles took us as long as the first thirty-five had.

Dad flicked on WJR to listen to the pregame show out of Detroit. All week, legendary Ohio State coach Woody Hayes had been complaining in the papers about the Big Ten rule that didn't allow a team to go to the Rose Bowl two years in a row. Ohio State had gone to Pasadena and won the national championship in 1968 with players like quarterback Rex Kern and cornerback Jack Tatum. The Buckeyes were undefeated again and ranked No. 1 in the nation heading into the game with Michigan. The Wolverines were having a more modest season with a 7–2 record under first-year coach Bo Schembechler, a Hayes disciple from Miami of Ohio. But because of the no-repeat rule, either Michigan or Purdue was guaranteed a trip to the Rose Bowl. Ohio State was shut out.

On the drive up, Dad started mimicking Hayes. "The best team in the country can't go to the Rose Bowl. . . . Blah-blah-blah-blah-blah . . . Isn't that a shame? . . . The best team in the country has to stay home New Year's Day."

We giggled.

"What a bunch of bellyaching," Dad continued. "Let's just see who the best team in the country is today. Kids, we're going to see who the best team in the country is today."

We nodded. Until that week, I barely could have told the difference between Michigan and Ohio State. That weekend, and forevermore, I knew. That day I became a Michigan fan. Not because of any particular love for Michigan, or because of their uniforms or helmets or a star player, the way most kids pick a favorite team. I loved Michigan because Dad couldn't stand Woody Hayes.

I figured out why Dad felt this way when I became a little older. Dad loved underdogs because he could identify with them, because he had been one himself as he and his family struggled through the Depression when he was a boy. He could not stand pomposity, and, to him, Hayes in 1969 was the very essence of ego, of arrogance, of bravado. Hayes, in his whining, already assumed his team would defeat Michigan that day. Dad didn't like that presumption. "Kids," he said, "you have to play the game." He so wanted to see Hayes get his comeuppance.

It might sound like blasphemy to live in Ohio and root against Ohio State, but it made sense to us. Dad liked the University of Michigan very much and thought it was a classy place. He always wondered aloud if any of us kids would go there. We never did, but it remained our favorite Big Ten football school, which hardly made us stand out in Toledo, the one true border town in the Michigan–Ohio State rivalry.

That day in 1969, Dad had us all revved up before we even got to Michigan Stadium. This place was legendary, Dad said, and I couldn't wait to see it. But as we walked toward it, something was wrong. All we could see was a low outer wall, just eighteen rows high. I was disappointed. The walk to the Glass Bowl was far more majestic. Dad had been talking in the car about how there would be more than 100,000 people at the game.

One hundred thousand people, here?

"Just wait," Dad said.

Soon, we walked through the stadium tunnel into our section in the end zone. And then, I couldn't believe my eyes. I gasped. We had entered the stadium on the seventy-second row. The stadium was a "soup bowl," Dad said, built into the ground. Down below us, past rows and rows of still-empty benches, was the field. For a moment, I didn't move. I couldn't move. I had to look around and take it all in. I had never seen such a place.

We found our seats in the fiftieth row, section 32, in a corner of the north end zone. Michigan Stadium was filling up quickly as the 1:30 P.M. kickoff approached. We knew some of the people sitting near us; they were the parents of our friends. I kept looking for other children, but I saw none. Yet there we were, an eleven-year-old, an almost-ten-year-old, and a seven-year-old, looking down on the grandest stage in college football with the "Biggest Kid on the Block," as Dad laughingly called himself.

My ticket for the big game.

As I sat, my legs bounced up and down. It wasn't the cold, although mounds of snow were piled in the corners of the end zone from a storm earlier in the week. It was the excitement. It was impossible for me to sit still. After the drive up and the hours spent talking about the game, I couldn't wait for it to get started.

Soon, the teams were running onto the field. When Ohio State came out, and the OSU band blared its fight song, Dad screamed out amid the boos: "Too bad the best team in the country can't go to the Rose Bowl!"

"Dad!" I said, elbowing him in the ribs. I was embarrassed, just a little.

Dad winked and elbowed me, ever so softly, from his thick jacket through mine.

The Buckeyes were a 17-point favorite, so it was no surprise when they scored the first touchdown. It was a surprise that they missed the extra point. Michigan answered and went ahead, 7–6.

It was the first time Ohio State had been behind all season.

Ohio State scored again, but missed the two-point conversion, then Michigan came right back to lead, 14–12, early in the second quarter. We sensed that something big was happening, even so early in the game. When radio announcers talked about feeling a sense of electricity in a stadium, this had to be what they meant.

I had never looked at a game from this vantage point, from high in the end zone, where plays developed, where the offensive line opened holes that I could see right along with the running back. When the ball was near our end zone, we had the best seats in the house—although the seat next to Dad in any stadium always was the best seat in the house. But when the ball was all the way across the field near the south end zone, we needed to rely on the fans to tell us what was happening. All sense of perspective was lost. The 20-yard line blended with the ten and the goal line.

There were 103,588 people in Michigan Stadium that day, a stadium that at the time seated 101,001. This was a math problem we quickly grew to understand. Every time we stood up to cheer, we lost more of our seats. Kate stood up and pointed to the seat numbers. We had started with four seats, each with a number painted on the bench. We each sat down on our number. By the end of the first quarter, the numbers were between us. We had just three seats. We were being moved by that massive crowd, and we hadn't even realized it.

"Don't stand up," Dad said, laughing.

But how could we not stand up? Every time we sat down, Michigan gave us something more to cheer. We felt like we were personally pushing Michigan punt returner Barry Pierson when he ran sixty yards away from us to set up another Michigan touchdown in the second quarter. Of course we stood up to cheer, then wedged ourselves back into what remained of our seats. This happened again and again, and at the end, as the clock wound down and the unthinkable (except to Dad) was about to be finalized, we stood and bounced around like jumping beans.

We three Brennan children and our father witnessed the absolute best from sports that day, throwing our hearts into a team and its cause, and seeing it turn out exactly as we had hoped it would. In the mother of all college football upsets, the final score was Michigan 24, Ohio State 12. It's a score I never have to look up.

The next football season, in 1970, our Toledo Rockets looked invincible again. We beat East Carolina, Buffalo, then Marshall to run the winning streak (including the 1969 Tangerine Bowl) to fourteen. In the Marshall game, played on a rainy night before just 12,804 fans (Dad, Kate, Jim, and I were the four), junior Chuck Ealey tied a conference record with four touchdown passes, and Don Fair, our six-foot, 165-pound wide receiver, had a school-record eleven receptions. They were becoming quite a duo; Ealey-to-Fair was our Unitas-to-Berry, our Lamonica-to-Biletnikoff, even if most of the nation had never heard of them because their games were never shown on national TV.

Ealey, the unflappable five-eleven, 195-pound quarterback from Portsmouth, Ohio, had been dubbed "the Wizard of Oohs and Aahs" by the *Blade* for his ability to throw strikes downfield with a defender crawling over his back or hanging on to his other arm. He was a rarity, a black man playing what was still a position almost exclusively reserved for white men. Meanwhile, Dad had given Fair, the quick receiver from Canton, Ohio, a nickname: "Sticky Fingers." Midway through the season, Kate said she got so used to calling him Sticky Fingers that she couldn't remember his real name. Fair will always be frozen in time in our minds in one position: on tiptoes just inside the sideline, arms outstretched, the ball resting safely in his fingertips, as if someone had walked up and placed it right there, just so. As best as we all remember, Sticky Fingers never dropped a pass.

Every time Toledo scored, the students fired off a cannon in one of the Glass Bowl's two Gothic towers in the end zone. We watched the smoke waft over the stadium and listened to the band play the Toledo fight song. We didn't know the words, so we simply sang, "Go, TU Rockets," over and over, until the band stopped playing. Somehow, our words melded to the melody of the music.

We were a constant foursome; Mom and Amy joined us for only one game a year, the afternoon homecoming game. Amy was just three and too young to become one of Dad's regulars. But she and Mom did play a big role in our strategy for getting back and forth to all the other home games. We had moved from the neighborhood right across the street from the campus to a suburban village called Ottawa Hills, which meant our walk to the stadium had turned into a two-mile drive. Before the game, Mom and Amy dropped us off along Bancroft by the stadium. Back at home, Mom would turn on the radio to listen to how the Rockets were doing, but also to find out when the game was ending.

When time ran out, she would hustle Amy into the car and drive to our appointed meeting spot: the parking lot of a Lutheran church that was a ten-minute walk from the stadium. Mom had her timing down perfectly in that pre–cell phone world of ours, often scooping us up in the lot just as we had arrived.

As the 1970 season moved along, Toledo kept winning convincingly. The last game of the regular season was at home, a 24–14 win over Colorado State, which was led by Lawrence McCutcheon, a future NFL star.

But we could not be delighted in victory. A week earlier, a chartered plane carrying Marshall University's football team had crashed on approach to the airport near Huntington, West Virginia, after returning from a game. Seventy-five people—players, coaches, university officials, fans, and crew—were killed. It was the worst disaster in U.S. sports history. We heard about it on the news on the radio and read the story on the front page of the *Blade* the day after it happened. Those players from Marshall had played in the Glass Bowl in late September; their bench was just a few feet in front of us. Now they were all dead. It was hard for me, for any of us, to fathom.

At the Colorado State game, the TU public-address announcer asked for a moment of silence and said volunteers would pass around containers for donations for the families of the players. When they came to our row, Dad put some money on the pile.

I remember the blackness of the November sky that night and the chill of the late-autumn air. But mostly, I remember feeling an emptiness that I had never felt before. All those players in white uniforms who stood so near to us earlier in the season were now gone. I looked up and down the Colorado State bench, trying to pick out every player—then closed my eyes and pretended they all had suddenly disappeared. For the first time in my life, at the age of twelve, I had a working definition of death.

Toledo won the Tangerine Bowl again to finish the 1970 season undefeated and run its unbeaten streak to twenty-three games. The Rockets were ranked twelfth in the nation by the Associated Press, seventeenth by United Press International. I was thrilled when I opened the paper and saw the final polls. Nothing like this had ever before happened to our city, to our team.

As the 1971 season opened, people around the country were starting to notice. CBS came to town to do a feature on Ealey, now a senior. *Sports Illustrated* devoted one and a half pages to him, including a photo of Ealey in a classroom. I was ecstatic; Ealey was in *SI*. I saved the magazine along with all the programs from every home game. The souvenirs were stacking up in my room.

Ealey was attracting attention because he had never lost a game he started in high school, nor in college. It seemed he was incapable of losing now. But everything that he had achieved, everything we hung our hopes on, two years of nothing but winning, was placed in jeopardy when the Rockets ran into trouble in the second game of the 1971 season, the first home game, our first chance to see Ealey and Fair and the rest of the stars of the team as seniors.

Toledo was playing Villanova and Ealey was having a bad game. "He's rusty," Dad said, shaking his head after an interception. The game was tied, 7–7, in the fourth quarter, and I was fidgeting in my seat, worried about the Rockets' winning streak.

"Does it count if we tie them?" I asked Dad.

"Well, it's not a loss, so you can say it's an unbeaten streak, but you can't say it's a winning streak anymore."

"But a tie is better than a loss, right?"

"Absolutely," Dad said. Just hearing him say that made me feel a little better.

I had almost given up hope when the Rockets took over at their 29-yard line after a punt with only twenty-nine seconds remaining in the game. But Ealey stepped back into the pocket and threw the ball deep toward our sideline for a fifty-seven-yard completion to the Villanova 14.

We leaped from our seats. Dad slapped me on the back.

Ealey threw the ball out of bounds to kill the clock, then sophomore kicker George Keim, who had already missed field-goal attempts of thirty and forty-four yards, came on the field to try another thirty-yarder.

I crossed my fingers and held my breath as Keim, part of the last generation of straight-on kickers, stepped toward the ball. It flew over the Villanova linemen and headed for the left upright of the goalpost.

"Oh no, don't miss," I said. "Please be good. Please be good."

My eyes darted to the referee standing in the end zone. At the moment of truth, he looked up, then threw both his arms into the air.

It was good.

Fans stormed the field while we jumped out of our seats. I hugged Dad. A few Villanova players argued that the kick was wide, to no avail. Toledo had won its twenty-fifth consecutive game.

"See, there was no reason to worry about that tie," Dad yelled over the screaming crowd.

Two years later, a handsome young student teacher appeared in our high school study hall. He wrote his name on the blackboard: Mr. Keim.

I had to know, so I walked to the front of the room. "Are you George Keim?"

"Yes."

"The man who kicked the field goal to beat Villanova?"

"Yes."

"Well," I said as I stood in front of him, my eyes wide, "thank you for doing that."

I was caught up in the most magical of relationships between a fan and a team that 1971 season. At thirteen, I threw everything I had, my heart and soul, into the Rockets, and they were repaying me—repaying Dad, Kate, Jim, all of us—in ways I never could have imagined. The louder I cheered, the more the team won. The Rockets never, ever disappointed me. They never let me down. They always rewarded my devotion with more victories, with more happiness. How often can a fan say that about a sports team?

Years later, I met the two head coaches in charge of the team over those three years, Frank X. Lauterbur and Jack Murphy. I told them that I had come to believe that the success of their teams, the way they rewarded a young girl's cheers over and over again, had led to my eventual decision to make a career out of sports. I also believed that their perfection led to my desire once I had embarked on that career to expect, even demand, the very best from athletes, from teams, from sport itself.

A few weeks after the Villanova game, Mom and Amy joined us for the afternoon homecoming game against Western Michigan. Toledo fell behind, 21–7, in the third quarter. In the past three seasons, we had never before been behind by two touchdowns. I was scared to death that we were going to lose. We didn't. Ealey threw two touchdown passes to Sticky Fingers and the Rockets stormed back to win, 35–24. The Western Michigan coach, Bill Doolittle, was so bewildered by Ealey's performance that he said, "I think God was throwing some of those passes."

The next day, the *Blade*'s Jim Taylor opened his story by saying that Ealey "surely invented the happy ending."

If Ealey invented the happy ending, by the time the season was over, he had cloned it as well. The Rockets reeled off five more victories in that 1971 season. None of those games was close. A third consecutive perfect regular season was over. The Rockets had won thirty-four consecutive games and were heading to one more Tangerine Bowl when I tore open a small present from my parents under the tree Christmas morning of 1971. I went numb with surprise. It was two tickets to the game, Ealey's final college game, the bowl game against the Richmond Spiders on December 28, 1971.

I couldn't believe it. Dad and I were going to Florida.

Chuck Ealey received many awards in his illustrious career.
(Courtesy of the University of Toledo)

We sat side by side in the section with the Toledo fans who had made the trip to Orlando. I wore a blue and yellow Toledo button. The Rockets won easily, 28–3. I never stopped cheering. But as the clock wound down, I strangely started to wish time would go the other way. Could we turn the hourglass over and let it start again? I wanted to add time to the clock to watch this team, not subtract it.

When the game ended, I could feel tears welling in my eyes. I looked at Dad. He put his arm around me.

"That's the end of an era, honey," he said.

"Dad, we'll never see them play again."

He nodded. "But you'll have a whole new team to cheer for next year."

The thought of next year, without these players, sent tears streaming down my cheeks. As the crowd began to file out around us, we remained in our seats, Dad's arm pulling me tighter toward him, his other arm reaching for a handkerchief in his pocket. All those great times we had had with our incredible, unbeatable team had come to an end.

"There will always be another kickoff," Dad said, trying to reassure me, but it seemed far away that late-December evening in Orlando. I was caught up in the memory of those three years of football. Thirty-five games I had watched, or listened to, or worried over. Three consecutive years of football games. The Rockets had won them all.

Even though Chuck Ealey's Rockets had played their last game, he still was ours. The NFL draft was coming up, so I asked Dad what he thought of Ealey's chances. I knew he was small by NFL standards at five-eleven, although other quarterbacks his size had made it in the league.

Dad shook his head. "Honey, Chuck Ealey probably won't get to play in the NFL," my father told me. "The NFL rarely lets black men play quarterback."

"But why not?"

"I wish I could tell you."

I was crestfallen, but Dad was right. In seventeen rounds of the 1972 draft, no one picked Ealey. He had been eighth in the balloting for the Heisman Trophy in 1971. But in the draft, twenty-six NFL teams continually passed on him. Four hundred forty-two players were selected by NFL teams, but not Chuck Ealey.

At the time, James Harris was playing quarterback for the Buffalo Bills and Joe Gilliam was Ealey's age and about to join the Pittsburgh Steelers, but that was it for black quarterbacks in the NFL.

Ealey spoke to the Kansas City Chiefs and Denver Broncos, but they wanted him to move to defensive back or wide receiver and he didn't want that. Amazingly, he never played even one down in the NFL, a place where most black athletes were still not viewed as being smart enough to lead a team. Dad tried to explain that to me, but I didn't understand.

"Chuck Ealey is brilliant," I said. "He always was the smartest player on the field."

"Unfortunately," Dad replied, "other people don't know that."

Ealey went to the Canadian Football League and won the championship, the Grey Cup, in his rookie season with the Hamilton Tiger-Cats, then played six more years in the league before settling into a successful career in business in the suburbs of Toronto.

The *Blade* printed small stories each week on the Tiger-Cats, keeping up with Ealey.

I read every one.

3

"STAND UP STRAIGHT, SHOULDERS BACK!"

Dad and Mom encouraged me to find my refuge in sports because, in the real world, I was a bit of an outcast.

"The boys at school have called me Frankie (short for Frankenstein) for some time. I'm the tallest in the class at 5 feet 3 1/2 inches and I weigh 110 pounds."

That was my diary entry for November 24, 1969. I was eleven and a half years old.

Frankie. I didn't like the name, and I cringed the first few times I heard it in sixth grade at our new school, Ottawa Hills. But I never shed a tear over it, even when my mother asked me how I felt about it at home one day.

"I wish they would call me Chris," I told her, "but other kids get called names too."

Mom smiled. There was nothing I could do to stop them, she told me, so I might as well act like it didn't bother me and see if the boys eventually just dropped it.

They did, but not for many months. I grew to answer to Frankie—and even accept it. The funny thing was, I actually liked most of the boys who called me by that name.

My Frankie days.

In some ways, I could hardly blame them for teasing me. I was an inviting target, and I remained so throughout junior high and high school. By early 1972, not yet fourteen, I was five-foot-nine-and-a-half-inches tall and weighed 140 pounds. I was growing so fast I had stretch marks on my knees. I towered over most of the boys all the way through high school; some were a head shorter than I even in our senior year. Mom never let me know her fears until I was an adult and had finally reached my full height of nearly six feet, but she had been worried I wouldn't stop growing until I reached six-one or six-two, and in the 1970s, that would have made it almost impossible for me to fit in.

As it was, it was difficult. Shopping for pants wasn't just a challenge, it became an ordeal. They all were flood length on me. Everything was short. Mom always was looking to see if there was enough of a hem to lengthen them. And shoes! My feet were size 10, same as Mom's, but there were very few youthful size 10 shoes in Toledo—and we felt lucky when we found a pair.

Because I was the supersize version of a 1970s girl, I became one of the very few teenage girls in the country who despised shopping for clothes. I developed splitting headaches in shopping malls. Within minutes of walking into a department store, I'd want out. Mom asked me to give it a few minutes. I did—then I asked when we were leaving.

I remember salesclerks trying so hard to be nice to us, but finally scrunching their noses and giving up. Soon, I was giving up as well. Mom would go shopping for me when I was in school, sparing me the agony. Whatever she brought home, I wore. She did her best, but size 14 dresses and pants often were designed to suit the tastes of older women, not young teenagers.

Dad too had his concerns, and he addressed them in his own unique way: "Stand up straight, shoulders back! There will be no slouching in this family."

Dad sounded like the army sergeant he once was. I heard those words at least a hundred times as a teenager and young adult.

"People are going to notice you when you walk into a room," he explained. "They're going to think you're older because you're so tall. So stand up straight, shoulders back!"

Who knew he was preparing me for a career of walking into men's locker rooms?

My height was not the only reason the boys called me Frankie. My hair was dark brown, nearly black, and I wore it very simply, in a shaggy pageboy, with bangs brushing my eyebrows. Before I got contact lenses my sophomore year of high school, I wore glasses with heavy black frames. I didn't wear makeup until my senior year of high school, and even then, it was only for big occasions, and only blush and lipstick. I never thought of putting on earrings. My ears weren't pierced—nor, for that matter, were Mom's, Kate's, or Amy's. Jewelry was barely on my radar screen. And let's not even talk about nail polish. I was throwing too many baseballs to worry about that.

Years later, looking at old pictures, Mom and I shook our

heads. "Why did we ever let you look like that?" she asked. We both shrugged. All we could figure was that neither of us thought it was important back then.

As unflattering as many of the pictures were, I never remember thinking of myself as unattractive when I looked in the mirror. I didn't even bother to attach a word to what I saw. I had other priorities, like school and sports. I was not reading teen magazines, I was not noticing the latest fashions on television, I obviously was not lingering around a makeup counter or wandering through racks of clothes as many young girls were. I wasn't even learning to cook with Mom as Kate and, later, Amy were. I was known around our house as the Home Ec Wreck, although I did become the family's go-to person for making Toll House cookies. I wouldn't necessarily call that cooking, though, because we often ate more than half the dough.

In short, I was completely out of step with my gender in the 1970s, but because I paid absolutely no attention to what most girls my age were doing, I didn't know how out of step I was.

I did fall in line with the rest of the world one Saturday night every September to watch the Miss America pageant. We had a running joke in our house about what would happen if I, the gawky teenager, somehow grew up to become a Miss America contestant.

What would I do in the talent competition?

"Dad would come onstage with you," Mom said with delight, "and he would pitch baseballs to you, and you would hit them into the audience."

My father, Jim Brennan, was built like a block of granite, hammered out of the sidewalks of Chicago. At six feet and then 185 pounds, he had been a fine tackle at Hyde Park High School on the South Side of Chicago, good enough to earn a scholarship to Drake University in Des Moines in 1944. Dad always shrugged when my siblings and I asked him how good he was, telling us that he didn't even start in his senior year and basically, as he put it, "collected splinters in my can." This was the 1943–44 school year, when so many American boys were fighting overseas in

World War II that colleges gave scholarships to anyone who showed the slightest bit of talent, which my father clearly did.

I knew this to be true because of the little scar under his lip, a sliver of a line, barely visible except when he smiled broadly and got ready to tell us his story once again. Buddy Young, a future NFL standout who played for a rival Chicago high school, had broken through the line and was "moving like an express train," Dad said, toward the goal line. How Dad got down field he never really said, but he lunged and "got a piece" of Young— "his knee, shoulder, whatever"—and the next thing Dad knew, blood covered his uniform. He had bitten down so hard, his teeth had sliced right through his lower lip.

"But guess what? I stopped him!" Dad said.

For one play.

"The very next play," Dad admitted, "he went in for a touchdown."

My father also was a shot putter, the second best at Hyde Park in those days. He felt a sense of pride in being number two because when he was a senior, Hyde Park had a junior named Jim Fuchs who went on to win the bronze medal in the shot at both the 1948 Summer Olympics in London and the 1952 Summer Olympics in Helsinki.

Dad was born in 1926 and grew up during the darkest days of the Depression. His parents lost everything they had—which wasn't much—on Black Tuesday in October 1929. His father, whose parents were first-generation Irish Americans born and raised in Indiana, had worked various jobs on the railroad in Indiana before Dad was born, then started selling stocks and bonds. My grandfather's timing was terrible; once the Depression hit, he was out of a job. Throughout the 1930s, he was away looking for work, as many men were. Dad saw him only occasionally.

Dad's mother was part of a big family that originated in Germany's north Rhineland and came to the United States in the 1870s, before she was born. She worked as a stenographer in downtown Chicago but wasn't making enough money to support her three children and pay for an apartment, so they moved into her parents' house. Often during the Depression, four or five different families—cousins of Dad's, or aunts and uncles—were living there under one roof, with my father's family occupying a room in the third-floor attic.

Once, Dad's family cobbled together enough money to rent an apartment, only to find themselves headed back to the third-floor attic a few months later when they were evicted and their belongings were out at the curb.

Years later, when my father told us these stories, his voice was tinged not with sadness but pride—pride that he was able to overcome such a difficult start to live what anyone would call the American Dream. Dad constantly deflected the credit for his rags-to-riches story from himself to his country; it was the great United States of America, he said, that allowed such things to happen. Dad also always found a way to smile about the hardships of his childhood. He used to tease my mother that her family, also from the South Side, must have been rich because they not only had their own apartment, they also owned a car.

In 1934, with money scarce for his family and his father gone, Dad started selling magazines. He was just eight years old. He sold the *Saturday Evening Post, Ladies' Home Journal, Liberty,* and *Country Gentleman*. He made $3 or $4 a week, which was enough to buy the milk and bread to put on the table for his family, with a bit left over to buy clothes and a used bicycle—on a 50-cent-a-week installment plan from a friend of his older sister, Peggy. He later added two paper routes to his duties, even hiring another boy to help him deliver the newspapers in apartment buildings. Before he became a teenager, Dad was a businessman, and a boss.

He was a precise young man. He was an excellent student with a nearly photographic memory. He kept meticulous records for his magazine and paper routes. As he grew up, he became tall and broad-shouldered, with dark, wavy hair, and because he wore glasses, his friends called him Clark Kent. His discipline and his surging sense of patriotism in wartime led him to the ROTC program in high school. His younger brother, Bob, remembered that, without fail, every Thursday night, Dad polished the buttons on his uniform, which he then wore with shoulders-back pride every Friday.

When times became a bit better economically, Dad turned to sports in high school, then stayed at Drake on his football scholarship for just a year before yearning for the excitement of the U.S. Army as the war was ending. He joined up and served as a sergeant in the First Infantry Division during the occupation of post–World War II Germany. During a review for the Joint Chiefs of Staff in Grafenwoehr, Germany, Dad was selected to hold General Omar Bradley's four-star flag. Dad had to stand perfectly still throughout the ceremony, which lasted more than three hours.

When Dad returned from Germany in the late 1940s, he went home to Chicago to a series of good jobs in sales, but he never entirely forgot about football. One day, he showed up for a tryout with Coach George Halas of the Chicago Bears. Halas watched my father run and block, then told him to get into better shape and come back next year.

Selling heavy equipment, Dad was making more money than an average NFL player at the time. He never went back.

My mother, Betty Anderson, was born in 1928 and grew up in an apartment just two miles from Dad. They didn't know that then; only when they met in their twenties did they learn they had lived no more than a six-minute drive apart. Mom's family struggled during the Depression, though not as severely as Dad's. It was true they had a car, although, one Christmas, they were in a bad traffic accident on the snowy Chicago streets. No one was seriously injured, but Mom told us that as they were being taken to the hospital, she looked back to see her only Christmas present that year, a glove-and-scarf set, laying in the street, splattered with blood. It was several years before they were able to buy another car.

Mom's mother was born in Lapland, in the north of Sweden. Her father, a house painter, was the first of his generation not to be born in Sweden, but in the United States, specifically in Chicago. Because they owned a car, Mom and her three siblings had the opportunity to see much more of Chicago than my father's family did. During the holidays, they would drive up to the North Shore to look at the Christmas lights sparkling on the homes in the wealthy suburbs of Evanston, Winnetka, and Wilmette. Mom's family never had the money to put up lights of their own.

Although Mom swam in Lake Michigan in the summer and played club basketball and softball with the girls in high school, she never thought of herself as an athlete. I don't think she ever used the term to describe herself. Few women born in the 1920s did. But she was tall for her generation, five-seven-and-a-half, with broad shoulders and stylish dark hair. She even suffered a sports injury once; playing Red Rover as a girl, she broke her collarbone when another child crashed into their human chain as Mom refused to let go of her friend's hand.

As an adult, Mom swam laps religiously during the summer, but her grandest season was winter. We used the garden hose to freeze our patio so we could skate and play hockey. Mom had the best skates, blue patent leather with gray faux fur.

Dad would always herald her arrival: "Here comes Sonja Henie!"

"Who's Sonja Henie?" we would reply in unison.

After high school, Mom went to business school, then became a clerical supervisor with Illinois Bell, dressing in a trim suit and pumps and taking the train to downtown Chicago every morning from the apartment she shared with her mother and father. Although Mom was only in her mid-twenties, her aunts already had written her off as an old maid when she met Dad at a Chicago community church's Sunday Nighters singles party in 1953. Typical of the era, the group adjourned to a bar to continue to socialize over drinks and cigarettes.

Little more than two years after they met, Mom and Dad were married. On their wedding day, my father was twenty-nine and my mother was twenty-seven, ancient by the standards of the day. The two of them made a handsome couple, smiling at the photographer who was taking pictures in black and white that warm September day in 1955.

Mom and Dad on their wedding day, September 17, 1955.

—

Mom and Dad were living, breathing oxymorons: they were Chicago Republicans. Dad's boyhood friends knew he was headed into politics. One wrote in Dad's high school yearbook that he expected him to become governor of Illinois someday. That never happened, but he did become the Republican party chairman in Lucas County, which includes Toledo, three times from 1977 to 1998. He also was vice chairman of George H. W. Bush's 1988 Ohio presidential campaign. Dad was a 1950s-style, never-vote-for-a-Democrat party man, a conservative in his day with views that would be considered extremely moderate today. When he said he wanted government out of his life, he meant completely out of his life—and the lives and choices of his wife and children too. As someone who pulled himself up by his bootstraps, he did not like the concept of the welfare state, the notion that government could solve everyone's problems. In another life, he could have been a Libertarian.

No one who ever met Dad was uncertain about where he stood on any issue, especially a political issue. Dad gruffly spoke his mind. "Are you a taxpayer," he would ask my liberal college friends, "or a tax taker? If you're a taxpayer, you should be a Republican."

He didn't care one bit if no one else agreed with him, or if he was too brusque, or if he was in the minority, or if his cause would ultimately be a lost one. You often stood alone when you started out as a Republican in Chicago, the city of Richard J. Daley, his Democratic machine, and the time-honored phrase "Vote early, vote often."

Dad's first significant political race was in the spring of 1955, the Chicago mayoral election between Daley and Republican Robert E. Merriam. It was Daley's first race for mayor. It would not be his last. Dad was one of six people who had gathered nearly two years earlier to support Merriam; by Election Day there were fifteen thousand volunteers working for the Republican, including Mom.

It didn't matter. Dad went to one polling place at lunch to see how things were going. He was told that more than five hundred Democrats had been in that morning to vote. He asked how many Republicans had voted.

"Two."

And that was before the cemetery vote came in, Dad said with a laugh.

When Mom and Dad moved to Toledo, as Democratic as Chicago but on a smaller scale, they found themselves on the outside looking in once again. When Mom voted for the first time, a kindly precinct worker reached to take her ballot from her. Mom pulled her hand back and refused to let go of the ballot until she alone had pushed it through the opening in the ballot box. In Chicago, you learned early on that if you were a Republican and let go of your ballot before it made it into the box, it probably wouldn't make it into the box at all.

Used to having to defend their positions against the majority, and already having lived substantial lives before marrying and having children, Mom and Dad were very comfortable in their own skin. If everyone else was going the other way, so be it. By the time I became an adult working in journalism, I began to appreciate this way of attacking life, of standing up for what you think is right, of speaking out, come what may. Actually, I think it's the job description of a columnist.

Dad, especially, lived for the next challenge. He always had a full head of steam built up, ready to unleash on something or someone. He used to tell us that when he was in the army, he slept standing up to save time. He lived as if he had a lifetime to-do list and couldn't wait to check off the next item. He also possessed a sense of insatiable inquisitiveness; there wasn't a cabdriver who took us anywhere on vacation who didn't end up telling us his life story at Dad's urging.

He was driven, and he was intimidating. Invincibility had a sound, and that was Dad's voice. If it was possible, he looked even tougher than he sounded, with that crew cut throughout most of the sixties, his answer not only to convenience, but also to the growing cacophony of antiwar protesters in America. He definitely came across as a "love it or leave it" guy. Adding to the image, as if it needed further enhancement, was his omnipresent cigar, always at the ready to be fired up. This was a man in charge, always.

Years later, talking to men and women who worked with Dad in business or politics, I was struck by how they spoke of him: as army men and women speak of their commanding officer. They were afraid of him, in awe of him, cowed by him, inspired by him. He was the ultimate man's man, his heels clicking, his pockets jangling with loose change, his shoulders back, his eyes unyielding.

To me, Dad was indestructible. He was rooted like a big oak tree. We always "made muscles" to see whose were stronger, not that there was ever any contest. Punching his biceps was like hitting a brick wall, even when he was seventy-five.

One night when I was little, I remember being afraid as Dad left the house to walk to Ace Drug to pick up a few items. I knew he had to cross busy Bancroft Street, which we little kids never were allowed to do without a parent. I wondered if I should worry about him, then thought, no. If a car hit him, I pictured the car bouncing off Dad, not vice versa.

Mom and Dad left Chicago for Toledo simply because a Yale forklift-truck franchise opened there. Dad wanted to be independent, to run his own company, and Toledo gave him his best shot to do it. He formed what would eventually become the Brennan Industrial Truck Company: selling, leasing, renting, and repairing forklift trucks. Toledo was, in many ways, a miniature version of Detroit. As Dad said, if Detroit caught a cold, Toledo got pneumonia.

It would be an understatement to say Mom and Dad both were in culture shock when they left their lifelong home in Chicago and headed east. Dad set up shop with a card table and a telephone in a one-room office in South Toledo. The first time my mother, pregnant with me, visited his office, she burst into tears—and she was not one to cry over just any old thing. Mom had quit her job after their wedding, a common custom in those days, and became a full-time homemaker. (Dad despised the term *housewife*. He found it demeaning. When I once wrote it on a school form for Mom's occupation, he made me erase it and write in *homemaker*.) Dad was a true-blue Republican, to be sure, but he also had a strong feminist streak. Not that we used that word—*feminist*—in our household to describe any of us, ever. But that didn't matter. Because of the way we were growing up, so open-minded in the most strident of Republican households, we also didn't have much use for labels or stereotypes.

Mom didn't need Dad to fight her battles, however. She was neither a shrinking violet nor a pushover; on the contrary, she was strong-willed and aggressive. With Dad working twelve-hour days to get his business up and running, Mom learned all about Toledo on her own, and then was ready to explore it when we children came along. She had the world's fastest walk, or at least I thought so when we were young. "Come on, kids!" she exhorted if we dallied along a sidewalk or in a store. And with that, she was off, and so were we, trying to keep up with her long, purposeful strides.

Mom spoke resolutely, with a deep, rich, textured voice. She smiled at almost anyone with whom she crossed paths, and she encouraged us to do the same. She always said thank you, even for the littlest thing. Mom, like Dad, was eternally optimistic, always believing good things would happen with hard work and a little luck. While Dad was brazenly outgoing, always enjoying a crowd, Mom was more personal, at her best one-on-one with a friend at church or in a store. As they grew older, he craved political dinners while she retreated to her volunteer work and her garden. When Mom was obliged to accompany Dad to important political dinners in Toledo, she was seated at the head table next to high-profile, national political wives. Never one to be impressed by celebrity, Mom often struck up a conversation with the waitress.

Mom was the personification of the past, present, and future of American mothering; she very much wanted to stay home with her children full-time and care for her family as her life's work, but she refused to be the window dressing of our family. She taught us all to be serious, substantial, productive human beings. This went not only for her son but for the daughters she was raising as well.

I wore Mom's blue patent-leather skates to join Amy
and Kate on our frozen backyard patio in 1970.

* * *

Looking back on it, I was comfortable being so different—
Frankie, for instance—because of the simple lessons Mom and
Dad were teaching me. Dad gave all of us some demanding
ground rules for life. We played by his rules, not society's. His
were much tougher. He never quite said this, but I knew he was
thinking it: You play by my rules and you'll find life's rules to be
a piece of cake.

It started with school. We were not allowed to get a grade in
junior high or high school lower than the first letter of our last
name. If it happened, and it did once or twice for me, we had a
meeting with Dad to discuss it. My freshman year of high
school, I could not figure out how to break the news to him that
I was about to receive a horrifying *D* for the quarter in geome-
try. I didn't tell him for several days until I nearly burst—then it
came out in a flood of tears in our kitchen.

Dad immediately took me into the den, closed the door, told
me he was very disappointed, and then came up with a plan. He
would call my teacher. He would arrange for me to meet with
the teacher as well. He told me he would stay on top of the situation, go to the school if necessary. "I'm going to help you make
sure this doesn't happen again," he said. He never yelled, never
raised his voice. For a moment I thought that I detected just a
touch of sympathy in his bright blue eyes. I received the grade
associated with our last name in that class the next quarter.

Dad's rules covered church as well. We had to pledge money
to Christ Presbyterian Church every week—not a fortune, just a
little—and put it in the offering plate every Sunday. Whenever
there was a collection for canned goods or money to help the
poor, we were donating, and, on occasion, even delivering, to
the needy people in Toledo. Whenever a charity was looking for
someone to help children in particular, it seemed Dad was involved.

"Come on, kids, we get to play Santa Claus!" Dad would yell
as we piled into the car to go shopping for toys for a family we
did not know. Dad would drive the toys to the children in a
poor, sometimes crime-ridden neighborhood in Toledo, and we

would wait expectantly by the door for his return home to hear what the kids said when they saw their gifts. Dad told me later that like others his age, he just couldn't say no to a child, especially a poor child. Even though he had never before met these children—kids often without a permanent home, kids sometimes without a father in the house—he definitely knew them.

Almost every day, Dad reminded us how lucky we were to be born in the United States. The two times we moved as a family, the first thing Dad did was have a flagpole installed so he could fly the U.S. flag every day of the year. And we did have to use that term: the U.S. flag. It was not the American flag. The Americas included Canada and Mexico, and the nations of Central and South America as well. How presumptuous of us, Dad said, to appropriate the hemisphere as all ours and take the name for our own. (This was one rule Dad cut me some slack on after I became a journalist and explained that there were times I needed to vary my adjectives when covering American, er, U.S. athletes.)

What's more, Dad bought only U.S.-made cars and strongly suggested as we grew older that we do the same. To this day, I've never even considered buying a foreign car, although many of those cars are now made in the United States. As foreign and domestic car companies started to merge, I asked Dad about his rule, and he stuck by it. "I believe we should support the companies that are headquartered in the United States," he said.

Patriotism was serious business to Dad. On a family vacation to Hawaii in 1974, when I was sixteen, we took a day to visit Pearl Harbor. After spending some time on the *Arizona* memorial, we were ready to catch the boat back to shore—all of us, that is, except Dad.

We found him standing ramrod straight, hands clasped behind his back, staring at the wall of names of those who were killed on December 7, 1941.

"Dad," I said, agitated and ready to leave, "what are you doing?"

"I'm reading every name and saying thank you."

We didn't leave until he reached the last one.

Patriotism also could bring confusion. A few years earlier, Dad and I had been watching the 1968 Democratic convention together in our family room. The streets of Chicago were filled with students protesting the Vietnam War. We saw police hitting the demonstrators over the head. For a moment, not understanding what I was seeing and being all of ten, I thought the police were doing the right thing.

Then Dad spoke up.

"This is awful," he said. "The police can't hit kids like that."

Although Dad was a patriot, a true-blue U.S. citizen, he at times defied description because he never went with the pack. If the crew-cut types went one way, he might go their way—or he might go another. In this case, what was happening in Chicago under the iron fist of none other than Richard J. Daley was terrible, Dad said. He thought through his every belief. He did nothing blindly. I learned that firsthand the night he worried about the way the police were treating the kids who were protesting the war he strongly supported.

From that moment on, I started to follow politics with Dad. It was a tumultuous time. During Watergate, Dad supported President Richard Nixon until near the bitter end. But when the facts became apparent, Dad gave in. "He lied to me," Dad said disgustedly. We were on our family vacation in Hawaii the day Nixon announced his resignation. At 5:45 the next morning, August 9, 1974, Dad woke Kate and me up in time to watch Gerald Ford take the oath of office at noon in Washington, 6 A.M. in Hawaii. No matter what time it was, we were not going to miss something so historic.

If patriotism was part and parcel of being a Brennan, precision was too. No one worked *for* Dad at his company. Everyone worked *with* him. If I ever got it wrong, he'd correct me.

We had to learn and recite all the U.S. presidents in order. Next came the books of the Bible and the Gettysburg Address. Gettysburg was special to Dad. We walked the battlefields with him for the first time on spring break in 1969. It wasn't the last time. Before that trip, Dad assigned Kate and me to write a report on the battle.

There was detail in every phase of our lives. My name grew shorter as I grew taller. Named Christine Elizabeth Brennan in honor of my grandmothers, I was called Christy until the second or third grade, when I started to favor Chris. When Chris Evert came on the scene a few years later, and I had begun playing tennis, I thought my name was perfect. Chris is the name many friends call me to this day, although I began answering to Christine once it began appearing as my byline after college.

I use the byline Christine Brennan because of Dad. When I was filling out my application for Northwestern University in 1975, I wrote my name as Chris. As Dad checked my work before I sent it in, he called me over.

"I think you should change this," he said. "Use your formal name."

Dad was a stickler for everything, but most of all dates. He remembered everyone's birthday and anniversary. He would startle a casual acquaintance at a party by saying, "Happy birthday last Wednesday."

Dad often called our attention to the obituaries in the *Blade*.

"Look at this," he would say. "This man was born in 1906, yet they say he was a veteran of World War One. He was twelve when the First World War ended."

We also had to date every piece of paper we used, preferably in the upper-right-hand corner.

One day in the kitchen, having become a teenager who was getting slightly exasperated with her father, I told Dad I didn't need to put a date on a piece of paper because I was only going to write down a phone number, call it, then throw the paper away.

"I don't care," he replied. "Put a date on it."

I furiously scribbled the date, dialed the number, then balled up the paper and dramatically threw it in the wastebasket, scowling at my father. Dad didn't say a word. He didn't have to. I've dated every piece of paper since. Dad's obsession has become mine, with the most serendipitous of results. Whenever I reach for one of the old notebooks I have stashed in a cabinet and wonder when I conducted an interview—sometimes a very important piece of information as I'm researching a story or column—I simply open the notebook and there is the date at the top of the page.

The discipline to put a date on everything followed hand in hand with my interest in keeping a diary. Mom and Dad gave me a new one every Christmas and they encouraged me to write in it every day, which I did. Throughout high school, into college, and all the way into the mid-1980s, I didn't miss a day. It was like a game to me, to see if I could keep it up and not break the streak. I became the Cal Ripken Jr. of diary writers.

Dad also enjoyed relating our world to the facts in the news. If 100,000 people were left homeless by a flood or hurricane, to understand how many people that was, Dad would have them filling Michigan Stadium. The number of G.I.'s killed in Vietnam—58,000—would have more than filled Tiger Stadium, Dad reported to us. When Neil Armstrong and Buzz Aldrin were descending to the moon's surface in July 1969, a NASA announcer dramatically counted down the distance remaining until touchdown. Dad quickly translated for us. A mile from touching down was the distance from our house to the school. At two thousand feet, Dad announced, "They're only as far away as the tennis club." Pretty soon, it was the next block. Then they landed.

Dad with us kids in 1969.

Dad also used our everyday games to teach us his life lessons. Monopoly was his favorite. He never went easy on us and let us win; he believed playing fair and square as an adult was a far better lesson for his children. As we played, his advice to us was simple: "If you land on it, buy it." Sometimes he mortgaged property just so he could buy more. This was a metaphor for the way he lived: Make a decision and never look back. Never second-guess. Be confident and bold. "There will be no shrinking violets in this family," he said.

Some children rebel against fathers like mine, against all the detail, the minutiae, the rules. I drew closer. I wanted him to quiz me on my homework or about what happened one hundred years ago today. I wasn't afraid not to know the answer; if I didn't, I knew I would learn it from him right away. I was my father's willing disciple. He encouraged me to ask questions of anyone about anything, and he did so early on. At Thanksgiving dinner in 1964, when I was only six and a half, I polled my cousins about who their parents had voted for in the presidential election, Lyndon Johnson or Barry Goldwater. Then I reported the results back to Dad: "You and Mom are the only ones who voted for Goldwater." Every one of his siblings and in-laws had voted for LBJ. As I left the room to return to the other children, I heard Dad begin a conversation that would turn into quite an argument.

Sometimes Dad would grab one of our green and white volumes of the World Book Encyclopedia and start reading it just for fun; soon, I would be reading the encyclopedia too, "just for fun." My light reading also included the Warren Commission report. Dad piqued my interest in the controversy over the assassination of President Kennedy by showing me the coverage in *Life* magazine, buying me books by Warren Commission critics, and even taking me to hear one of those critics, Mark Lane, speak at the University of Toledo. I was on my way to becoming an assassination conspiracy buff. I studied the Zapruder film frame by frame in *Life* magazine and wrote a forty-four-page term paper my senior year of high school calling for the matter to be reopened and reinvestigated. I wasn't at all convinced Lee Harvey

Oswald acted alone. In fact, I was pretty sure he didn't. Any time I'm in Dallas to cover an event, I make my way to Dealey Plaza and roam around until I have to dash to my assignment, trying to imagine what it was like there during those horrible few seconds on November 22, 1963. If time travel ever becomes possible, that's where I'm going.

I quickly became as caught up in precision as Dad was. In the days leading to my tenth birthday, I asked Mom what time exactly I was born. She told me 7:58 P.M.

On May 14, 1968, as the minute drew near, I camped out in front of the clock in the kitchen until the second hand reached twelve at exactly two minutes to eight.

"I'm officially ten," I announced.

Mom gave me a look that said only one thing: Oh, no, not another one.

This love of detail, this quest for knowledge, led right to the dinner table every night at six, when we always turned on the local news on the NBC affiliate WSPD, then watched NBC's *Huntley-Brinkley Report* at 6:30. In a couple of years, it would be John Chancellor's newscast. We were an NBC News family. We never watched Walter Cronkite; I don't know why, although Chancellor was a Chicagoan, Mom and Dad told us. And if it was the top of the hour and we were near a radio, Mom or Dad flicked it on. They loved the news, so I loved the news.

As strong and demanding as Dad could be, he really was an old softie at heart. The legendary Kodak commercials, the sentimental ones asking us to "remember the times of your life," were one of our first clues that Dad wasn't as tough as we thought. A few seconds of watching a family grow up before his eyes and Dad was in tears. Every single time, those commercials got to him.

Dad rarely watched TV, but when he did, he often got emotional over some program or other. One day we came home from choir practice and found Dad teary-eyed by the television. We wanted to know what was wrong. Nothing was wrong, Dad said. An episode of *The Waltons* had just ended. The show reminded Dad of his childhood; the Waltons' struggles during the

Depression were similar to those of his own family. He watched only a few episodes of that popular show over the years, but he was sniffling after every single one.

When I was just seven or eight years old, I enjoyed going down to the basement on Sunday nights to watch Dad write checks to pay the bills. One time, he put aside the checkbook and pulled out a scrapbook filled with black-and-white pictures of his childhood. As he talked about his wonderful mother, who had died four years before I was born, tears started running down his cheeks. Soon, they were streaming down mine.

One afternoon, a teenage boy who lived across the street made a huge mistake as he was practicing driving with the family car on the driveway; he plowed into the brick partition between their two garage doors. We all came out to see what had happened. The boy was crying, his parents were furious, and to make matters worse, he wasn't yet sixteen, so he was not insured. After a minute or two of watching this, Mom and Dad shooed us inside.

A half hour later, Dad called our neighbors with an offer. He wanted to know if their son would come over and play chess with him. For the next few hours, Dad put aside the chores he planned to do that evening and played game after game with the neighbor boy to help him calm down.

As I watched Dad in action, I slowly started to figure him out. Anyone who was afraid of him just never understood him, I thought. The tough exterior melted around children, especially his. In the dead of winter, when he came home and hugged every one of us, I always was comforted by the chill of his face as he gave me a kiss. And when it was summer, we would wait on a small hillside at the corner for him to make the turn for home after work. We jumped up and down and waved like this was something new and a big surprise, even though we went through this routine almost every summer day. And, every day, Dad acted as if he wasn't expecting us to be there, honking the horn and waving back, feigning shock and surprise.

When he was with us, he became a kid himself, that "Biggest Kid on the Block," as he said. He would tell us stories that made our eyes grow wide. Once as a young man in his twenties, he fell asleep at the wheel on an Illinois highway and woke up just in time to see that he had driven under the body of a long truck. "I was lucky to live through that," he said. Dad's hand was broken in the accident; we all gathered around to see the scars where the wires had been inserted.

We recoiled in a mix of squeals and horror every time a wasp alighted on the pool deck and Dad summarily killed it—by stepping on it with his bare foot. I witnessed this dozens of times. We offered Dad a shoe to stomp on the next wasp, but he declined.

"It's better with your bare feet," he bellowed.

Dad loved getting a rise out of us. He sometimes swam with a lighted cigar in his mouth. He even water-skied on family vacations while puffing away. People we didn't know came running to the boat dock to take pictures of him.

Dad certainly was a man of regimentation and rules, but every now and then, he decided to color outside the lines. On an October Sunday evening in 1969, Dad picked up Kate and me from choir practice at church. Instead of heading straight home, he decided to take a detour. A new interstate was being carved out of the earth near our church, twisting like a ribbon through the suburbs toward downtown Toledo. We watched the progress of the construction from week to week, wondering when the highway would be finished.

Dad decided it was high time we found out for ourselves. We drove up a deserted entrance ramp, past barriers and signs warning us not to enter. Dad assured Kate and me that he would be careful. Once we cleared the ramp, it was smooth sailing on the pristine concrete.

"We're the first people to drive on the new expressway!" Dad howled as we moved along at no more than 30 miles per hour.

We laughed in the darkness until we heard a loud thud under the car.

We lurched forward. The car had stopped.

Dad opened his door and looked out.

We had run out of road and were stuck in the mud.

"Well, girls," Dad said, "we now know where the construction ends."

We were stuck very close to another entrance ramp, so Dad told us to sit tight and locked us into the car, trudged down the ramp, and walked to one of the stores on the street below to call Mom. He then came back and got us.

As Mom drove up, she glared at Dad, hustled us into her car, and took us home. Dad stayed behind to wait for someone from his office to bring a tow truck to drag the car out of the mud.

This mishap might have shaken some men, but not Dad. A week later, visiting a friend's farm, Dad decided to venture off the dirt road—and got us stuck in the mud again.

Even when we became adults with our own homes, Dad always had something up his sleeve. April Fool's Day was Dad's national holiday. He'd sneak out at about 4 A.M. and place yard ornaments and FOR SALE signs in the front yards of the two children, Kate and Jim, who lived nearby.

One year, Dad considered the joke a complete success when Kate called later that morning to say a neighbor had phoned to ask when they were moving.

Seeing Dad in action, watching the world's toughest son of a gun become the kindest, silliest, and gentlest man I ever knew, was a lesson that for me and my siblings would reap great benefits. That Dad's tough-as-nails exterior hid such a soft, sentimental, childlike interior gave me invaluable insight into the strong men I would run into later in my career in sports journalism. If I knew that my father, a man who could overpower almost anyone, cried over *The Waltons* and got cars stuck in the mud twice in seven days, how could I ever be intimidated by the likes of George Steinbrenner, Jack Kent Cooke, or Don Shula? The sports world was full of these characters, of men like Dad. I found myself undaunted by them, intrigued by them, even entertained by them. Deep inside, I knew that I knew these men. I told myself they were like my Dad.

Like some of these famous sports figures, Dad was a rugged individualist, and that was reflected in his attitude toward having a girl jock in the house. At a time when most girls were not being encouraged to play or follow sports, Dad, and Mom too, never said no to me, even if the rest of the world was thinking that we were rather strange.

If my parents had had their way, it would have been just as acceptable for a girl to play organized team sports in the 1960s and 1970s as it was for a boy. But they were a little ahead of their time.

These days, we see big, strong girls—girls like me—playing on organized teams in every neighborhood. Those girls dash from game to game and field to field wearing jerseys and uniforms and baseball caps. Count their sports: soccer, basketball, softball, field hockey, lacrosse, Little League baseball.

A girl like that, today's young female athlete, plays on as many as twenty-five organized teams before she reaches her freshman year of high school.

I have no trouble remembering the number of organized teams I played on before my freshman year of high school.

Zero.

I never wore a uniform or jersey until I entered high school. I never wore a baseball cap while playing an organized sport. With my size and passion for sports, I would have been a natural to play on every team. But there were none.

Back then, no child was playing organized sports the way girls and boys are playing them now. But at least the boys had something: Little League baseball and peewee football. In the summer of 1967, David Hansen and some of the other boys started playing Little League. Girls weren't allowed.

Playing fields full of girls? We couldn't have imagined it back in the sixties and seventies. I was born a generation too early for that. Title IX, the landmark law that would eventually provide unprecedented athletic opportunities for girls, was signed by President Nixon before my freshman year of high school, but had no impact for several years. I was actually coming of age as women's sports were coming of age. I just didn't know it yet.

But no one got angry, no one complained—not even the parents of the best-known tomboy in the neighborhood.

Instead, Mom and Dad created a diversion for me. Unfailingly positive, Dad said it was a big world out there, so if one door closed, another had to open. Not coincidentally, in that same summer of 1967 that the boys started Little League, Mom signed me up for tennis lessons. I took to the game immediately. Playing all that baseball had helped me have the kind of hand-eye coordination needed for tennis, and the sport became one of my favorites. I kept going back for more lessons and challenge matches every year until, by the time I was in junior high, I was spending most of my summer days with my friends on the clay courts at the tennis club in our neighborhood.

Dad told me that there were three sports that girls could participate in for a lifetime: tennis, swimming, and golf. "You should be able to do all three," he said.

Mom and Dad were obviously compensating for the sports I couldn't play. They looked for another outlet for me. It was the old bait and switch; if I couldn't play baseball, I'd play tennis. That was a sport we all knew girls could play. I watched Wimbledon every year. I saw women playing there, and I saw women on television from the Olympics, but they mostly were figure skaters, swimmers, skiers, gymnasts, and runners. It was thrilling for me to see women competing in international sports, but it was hard for me to identify with some of them, figure skaters and gymnasts in particular, because so many were small and thin, and I was neither.

Tennis was different, and I embraced it as my next big sport, but I wasn't entirely happy with this situation. I still loved baseball—batting, playing catch, running bases—and even though I was gradually losing my playmates to Little League, I wanted to keep playing.

So, one day, I wrote in my diary: "I played catch with myself today." I threw the ball into the air, then ran under it and caught it. I did that for at least a half hour. That wasn't the only day either.

David Hansen and I still played sports together on occasion, but after we moved away from Old Orchard to Ottawa Hills, and the Hansens moved to another suburb, a parent had to drive one of us to the other to do it.

But the good news was I had found a replacement for David

and the other boys. He was right under my nose. It was my brother, Jim. I couldn't wait until Jim grew old enough to play with me, and then when he did, we never stopped. From those earliest days, when I was about eleven and he was about seven, all the way through high school and even my college days, we played everything together. People have always assumed that because I am a sportswriter, I must have had older brothers. No, just Jim, and Dad, and David, and the other boys in Old Orchard.

Jim and I made up baseball games with a tennis ball and a bat on the driveway in which the number of times the ball bounced when we hit it indicated whether it was a single, double, triple, or home run. We drew a strike zone in chalk on the outside of our house. Mom and Dad didn't mind. Sometimes Kate and Amy and their friends joined in. Dad and Mom even played the "outfield" on occasion. Mostly, though, it was just Jim and me.

I also played tackle football with Jim and his friends in the side yard. I towered over the boys, but they were good little tacklers, and when I came down, I came down hard. We froze the patio, put on our skates, and played hockey in the winter. We shot baskets for hours, even in the winter. When the ball grew cold and flat, we'd dash into the house and douse it with hot tap water until it became all bouncy again. Then, when we were ready to go inside for good, we had to hit our last five shots before quitting. Just like the pros, we had our rituals.

Sometimes I shot baskets on the driveway alone. I would make up game situations: "This free throw is for the Ohio girls' high school championship," even though there was no such thing back then. I sometimes dreamed that *Sports Illustrated* would write up my mythical games, for which I always sank the winning basket.

Soon, Jim was playing organized team sports, but I, four years his senior, had to stay on the sidelines until high school. So I did the only thing that made sense. From the bleachers, I threw myself into Jim's games: Little League baseball, church-league basketball, peewee hockey. I knew most of the boys on his teams, and even some of his opponents. Watching them play, I analyzed the games with Dad, cheering loudly for my brother and his teammates. After Jim's games ended, I would practically interview the poor kid, so interested was I in what he was thinking. Who would have guessed that by not being able to play yet myself, I might find something else I liked to do, not quite as much as playing, but close.

One summer evening in 1969, Dad came home from the office and issued a pronouncement. He was taking Kate, Jim, and me to play golf with him that Sunday afternoon at a municipal pitch-and-putt just two miles away called Par 3.

"I want you to learn to play this game," he said. It was the only one of his Big Three—tennis, swimming, and golf—that I hadn't tried. Duly inspired, I dashed off to our World Books, grabbed the G volume, and started reading. I soon was armed with an array of facts that I wanted to share with my father.

"Dad, did you know getting ready for a shot is called addressing the ball?"

Dad played golf but was not very good at it. He never took a lesson to correct the choppy half swing he took at every ball. He never even considered it. He was too busy running his business to spend enough time at golf to get better.

But he did want to use golf for one specific purpose: to spend summer Sunday afternoons with his children and expose us to one of those lifetime sports. Soon, trips to Par 3 became part of the family routine. He would pop open the trunk to put on his golf shoes and pull out his bag. We would marvel at all the clubs he had: every number from two to nine. I threw a blue bag over my shoulder with Mom's Patty Bergs inside—two woods, a putter, and four irons: three, five, seven, and nine. Kate and Jim shared a flimsy white bag with five clubs between them.

We must have been quite a sight trudging to the first tee that summer: a father and his three kids, none older than eleven, two of whom were girls, all of us with a golf club in our hands and our names already scribbled onto the scorecard.

I looked forward to playing each summer Sunday; I lived to reach back and send the ball flying off the tee as if it were a baseball being pitched to me on Goddard Field. I fell in love with the *thwack* of the club meeting the ball. But this hardly was serious business. Kate and Jim stopped playing in the middle of a hole to look at the baby rabbits we came upon on the back nine one Sunday. Dad and I set down our clubs to look as well. A group of men played through.

On the greens, we had no sense early on of how hard to smack a putt. I once sent one barreling toward the hole. Dad could tell this was trouble. "Hit a house!"

"What?"

"We need that ball to hit *something* to stop."

We were little kids then, but on some level we realized what was happening to us, Sunday after Sunday. When many other fathers were hitting golf balls at the country club with their buddies, our father was playing golf with us. Years later, Dad explained to me that one of the reasons he spent so much time with us was that his father was away for much of his childhood, and, remembering that, he was not going to let that happen to our family.

I loved to hear Dad laugh, to watch him miss a shot nearly as badly as we did, to stand in the sun and smile with him. Surrounded by adults on almost every hole, we were learning a valuable lesson: there was no place on earth we couldn't go and feel we belonged.

The only other time Dad played golf was at 6 A.M. on the occasional spring and summer Saturday with some men from work. They played early so they were finished in time to put in five or six hours at the office. He and his colleagues always went to public courses, usually a beautiful municipal course called Ottawa Park, where we kids later played many rounds.

Dad did join a country club in the Toledo suburbs in the late 1960s for a couple of years. It was a rite of passage for him; the poor boy from Chicago who always was on the outside looking in finally could be on the inside looking out. Dad encouraged us to join the swim team and take golf lessons, and I did, but we didn't like the place and were gone in two summers.

We also were longtime members of a downtown athletic and

social club in Toledo that was slowly undergoing changes to allow women, African Americans, and Jews to be members. Those were different times in the 1960s and 1970s, but even then, I remember Dad and Mom feeling strongly that discrimination was wrong and that things should change at the club, and they did.

That seems like a lifetime ago. As Dad watched us grow up, he became more aware of restrictions based on gender, race, and religion at private clubs. They bothered him. He told me later on that he would never again set foot at a club where his daughters couldn't go. Another Dad rule. It sounded so logical, I couldn't believe any father would think differently.

Two decades later, as a columnist for *USA Today*, I criticized Augusta National Golf Club's restrictive membership policies toward women. Sitting on a plane, a woman named Martha Burk read my column and fired off a private letter to the club's chairman, a man named Hootie Johnson. Watching the ensuing controversy from afar, with a knowing smile, was a seventy-six-year-old grandfather in Toledo who never was much of a golfer.

4

IN THE GAME

Seven seconds remained on the clock. Our junior varsity girls' basketball game was tied, 16–16. We were playing in a small gym at Ottawa Hills High School, a multipurpose room also used for lunches and receptions, with basketball nets on either end and a small electronic scoreboard up high in a corner. The few parents who came for the Tuesday-afternoon game on February 13, 1973, found a seat on the end of our bench or leaned against the wall. Dad was the only father there.

It was my freshman year of high school and I finally was playing on a team.

I was the starting JV center, occasionally moving up to the varsity to play a few minutes in those games. This was the fourth game of my freshman year, the fourth organized basketball game of my life.

Our young coach, Sandy Osterman—we called her Miss O— signaled for a time-out. With those few seconds remaining, we gathered around her. She had a notepad and a Magic Marker in her hand. She was talking fast and scribbling even faster.

"We're going to try a trick play," Miss O began with a smile. "Cathy Collins is going to inbound the ball to Chris Brennan," she said, looking to me. "Chris, you'll be at half-court, and you're going to lob the ball to Susan Secor, who will be going toward the basket. You hit her here," Miss O said, marking a spot to the right of the basket on her notepad.

"Now here's the tricky part," she said, lowering her voice. "When you come out, Chris, you pretend you're going to throw it to the other side, and start saying it's going to the left, okay? Say that so they hear you. And Susan, you act like we're not throwing it to you, pretend you don't care where it's going, like you're not involved. Say it's not coming to you so the girl guarding you hears it. Make sure she hears you. And I'll keep yelling it's going to the left. Okay? Let's fake 'em out."

This is what qualified as sophisticated strategy in high school girls' basketball in 1973.

We broke the huddle. As Susan walked back onto the court, she sulked dutifully. Our opponents from rural Lake High School seemed to be paying attention to her, I noticed.

"Look to the left!" Miss O yelled, following her rudimentary script. "Look to the left!"

Cathy took the ball from the referee on the sideline and threw it to me at midcourt. True to the plan, I heaved it to Susan, whose defender—just as we hoped—was nowhere to be found.

Susan laid it up. The ball bounced around the rim one, two, three times—then fell through the net as time expired.

The master plan, perfectly executed. Victory for Ottawa Hills!

Miss O bounded onto the court in huge, loping strides and hugged Susan, then me, then Cathy. We jumped around in one another's arms for several moments. "It worked!" we screamed. "It worked!"

I looked over at Dad, who was standing and cheering with Mom and the other mothers. He pumped his fist. I pumped mine back.

I had been so nervous to make that team. I had dreamed almost my whole life, all fourteen-plus years of it, for the moment I could try out for a team. All those days spent playing with the boys in the neighborhood, all those hours spent on the driveway, shooting baskets with Jim or by myself. And then, finally, the day arrived. Two nights of tryouts to make the Ottawa Hills High School girls' varsity or JV basketball teams.

About thirty-five girls walked through the darkened school hallways into the main gym. We ran sprints, made layups, and worked on basic plays until someone finally gave up on whatever it was we were trying to do and just shot the ball.

I jammed my ring finger on my left hand going for the ball the first night but didn't miss a play. I wouldn't let myself miss any playing time. This was too important to me. When I got home, I plunged my hand into a bucket of ice to keep the swelling down. Even though it hurt badly, I was back the next night, playing every time Miss Osterman called on me.

After that last tryout session in the main gym, Miss O told us she would post the names of the girls who made the teams on the door to the girls' locker room the next morning. I was so nervous going to school that I made Kate walk with me to the door to see the list. When Kate and I saw my name, I think she exhaled louder than I did.

A typical crowd in the main gym at one of our high school basketball games. I'm in the middle, running through the key without the ball.

Practice soon started, and I, one of the two tallest girls on either the varsity or JV, and the tallest freshman, soon became the whipping girl for the good-natured ribbing of the juniors and seniors I barely knew. They called me "Hodak," after a University of Toledo guard named John Hodak who loved to shoot from way outside in the days before the three-point shot. Even though most of my points came inside off rebounds, I occasionally gunned one from twenty or twenty-five feet. "Hodak!" the girls would yell. I smiled. It sure beat Frankie.

They loved to tease me, and I didn't mind. As Dad said, "You're a big target. But you can handle it."

One day, we were doing a drill in which we had to jump up and down in squares. "Jump higher!" Miss O yelled.

"Brennan's already touching the ceiling!" screamed one of the older girls.

I laughed. Even though the joke was on me, I was flattered by the attention. I didn't think upperclassmen noticed freshmen. So this was what being on a team was like, I thought to myself.

For the first time in my life, I was around a couple of dozen girls who were like me. They had not been keeping score of Mud Hens games; they weren't that nutty. But they could talk about the Tigers. They argued about Michigan and Ohio State. They were not into makeup and clothes and cooking, but fast breaks and jump shots and pick-and-rolls. This was almost too good to be true.

One of the first orders of business that season was picking a jersey. After some of the older girls chose the numbers they wanted, I grabbed 27. (When we got new jerseys a few years later, there was no 27, so I went for double that, 54.) How I loved that first jersey. It was a forest green nylon shirt with white numbers and letters bordered in yellow and the words *Ottawa Hills* written on the front. Unfortunately, Ottawa Hills' colors were kelly green and white, so the shade of this jersey was a little bit off. But it hardly mattered. This was the first jersey I ever put on, and I cherished it so much I still have it tucked away in a dresser drawer.

To round out our "uniforms," we wore gym shorts and had

to buy our own socks and shoes, so few of us matched. Some girls had wider stripes on their tall socks than others did. And the shoes were little more than street sneakers, hardly the standard basketball shoes the boys wore. As a team, we looked more like the Bad News Bears than the Ottawa Hills Green Bears.

It was a good thing I liked my jersey because it was the only one I had my freshman and sophomore year. I wore it for basketball, volleyball, and softball, which meant that my mother was washing it nearly every night. High school girls' sports were such an afterthought in the 1970s that even the cheerleaders had better uniforms than we had. But I was so happy to be playing that I never even thought about what we didn't have.

There wasn't much to girls' high school athletics in those days. We played only a handful of games in most sports, and until my junior year, if there was a league, or standings, I certainly don't remember. I do remember that we were mediocre, about .500 in most sports. We kept a score book, but no one compiled our statistics until my junior year, except for whatever scores and point totals I wrote in my diary. While the boys had buses taking them to their games, either our mothers or older students drove us in cars to away games, because there were no buses for us. If there weren't enough drivers, our games were postponed.

There never was talk of being good enough to win a tournament or a state championship. That's because there were none for girls until basketball my senior year. What's more, few girls thought about playing in college. There were no scholarships for women as far as we knew.

As bad as things sounded, girls' sports were emerging enough so that within a few years of my graduation, there would be all of this for the girls in Ohio: tournaments, state titles, buses, uniforms, scholarships. But back then, girls' teams were relegated to club status, no better or worse than the drama club. Girls who played sports were members of the Girls' Athletic Association (GAA), which was like any other high school club. We had an active social calendar, and I threw myself into it, volunteering to run the father-daughter softball game in the spring of my freshman year. Later on, I became treasurer and president of the club.

The highlight of each year was the GAA spring canoe trip in Michigan. We paddled down the Rifle River, watched people fall overboard, and even got to spend the night at a lodge.

I was with all the teammates whom I liked and admired, all the people I looked up to my freshman year. But the canoe trip turned sour for me when a number of my teammates were caught drinking beer. To me, this was horrible. The perfect little sports world that existed in my imagination crumbled to pieces that weekend. The girls were suspended from school for one day, the father-daughter softball game I'd put together was canceled, and I was crushed. I had put my teammates on a pedestal, naively looking up to them as older versions of goody-two-shoes me. I was so disappointed in them, and in myself for believing in them. We all have our loss-of-innocence moments in life, and we all get over them. That day as a freshman in high school was one of mine.

Mom filled Dad in on the news before he came home from work that night. After dinner, Dad took me aside.

"You know," he said, "you're a good kid. A really good kid. And that means if you keep living your life this way, there always will be people who disappoint you."

I nodded. Dad put his big hands on my shoulders. We stood almost eye to eye.

"So you have two choices," he continued. "To let these kinds of things get to you every time, or to let them bounce off of you and keep moving. I'd suggest to always try to help those people who disappoint you, definitely take the good things you can learn from those people, and don't let the bad get you down. Okay?"

"Okay."

While my parents encouraged my interest in sports, they demanded I perform in class. That was no problem for me. I loved school.

As a freshman, I couldn't yet see down the road to what I would become, but I took a step in that direction when I walked into Richard Sanzenbacher's classroom my freshman year and discovered the magic that existed in the written word.

Mr. Sanzenbacher, then in his late twenties, with a shock of blond hair and piercing blue eyes, taught my honors English class. He was an eccentric. Often he sat facing us and ran the class from one of our wooden, one-piece desks. When we were studying *The Turn of the Screw,* he turned off the lights in the classroom to make it as dark as possible and lighted a candle on top of the small desk. Then he started reading to us. His quaint idea to read by candlelight was going well until the book caught on fire.

Mr. Sanzenbacher read aloud the disjointed poetry of Rod McKuen, whom he called "Rod McPuke-in," picking out especially bad parts that made us giggle. He danced around the room like Tina Turner, his favorite entertainer. When the movie *The Great Gatsby* opened in Toledo, he came to school one day dressed in a white suit, just as Robert Redford had worn in the film. He wore plaid suits and bow ties on other days.

One day as we were studying vocabulary words, he asked a boy to get out of his desk, lie on the floor, and slither around. "Get that shirt dirty," he shouted. None of us would ever forget the definition of the word *sullied.*

As luck would have it, Mr. Sanzenbacher was also the faculty adviser for the student newspaper, the *Arrowhead.* He taught a journalism class to juniors and oversaw the senior staff of the newspaper. Early in our freshman year, after absorbing just a few weeks of his mesmerizing act, my friend Shelley Wolson and I made a pact that we would be in that journalism class in two years and be on the staff of the paper in three years as seniors. I had my diaries and my newspapers and my baseball games on the radio, but no one had ever shown me how words and imagination could come together—and come to life—the way Mr. Sanzenbacher did.

Unfortunately, by the time we were juniors, Mr. Sanzenbacher was gone. His unorthodox approach to teaching was too controversial for some parents, so he left to become a college professor. Several of my friends and I mourned his departure, but he left an endearing legacy. With his inspiration, I went on to become coeditor of the *Arrowhead,* and Shelley became one of our top editors.

In the year we ran the high school paper, we decided to push the journalistic envelope whenever we could. We published an anonymous letter from a student attacking our new assistant principal. My coeditor, Kim Young, and I were immediately summoned to the office of principal Jim Casper, who demanded we name the author of the scathing letter. We sat in silence for a moment before I said, "Journalists don't reveal their sources." Where did I come up with this? It was the fall of 1975, and all of us budding journalists—even those of us who were Republican—were living in the glow of Watergate. Bob Woodward and Carl Bernstein were heroes to us. Their reporting had brought down a president.

I happened to mention Woodward and Bernstein to Mr. Casper. To his everlasting credit, he nodded and let us go.

That same autumn, amazing news fell into our laps. A thirty-seven-year-old Ottawa Hills graduate and his wife were charged with murdering his mother and grandmother in their home in our village. This was big news in Toledo, and bigger news for us. This kind of event never happened in tiny Ottawa Hills, population 4,270, where the school had only one hundred students in each graduating class.

In the school hallway the next day, a classmate who worked for the yearbook came toward me waving an old picture of the suspect pointing a rifle at a snow sculpture. I couldn't believe our good fortune. Of course, we published it—on the front page of the next issue.

Naturally, Kim and I wound up back in Mr. Casper's office. The suspect's attorney had called, demanding that Mr. Casper confiscate as many of the papers as possible. We surrendered some, but mostly, it was too late. Many of the copies had already gone out, I told Mr. Casper. He nodded. I think I saw him smile, just slightly.

This was not the last time we visited Mr. Casper's office. The greatest creative mind on our *Arrowhead* staff belonged to Mike Schwab, who later became a Toledo radio host. We gave Mike a column, and one week, he decided to rate the local television news. I urged him to be brutally honest, and he was, quoting from an industry report calling the local ABC affiliate, WDHO-Channel 24, "the worst television station in America."

We chuckled over Mike's line as we put that issue to bed.

When the paper came out, Mr. Casper received another phone call, this time from the station manager at Channel 24. We were summoned to the principal's office again. Mr. Casper looked at me. I looked at him.

"Freedom of the press," I pleaded.

"You're going to have to visit Channel Twenty-four," he replied.

Mr. Casper told us we had to take a tour of the station, meet its executives, and print a correction. Why? Channel 24 was maintaining it wasn't "the worst television station in America."

I couldn't believe a professional news organization cared this much about what was written in a little high school newspaper, but I was flattered. They were treating us like big shots.

We took the tour, met everyone, and then came back and mustered the best apology we could—one that managed mostly to exonerate us, and stick it to Channel 24 one more time, as only high school kids could.

Under the headline CLARIFICATION!, we wrote that the "worst station" comment referred "only to news and public affairs programming quality and not to overall station quality. . . . Inaccurate reporting is inexcusable; the ARROWHEAD offers its sincere apologies to TV-24 for committing such an error."

"That's a correction?" Dad said when he read it, laughing heartily. "You kids have called them lousy two times now."

If this was the way real journalism worked, I wanted to sign up immediately.

But most of my emotional energy was consumed by sports.

Sandy Osterman was the first woman I knew who made a career for herself in athletics. Her job description was to teach gym and coach the girls' teams—all of them in her first few years: field hockey, tennis, basketball, volleyball, softball, and track and field. Later on, other teachers started coaching tennis and a few other sports. But in those early years, Miss O received a total of $300 extra for her trouble, for the entire year.

Although she was in her mid- to late twenties, she could have passed for a mature-looking high school senior, and when she slapped the field hockey ball ferociously in practice and beat us in sprints, she fit right in. She even had her sandy blonde hair cut like we did, in a shag, and giggled with us when we talked about the single male teachers we wanted to fix her up with.

Miss O had been inspired by her high school gym teacher to go to Bowling Green State University in 1964 and study physical education. Before that, her career goal had been to become a secretary. She played six-woman basketball—in which three players from each team could play on only one half of the court—for BGSU in the mid-1960s. (We actually played that style of basketball in sixth-grade gym class before it was mercifully retired.) Even though Miss O's six-woman team represented Bowling Green and played other colleges, she never received a varsity letter.

When Miss O came to Ottawa Hills, she found similar inequalities. In academics, parents demanded the same opportunities for their daughters as they did for their sons. But not in sports. If equality was going to break out anywhere for girls in sports in the 1970s, it would have been in a progressive, educated place like Ottawa Hills. But it did not.

When Miss O first arrived, before I was in high school, she had to make numbers out of masking tape for her players' jerseys. Things didn't get much better during my playing days, or Kate's. During her senior year, Kate was on the field hockey team, but she wasn't given a team skirt to wear because they didn't have enough.

In basketball, every time our boys had a home game, we had to vacate our locker room so the visiting team could use it. The reverse never occurred. And we almost always got the worst practice times in the big gym: after the boys' varsity, the boys' JV, and even the boys' freshman team. Back then, I'm sure the rationale was that girls' sports were too new and unimportant to be treated equally with the boys'. I never even thought to ask why this was happening, which shows just how ingrained this was.

Everything was more difficult for us girls back then. Sometimes before field hockey games, Miss O and some of the members of the team had to race outside and put the white lines on the field. If the grass was too long to let the ball roll, Miss O would hop on the mower and cut it herself. She also had to schedule many of our games, line up referees, and take care of the team's medical needs. To do that, she fashioned a first-aid kit

On the high school field hockey team.

out of a shoe box. The boys' teams usually had a doctor at their games, sometimes a father of one of the players. We had a shoe box.

Our ritual after our home basketball games was also unequal, but not unpleasant. We invited the girls from the other team into the home economics room for milk and cookies. This was a tradition whether we won or lost. They often returned the favor when we played at their school. They don't do this at Ottawa Hills anymore; the social hour has been swallowed up by the necessary push for equality. It's competitive now in girls' sports; the stakes are higher and scholarships can hang in the balance. In that world, there is no room for milk and cookies, and while I'm all for what has happened in girls' sports, a part of me thinks that's too bad.

* * *

Milk and cookies were a perfect symbol for girls' sports back then, but things were definitely beginning to change. During the fall of my sophomore year, Billie Jean King, one of the very few female sports heroes I had, played tennis hustler and self-declared male chauvinist Bobby Riggs. Their "Battle of the Sexes" grudge match drew more than thirty thousand spectators in the Houston Astrodome and millions more watching on network TV. Miss O had us all worked up in the days leading to the match on September 20, 1973. In gym class and at our practices, if a boy came by, Miss O yelled out, "We know who's going to win the big match!" There were side bets worth all of a few dollars between Miss O and her male coaching counterparts. "We'll see who wins," she said with a mischievous laugh.

It was a carnival atmosphere that night as King, twenty-nine, and Riggs, fifty-five, came onto the court. Riggs, who had easily defeated Margaret Court a few months earlier, played the scene for all it was worth, and King played right along with him, even presenting him with a live pig wearing a large pink bow. She told me years later, when I got to know her, that she had been extremely nervous, that her hands had been shaking. But I never knew. On television, she looked calm and confident.

I finished my homework early to watch the match. Before it started, Dad and Mom pointed out the subtlety behind Riggs's bravado: while he was a blatant male chauvinist, they said he didn't seem to be a terrible guy. "He's acting bad, but in some ways, he's just playing along," Dad said. "He's the perfect opponent for Billie Jean. He makes you want her to win even more."

As it was, I already wanted her to win very badly. My first tennis dress looked like the kind King wore, sleeveless, with a zipper up the middle and a big striped collar. We took a small black-and-white TV set on vacation to northern Michigan every year so I could watch Wimbledon. King ruled women's tennis in the late 1960s and early 1970s with a demeanor on court that was a startling departure from that of the more demure women who preceded her. It was great to see a female athlete who was so aggressive.

There was no reason for any of us to worry that night. King routed Riggs, 6–4, 6–3, 6–3, throwing her wood racket into the air as we cheered in the family room. The next day, at our lockers in the high school hallway, I spotted Mike Kelley, one of the star boy athletes in my grade and a longtime rival and good friend.

"We won," I said to Mike. "The girls won."

"Yeah, I know," Mike said, grimacing and walking away.

Years later it became apparent what King's victory meant to girls like me. It was the first time I had ever seen a woman beat a man at anything.

In the many years since, a few men have told me they thought it was one of the more overhyped sports events of all time.

I always disagree.

"For you, maybe, but not for me."

I've talked to Billie Jean quite a few times in interviews, at dinners, at Wimbledon, even at a White House reception, where, nearly two decades into my career, she pulled me aside to get my thoughts on the women's sports movement. I smiled about that later: there was Billie Jean King asking me for my opinion on the topic that she pioneered and forever changed for the better.

No matter where we talk, I always make sure to thank her for what she did that night in Houston. It's surely overkill by now, but I can't help it.

"What you meant to a fifteen-year-old girl in Toledo, Ohio . . ." I tell her. I never complete the sentence. She knows.

Many link Billie Jean King's victory with the passage of Title IX fifteen months earlier in June 1972. The law contains just thirty-seven words: "No person in the United States shall, on the basis of sex, be excluded from participation in, be denied the benefits of, or be subjected to discrimination under any education program or activity receiving federal financial assistance."

While it applies to a wide range of education programs and activities, it has come to be known as the law that changed the playing fields of America by mandating that girls have the same opportunities in sports as boys.

King's victory personified Title IX for girls like me. A few months after the match, in my sophomore speech class, another girl and I debated the law with two boys, one of whom was Mike Kelley.

"Resolved, that high schools and colleges should allocate the same amount of money for the girls' athletic program as for the boys' in the United States."

The date on our brief was February 21, 1974. I wrote many of our arguments in favor of Title IX:

> If the opportunity exists, then interest will grow for girls.
>
> Girls need and deserve better coaching and equipment (like the boys get).
>
> In their respective sports, girls are just as competitive as boys and they deserve equal money (to pay) for these sports.
>
> Coaches of girls' teams should receive the same salary as the boys' coaches and if the boys' teams had assistant coaches, the girls' should too.
>
> Instead of taking money away from the good boys' programs to give to the girls', a gradual process could be put into effect annually to upgrade the female programs.
>
> Girls would eventually have equal facilities, equipment, rewards, and game times to produce more involvement and school spirit.
>
> With this involvement and spirit, the girls' sports programs would begin to financially sustain themselves.

In listing the benefits of our plan, we wrote:

> Women will become healthier.
>
> Female athletes will become well-rounded and will gain a sense of personal identity.
>
> The girls will bring more recognition to their

school by winning tournaments, being featured in newspapers and on the TV and radio, etc.

Girls will learn sportsmanship and will become more psychologically developed.

If more money was used to fund the girls, fewer girls would be "out in the streets," spending their time in the wrong way.

Rereading those arguments three decades later, I was surprised to see that many of them contain the same points, refined over the years, that I've used in columns for *USA Today*. We won the debate that day, but hardly against the greatest of adversaries. The boys didn't take the issue quite as seriously as we did. They quoted some experts whose names we were certain they had made up.

For all my interest in equality for girls and women in sports back then, Dad and I rarely talked about the issue. We never discussed what the boys' teams had and the girls' teams didn't; we never thought to bring it up, as surprising as it sounds now. I think that's because, where it mattered most, in our home, I felt equal.

Dad was a fan for all seasons. He came to almost all of my games, matches, and meets. If I didn't see him by the time one of my basketball games started, I knew exactly when he arrived. There wasn't much cheering at those games because almost no one was there. Our fans applauded politely, but there were no cheerleaders, so most of the noise in the gym came from our squeaky shoes on the floor, Miss O shouting instructions, and the occasional interruption of the referee's whistle. Therefore, the unmistakable click of the heels of Dad's black dress shoes gave him away every time he marched across the entryway to the gym.

Dad would stand on the opposite sideline, waiting for a timeout so he could walk around the outside of the court, under the basket, and sit in the bleachers just two or three rows behind our bench. From that spot, he would calmly urge us on. The man who screamed at Woody Hayes from fifty rows up spoke softly at our games. Sometimes Dad didn't say a thing. He would simply nod at me approvingly as I ran in, huffing and red-faced, for a time-out. I loved that he was there.

Dad watched me play more than basketball. I played all six girls' sports at Ottawa Hills because you didn't have to specialize back then. If it was the fall, he was on the sideline for a field hockey game or one of my tennis matches. In the spring, it was softball and track and field. One winter during volleyball season, after we came from behind on my serve to win a big match, I wrote in my diary, simply, "I played well for Dad."

My sophomore year, my parents bought me a green and white Ottawa Hills letter jacket. A few of us had been talking about getting one; many of the boys wore them, but none of the girl athletes did.

My teammate Carol White and I decided it was time for girls to start wearing them too, so she got one as well. Mom took mine to a seamstress to have the big *OH* patch sewn on. We picked it up right before leaving for Chicago on spring break, and I wore the jacket all that week. Among strangers, I was proud to wear it.

Back at home, Carol and I took the plunge and wore our jackets to school the week after vacation. A few of the girls from our teams said something nice about my jacket, looked it over, touched the sleeve. But most of the other kids simply stared. It made me feel self-conscious, and I didn't like that. I always stood out, but this time, I stood out too much. It wasn't like it is now in high school sports, where the homecoming queen also just might be the captain of the basketball team. Back then, you definitely were one or the other. You can take it from me, the captain of the basketball team.

Carol told me she didn't like how people stared either. It was one thing to play sports as a girl in the 1970s. It was quite another to call attention to that fact.

Carol said she wasn't going to wear her jacket anymore, that it just didn't feel right.

I too went home and put my letter jacket in the back of my closet.

I never took it out again.

* * *

Sports were my passion and my diversion. They also often were my social life because I never had a date in high school.

I was asked out only once. A boy from another high school whom I had met at a citywide school function my sophomore year called our house to ask me out, but I was so surprised that I got flustered and blurted out no before I had time to think about it. I then was so embarrassed by what I had done that I never told anyone about it.

Every time the homecoming dance came around, I hoped the phone might ring for me, but it never did. My junior year, I called David Hansen to see if he was doing anything the night of the dance. He was a senior at nearby Sylvania High School. He said he was free. So I asked him if he would join me—at the Toledo Rockets–Bowling Green football game at the Glass Bowl with Dad and Jim and his friends. He accepted. Sports had become my refuge, always there for me, even the night of the homecoming dance.

Most of my friends weren't dating or going to homecoming either, so I was never alone. Kate went to the homecoming dance from her sophomore year on, but never went out on other dates, so we spent very little time talking or worrying about boys in our house. I did wonder, however, what it would have been like to go on a date with David Cassidy from the TV series *The Partridge Family*. We did have similar hairstyles.

That was one of my rare schoolgirl dreams. Unlike many girls my age who were preoccupied with makeup and hairstyles, I never thought much about my looks. I focused on other things—grades, sports, getting into college. Faced with a daughter who wasn't running with the in crowd, Mom and Dad emphasized academic achievement, and I bought into it. What's more, while they were very active in charitable organizations in Toledo, Mom and Dad themselves were home many weekend nights. They told us they most enjoyed spending time with us, and we kids knew it was true.

In the age-old debate of substance versus style, my parents were not fence-sitters. They were all about what you did, not how you looked or who you dated.

Never going out on a date didn't bother me, except once. Ottawa Hills High School had a junior-senior prom, and my senior year, as the day drew near, it was clear no one was going to ask me. Kate, however, had been asked. As a junior, she was going, and I was truly excited for her. While we had our sisterly battles, we also had such different interests that we rarely competed.

On the Friday afternoon before the prom, the thought of not going to this final dance, of not going to any dances at all throughout high school, got to me, and I started to cry up in the bedroom Kate and I shared.

Soon, there were footsteps on the stairs. Kate had gone down and sent Mom up.

Mom sat beside me on my bed and put her arm around me. "I know this seems so important now, but this will be meaningless in your life."

I smiled through my tears. Mom reminded me that she had never had a date in high school either. "And everything turned out pretty well, didn't it?" I smiled and agreed that it had.

The next night, Kate's date picked her up at 7 P.M. I waved at the door as she left.

By 9 P.M., I was sitting in a movie theater with seven girlfriends who weren't asked out either. While the girls at the prom danced the night away, my friends and I watched the popular new movie about Watergate, *All the President's Men,* and I started dreaming about what it might be like to work at the *Washington Post.*

I played my last basketball game for the Ottawa Hills Green Bears on March 12, 1976. For that one day only, we were treated like the boys. We met at 4 P.M. at Ponderosa steak house for a team dinner. Then we took a bus, the first bus ever for an Ottawa Hills girls' game in any sport, for the hour drive to Defiance, Ohio, to play in the first Ohio Girls' Class-A Sectional Basketball Tournament.

When we arrived, our fans, including Mom, Kate, and Amy (Dad was out of town on business and couldn't change his plans), bought programs for 10 cents apiece. As we were practicing on the court, I noticed Kate waving to me. I ran over to her. She opened the program. On the page that listed our roster, there was the team nickname: Green Beans.

Green *Beans*?

I took the program to Miss O, who was standing on the court. She started to laugh. Soon, we all were laughing. The person typing the program obviously had misread Miss O's handwriting, thinking her *r* was an *n*.

"Go Green Beans!" Kate and a friend yelled throughout the game.

The Green Beans had about as much luck as the Green Bears. Our season ended at 4–5 with a 51–33 loss to Tinora, a school we had never played—never even heard of—until that day. I managed only nine points that evening. I remember coming out of the game at the end for the last time, the horn signaling a substitution, our fans cheering, and Miss O shaking my hand as I sat down hard on the bench. I wanted to be happy and soak up the scene, but that would have to wait. Frustration was all I felt, and Miss O knew it. She left me alone. We would celebrate another day.

I ended up leading the team in scoring that season with an average of 15.6 points per game. I was five-eleven-and-a-half by then, and 150 pounds, the biggest girl on the team. I played mostly on heart, not raw talent. Ottawa Hills would soon be pumping out dozens of girl athletes better than I was, but for my time, I wasn't bad. I was named the school's senior girl athlete of the year in 1976. My parents were thrilled, but they told me it made them prouder that I finished number two in my class—our salutatorian—and gave one of our two graduation speeches. I was nervous that night in the packed high school auditorium, but when I started my speech, a Bicentennial theme comparing a high school class of 1876 with the class of 1976, I glanced at Mom and Dad. When they nodded, nearly in unison, my spirits soared.

Even though I was playing sports as never before, I still carved out hours of my week to watch games on television, any kind of game, any chance I had.

I had two major preoccupations during high school: one old and one new. My passion for Michigan football grew during those years, though the results were not ultimately rewarding for one disheartening reason: Michigan could not beat Ohio State. Cheering for the Wolverines was not going to be like cheering for the Toledo Rockets from 1969–71, I was learning.

In 1973, Michigan and Ohio State were both undefeated heading into the big game, but it ended in a tie, 10–10. We were there that day, as we were most Saturdays for Michigan home games. Dad had started buying Michigan season tickets to go along with our Toledo season tickets; on some busy Saturdays, we actually fashioned unique "doubleheaders": Michigan games in the afternoon, Toledo games at night—six hours of live college football on the same glorious day.

After the tie in 1973, Michigan and Ohio State finished tied for the Big Ten title too, which meant the league's athletic directors had to vote to send one or the other to the Rose Bowl. The next day, the announcement of their decision came during the NFL games. I was watching TV when I heard the news: they voted to send the Buckeyes, despite the fact they had gone the year before. (The Big Ten's no-repeat rule had been abolished.) I dashed to Dad's den to deliver the crushing news. We stared at each other in silence.

The next year, we were heartbroken again when Michigan missed a late field goal in Columbus to lose, 12–10, as we watched on TV. Incredibly, the seniors on that team went 30–2–1 in their three eligible years and never went to a bowl game. After the third game of their sophomore season, they were never ranked lower than number six in the nation. This was one of the best teams in college football history never to go to a post-season game.

There was one more Michigan–Ohio State game before I went away to college, and one more loss. In 1975, in Ann Arbor, Michigan held the lead until two late touchdowns gave Ohio State a 21–14 victory. Jim and I sat on the 45-yard line—Dad got two great seats and gave them to us—while Dad and Kate used our season tickets in the end zone. Before the game, we had decided that instead of looking for one another in the stadium when the game ended, we would meet back at the car.

As Jim and I walked over the crest of a hill and spotted Dad and Kate, I burst into tears. I knew it was ridiculous for a seventeen-year-old high school senior to be so caught up in a football game that she couldn't hold back tears at the sight of her father, but if you were going to cry over something, Ohio State going to a fourth consecutive Rose Bowl was as good a reason as any. I buried my head in Dad's shoulder. He told me there would always be next year—"There will always be another kickoff"—but he admitted he too felt terrible.

I had recovered, mostly, by the time we walked in the door at home, only to find that there had been tears there as well. Mom had watched the game with Amy, then eight, and one of her best little friends. When it ended, both girls immediately started crying.

Oddly, Mom wasn't smiling when she saw me. She had a question:

"What have you done to them?"

My newfound passion was the Olympic Games. I barely remember watching the 1968 Games, but I fell hard for them in the winter of 1972. I loved the new sports, all those unusual events in ice and snow, but what fascinated me even more was how the Games dropped into my life for two weeks and then dropped out for four years. They were there every night, all evening, for sixteen days—and then they were gone. No other sporting event was like this. They played the Super Bowl again in fifty-two weeks. The World Series too.

But not this. This left for four years. *Four years?* It was hard for me, then just thirteen, to think one year ahead, much less four. It might as well have been a lifetime. How meaningful was a sporting event that came and went like this? How compelling were these athletes, training for four years, then appearing for just a few minutes of competition before leaving again, never overstaying their welcome? As I wrote in my diary in 1976, "The Olympics are the best, even better than UM-OSU in football." That was saying something.

I pulled out all the stops for the Olympics. In those days before VCRs, Jim and I made audiotapes of ABC's coverage. We kneeled next to the TV set and held our tape recorder close to catch the call of a big boxing match by Howard Cosell, or a swimming race by Keith Jackson and Donna de Varona. We then played the tape back over and over in the following days, just to relive the event. I saved the tapes in my desk. By then, I was saving everything related to the Olympics. I cut out and put in a file every wire story on the '72 and '76 Olympics, both winter and summer. I even kept my own medal count, updating it as I sat in front of the television.

Most of the Olympic events from Europe were tape-delayed, but sometimes I decided I couldn't wait until the evening telecast to find out what happened. The day Dorothy Hamill went for the figure-skating gold medal at the 1976 Games in Innsbruck, I did the math and figured we were six time zones behind Austria. I didn't have much patience to begin with, but what little I had was overwhelmed by the anticipation of this event. I wanted to know the result right away. So, starting at about 4 P.M. my time, I went up to my room, sat on my bed, and listened to Toledo's all-news radio station until a reporter at the skating venue, with music playing in the background, broke in to announce that Hamill had just won the gold.

I leaped off my bed in delight, making such a clatter that Kate, Jim, and Amy heard me from downstairs and came running to the bottom of the stairs.

"What happened?" they shouted up.

"Hamill won!"

They raced up to hear more details and dance around with me in celebration.

The Games that etched the Olympics into my soul, however, were the 1972 Summer Olympics in Munich. On September 5, the day before I began my freshman year of high school, we were on our way to buy school supplies when we heard the bulletin on the radio: Terrorists had sneaked into the Olympic Village. They had killed two members of the Israeli team. They were holding nine other Israelis hostage.

When we arrived home, I walked straight to the TV, turned it on, and sat on the couch in our family room. I didn't get up for hours. ABC's Jim McKay was describing the negotiations that were proceeding outside the Israeli dormitory in the Olympic Village at an address I would never forget: 31 Connollystrasse. The hostages were wrestlers, weight lifters, and coaches, blindfolded and bound to one another. Negotiations were ongoing. Terrorist deadlines were passing. I was amazed to be watching uninterrupted live coverage of a breaking story in West Germany from our family room. I felt pulled into this story as I had with no other news event in my life. I felt like McKay was talking directly to me.

As the day wore on, while everyone else played outside on the last day of summer vacation, I didn't move. I sat inside and watched the news from Munich. McKay talked about how ironic it was that the men who were being held at gunpoint inside the dorm rooms were big men with great muscles, unable to do anything to free themselves. As the names of the Israeli hostages trickled out, I heard that one was a twenty-eight-year-old American who had immigrated to Israel. His name was David Berger. He was from the Cleveland suburb of Shaker Heights. Mom was in the kitchen when this was announced. She walked into the family room to join me for a moment, shaking her head.

"Can you imagine what his parents are going through?" she said.

Just after 9 P.M. in Munich, 3 P.M. in Toledo, word came that the hostages were being taken by helicopter to a military airport outside Munich to be flown to an undisclosed location. Speculation centered on the Middle East. "This doesn't sound good," Mom said as she watched from the kitchen. My heart sank.

For hours, there was no definitive word on what was happening. At one point, around dinnertime, McKay said a report had come in saying the hostages were safe. He emphasized that the news was not confirmed.

After dinner, I went back to the TV. Kate, Jim, and Amy went to sleep early—it was a school night—but Mom and Dad let me stay up. It was nearly 10 P.M. in Toledo, nearly 4 A.M. the next day in Munich, when McKay interrupted a studio conversation with several of his colleagues to report the news that had just been relayed to him through his earpiece:

"When I was a kid, my father used to say our greatest hopes and our worst fears are seldom realized. Tonight our worst fears have been realized."

McKay took a deep breath. He looked like he was going to cry. Mom and Dad hurried into the family room to be near the TV set.

"Two [of the hostages] were killed in their rooms yesterday morning. Nine were killed at the airport tonight."

McKay shook his head.

"They're all gone."

I looked at Dad. He clenched his jaw and turned away.

"That poor family in Cleveland," Mom said softly.

I tossed and turned in bed that night, thinking of those eleven men who went to the Olympics because of their love for competition and now were heading home in coffins. I couldn't let go of the thought that night. In some ways, I never have.

5

"THIS AIN'T NO DRESS REHEARSAL"

It didn't matter how many sports I played. It didn't matter how many sports I watched. It didn't matter that I was the tomboy of the neighborhood. As I graduated from high school and left home for Northwestern University's Medill School of Journalism in 1976, I never seriously envisioned becoming a sportswriter. A journalist, absolutely. A political writer, most likely. But a sports writer? Did women do such things?

It sounds ridiculous now. But that is the power of role models, or in this case, a lack thereof. In 1976, I never knew women wrote about football, baseball, basketball—any sport really. I saw no hint of this in the Toledo or Detroit sports sections. I saw no women reporting sports regularly on TV except for Phyllis George, Miss America 1971. She was one of the stars on CBS's *The NFL Today*. It was an awe-inspiring role for a woman, but I never looked at George as a role model for me. Her career path was not going to be my career path. If you had to be Miss America to land on sports television, I knew I wasn't going to be on sports television. And if she was the only woman in all of sports media, as far as I knew, except for Olympic coverage every four years, then I wasn't going to be in the sports media.

Were there other women out there? It turned out that yes, there were. Some of the most esteemed pioneers of my future profession, the trail-blazing women who worked hard to open doors that I eventually walked through, were beginning their careers in Boston, New York, parts of the Midwest, and California. It was quite a lineup: Lesley Visser, Tracy Dodds, Julie Ward, Jane Gross, Robin Herman, Lawrie Mifflin, Jane Leavy, Betty Cuniberti, Mary Flannery, Diane K. Shah, and Melissa Ludtke, among others. Eventually, many of them would become friends and colleagues of mine. Another woman, the venerable Mary Garber, had been writing sports in Winston-Salem, North Carolina, since World War II, achieving a remarkable, unprecedented longevity and setting a high standard for us all. But in 1976, sitting in Toledo, Ohio, well before the Internet age, I had no way of knowing these women existed.

To me, sportswriting in the early to mid-'70s was (A) a man's world, and (B) a sloppy man's world. I say "sloppy" because the nation's most visible sportswriter was not a real sportswriter at all, but the fictional Oscar Madison in *The Odd Couple*. Madison, played by Jack Klugman in the TV sitcom, was a slob who couldn't find his telephone because it was buried under a pile of dirty clothes, but did once locate an old sandwich between the sheets on his bed. When you thought sportswriter, you pictured Oscar Madison. It should come as no surprise that the sports section was called the Toy Department of the newspaper.

I never actually walked up to Mom or Dad and uttered the words, "If that is sportswriting, count me out." There were no such momentous decisions, plus I enjoyed the show and often laughed out loud at Klugman's character.

But I felt certain that because I was heading to what I believed was the best journalism school in the land, I was going to become a serious reporter and writer—not the female Oscar Madison.

At the same time, Dad had uncorked a few new sayings, passing along two gems in particular. One was familiar: "To whom much is given, much is expected." The other was new to me: "This ain't no dress rehearsal." That one usually was followed by: "What are you waiting for? You don't get another chance at life."

I loved "This ain't no dress rehearsal" from the moment it first hit my ears in high school. If anything became my mantra for life, it was that saying from Dad. I extrapolated from it that I, his oldest child, should seek to embark on a significant, meaningful career that made a difference, not one filled with fun and games. I never asked Dad flat out, "Do you want me to become a sportswriter?" in large part because I wasn't thinking of becoming one myself. But if I had asked, I'm certain the answer would not have been yes.

On the other hand, I found myself dreaming—just a little, my mind wandering, almost a forbidden dream—about what it might be like to write about sports. On a tour of the *Blade* when I was in junior high, my heart raced as I walked through the bustling city room, with editors cradling telephones and reporters dashing between cluttered desks. When our guide pointed out the sports department, my head snapped to look. There it was. There, at those typewriters, were the men writing the words I would read the next day in the *Blade*. As our class moved slowly en masse along a hallway, I kept turning back to look. *Those writers at those typewriters—who were they?* My brain was quickly rifling through the writers' pictures I saw every day in the *Blade*. I was disappointed I didn't recognize any of them that day.

I took another kind of tour on our family's spring vacation to Missouri when I was in the eighth grade. We made a pilgrimage to Busch Memorial Stadium in St. Louis before the season started; it was cold and wet and we wore our winter jackets. We signed up for the tour, and when no one else came, we became the tour. I asked only one question: "Where's the press box?" Our guide said the press box usually wasn't on the tour, but Mom asked if it would be possible for me to see it—and off we went. As I leaned to look out of the press box window, I imagined the place entirely different: warm, sunny, full, a baseball game going on down below, and deadlines to be met up there, where I was standing.

If I had been able to see that a sportswriter could be a woman, I would have thought differently as I went off to college in the fall of 1976. But such was the nature of the time I grew up that a young woman as infatuated with sports and writing as I was did not even think seriously of putting the two together. If I, at eighteen, a sports nut and newspaper junkie, still did not think of sportswriting as a career choice as I was heading off to college, something must have been very wrong. I obviously was missing a female role model to show me the way. So, when I became older and thought back to these days, I vowed to do my best to become the role model that I never had.

But first things first. I had to find the front door to the *Daily Northwestern.*

I had been an emotional wreck getting ready to go to college that fall. I was very sad to be leaving home, but I also knew it was time to go, that I had to get to a bigger place.

Northwestern was that place. From the moment early on in high school that I found out about its prestigious journalism school, I was hooked. A Big Ten school, with Big Ten football? But a private school, with just sixty-five hundred undergraduate students? And in Evanston, Illinois, near Chicago, Mom's and Dad's hometown?

Every time I looked in a college directory and read more about it, I was more certain. I told Mom and Dad I was going to apply early decision, with no back-up school in mind.

"Are you sure?" they asked.

I was sure.

On a mid-September day in 1976, after a four-hour drive, Dad and I carried my possessions into my dorm room, a single room in a co-ed dorm full of singles. Then Dad took out a yellow legal notepad. Every time we spoke with another student, he wrote down his or her name, where they were from, and what room they were in. He left the notepad with me, with the date on it, of course: 9/18/76.

I fell in love with college instantly. I had never met so many people like me, and that was just in the hallway of my dorm that first night. I never felt homesick, not for a second. It turned out I was completely prepared for life on my own.

In my first days on campus, I walked into an open house at the *Daily* and asked to be pointed toward the sports department. I was stunned to see that the sports editor was a woman, Helene Elliott, a senior who gave me my first assignment as a sportswriter: intramural powder-puff football. So women did write and edit sports, I thought. I watched a few women's flag football games on the blustery fields beside Lake Michigan and wrote a short story, just a few hundred words. It wasn't very good. It never ran in the paper. I never asked why.

Helene not only was editing the *Daily*'s sports section, she also was writing part-time for the sports section of the *Chicago Sun-Times*. Her byline was the first female sports byline I had ever read. She graduated early and went to the *Sun-Times* as a sportswriter, later moving on to the *Los Angeles Times,* where our paths would often cross covering events. *People* magazine wrote a feature on Helene my sophomore year. I read it and kept it in a file. Helene later told me her guidance counselor at her high school in Brooklyn told her that women couldn't be sportswriters. Now she was showing me women could.

But the weighty issue of "to be a sportswriter or not to be" would have to wait for another day because I was distracted by other developments that fall. I decided that I wasn't going to go back to the *Daily* the rest of the quarter, and not because my first story bit the dust. I had a far more immediate concern: four demanding classes my freshman-year fall quarter, including a very difficult calculus class I had no business taking but stuck with nonetheless. I was heading for a C, I hoped, in that class. I called home and asked Dad what I should do.

"Study harder."

There would be no sympathy from Dad. Mom commiserated with me until Dad had had enough.

"Honey, you're at Northwestern. It's a tough school. You're a tough kid. You can handle it. Now let's get off the phone so you can get back to studying."

I did struggle home with a C and an ugly 2.75 grade-point average that first quarter. That led to another conversation with Dad.

"If you don't have at least a 3.0 after your freshman year, I'm not sure why you would be going back to Northwestern for your sophomore year."

"What?"

"You heard what I said. You're a better student than that, and if you can't do better this quarter, perhaps we're going to realize that Northwestern isn't the school for you."

I was furious with my father. Didn't he know how tough this was, getting used to college, being a freshman, taking difficult classes?

He didn't want to hear about it. Mom cheerily changed the subject.

But Dad knew exactly what he was doing. He scared me— and it worked. I buckled down. I spent more time in the library. I studied harder. Winter quarter, I received a 4.0.

My first journalism class was one of the four courses I took during that winter quarter of 1977. The class was called Basic Writing, and I was so nervous I almost threw up the first day. We were under enormous pressure for three hours every week. One day, we had to leave the classroom, find a feature story, report it, write it on a manual typewriter, and finish by the time the class ended. I dashed to the student center—something had to be going on there—and interviewed participants in Black Students' Career Day. Other days we interviewed the professor, wrote profiles on ourselves, and covered real live news, such as the el train crash that winter in Chicago's Loop. I loved the variety and added to it by making a brief foray into the Olympic world for one of my assignments: interviewing Northwestern professor Dennis Brutus, who had been an outspoken advocate of a boycott by African nations at the 1976 Montreal Olympics. I had read about him the previous summer in *Sports Illustrated*. When he and I spoke, we discussed civil rights and international politics, not split times in the 1,500 meters. Writing about the Olympics was so meaningful that it almost didn't count as sports, I thought.

This class was my introduction to an omnipresent rule at Northwestern's journalism school: if you misspelled anyone's name, you received an immediate *F*. Being my father's daughter, the "Medill *F*" remains to this day one of my favorite rules in journalism. It's such a simple reminder to get it right, a reverence for the facts that explains why many of us in journalism double-check, then triple-check, every column or story we write. It has been so ingrained in me that to this day, I sometimes open my computer at midnight to check once again. It's a cliché, but it's true: you're only as good as your last story. I believed it as a college freshman. I believe it today.

But there were other good reasons to try to be on top of my game as I started out at Northwestern. There was the challenge of keeping up with my peers, freshman year classmates who stood out then, and still do now.

I quickly became friends with a student from Bethlehem, Pennsylvania. I called him the Star of Bethlehem. He would later become a star of the *New York Times* national staff: Dean E. Murphy. My classmates also included three future sportswriters. One was a budding golf writer and editor named Peter McCleery, who would go on to work for *Golf Digest*. Another was from Ohio: Alan Abrahamson, who eventually would be headed to the *Los Angeles Times* to cover the Olympic beat. And another kid, a Chicagoan with a full Afro, was especially kind, soft-spoken, and friendly. That was Michael Wilbon, who would become the most famous of us all, from the *Washington Post* and ESPN's *Pardon the Interruption*.

There was a certain irony in the fact that we were on our way to becoming sports journalists by studying at a school that was known mostly for losing football games. I trooped to the first home game of our freshman year with friends from my dorm. The Wildcats (some called us the Mildcats) lost, 48–0, to Notre Dame. We went 1–10 that season. When we managed to get a first down during a lopsided game, we pumped our fists and chanted, "Rose Bowl! Rose Bowl!"

The next season, Northwestern again went 1–10. In our junior year, the highlight of the season was a 0–0 tie with Illinois. Then we lost ten consecutive games.

I witnessed one Northwestern victory in four years. My senior year, we beat Wyoming, 27–22. We danced on the field and cheered as other students tore down the goalposts. Could one afternoon of joy outweigh four years of angst? That day, I certainly thought so.

There were other losing teams in our midst. The Chicago Cubs, who had their own sad history, were just a forty-five-minute ride away on the el. In the spring of my freshman year, I went to a game at Wrigley Field with Rick Wamre, a classmate and fellow baseball fan. I pulled out a pencil and started to keep score of the game. "Where did you learn to do *that*?" he asked.

Going to those sports events represented nothing more than a delightful distraction for me and most of my peers. I never set foot in the press box at Northwestern's football stadium during my college days. In fact, the first time I walked into the press box was in 2000, during my twenty-year class reunion.

I also never took a sportswriting class in my four years of undergraduate study and one year in the master's program, for one very simple reason. There wasn't one. That was fine with me. I didn't need to learn about sports. I needed to learn about journalism.

After getting my grades in order, I walked back to the office of the *Daily Northwestern* spring quarter of my freshman year, spurred on by a good friend from the Chi Omega sorority I had recently joined. Christine Spolar, a sophomore from Pittsburgh, was already an assistant editor at the paper. Chris encouraged me to try her Off-Campus News Bureau, which covered city news, because of my interest in politics. That seemed as good a reason as any not to walk back into the sports department. Helene Elliott was already gone to the *Sun-Times* and a male student was the sports editor. But that wasn't why I didn't try sports again. I simply had a friend pushing me in another direction. I told Chris I was nervous. "So was I," she said sternly. "Now get in there."

My first day, I was given two printouts of UPI wire stories to rewrite for the *Daily*'s news digest. I handled four the next day. Four days later, I was planning and writing the entire thing. A week later, I had my first byline on a news story, on health-care costs. This was the lead: "Health-care costs in north suburban hospitals vary by as much as 420 percent, according to a survey released this week by 10th District Rep. Abner J. Mikva."

Included in the story were comparisons of the prices of appendectomies, hernia operations, and tonsillectomies.

The next day, Dean Murphy and I were sent out to survey the prices at grocery stores. A menial assignment, perhaps, but we were excited.

We shared a byline on this hard-hitting piece of journalism on April 15, 1977:

> There is nothing pleasant about the sound of a ringing cash register, especially if you are a penny-pinching Northwestern student.
>
> This third in a series of *Daily Northwestern* consumer surveys reveals what most NU food shoppers already know—food is expensive. . . .

The next day I bought a three-ring notebook to start saving my articles. "Clips" they were called, and they were the key to getting jobs, I had been told. So I began accumulating as many as I could.

Five weeks after I walked through the door at the *Daily*, I was made a senior reporter. I even was paid for my efforts, a whopping $25 a month. But my time there wasn't about earning money. I adored the excitement of not knowing what was in store for me when I walked through the door every day. I soon was spending hours there, most afternoons, and some evenings. Even when I finished writing, I stayed. I loved the energy in that little newsroom.

I also enjoyed reaching for the stack of newspapers in the lobby of my dorm every morning, especially when I had a story running. Writing for a newspaper was the greatest form of instant gratification I'd ever experienced. Something that had not existed the day before, a story I had typed from a manual typewriter on paper, which then was literally cut and pasted together in the pencil-and-paper editing process, was now published in a newspaper. There was no waiting. There was no wondering if what you were doing mattered. You worked on the story one day; you were holding it in your hands the next. This, I believed with all my heart, was the kind of substantial work Dad was referring to when he told me our lives were not a dress rehearsal.

I was learning about more than journalism in my first year at Northwestern. Mom and Dad had said that as soon as I left Ottawa Hills, the world would open up to me in ways I never could imagine. They didn't mention boys, but I think that's one of the things they were talking about.

Barely forty-eight hours after arriving on campus, I was dancing with boys—it seemed strange to call them men—at a series of freshman parties. They all were as tall as I was, or taller. This was a revelation.

I had the first date of my life the next weekend. I met him in that calculus class, proving there was something good about that subject after all. When he called my room to ask me out, I said yes, almost as if I was expecting him to call, almost as if I knew this would happen.

Within a month, I was invited by a different guy to a fraternity's dinner-boat cruise on Lake Geneva, Wisconsin, where the drinking age was eighteen. I asked my parents over the phone what kind of mixed drink I should order since I never had had one before.

They suggested a Tom Collins. "It's sweet," Mom said. "You'll like it."

I did. I had two.

I had thought I'd never join a sorority, but then I met girls—

women—who said they sat around their sorority house in sweat-pants and watched college football games and the World Series. I wanted proof of this; everything I had heard about sororities led me to believe this couldn't possibly be true. But then I saw it with my own eyes: a group of women gathered around the TV at Chi Omega for a Saturday Big Ten game. During sorority rush, when they asked me to join, I did, gladly, and I soon took over Chi O's sports programs, leading teams in everything from basketball to softball, flag football to floor hockey. I chose not to try out for any of Northwestern's varsity teams, which were some of the best in the Big Ten. Intramurals were just fine with me.

Football with my friends at Northwestern.

Before our fall formal that year, Dad flew in for a day—it was a forty-five-minute flight from Toledo—to take me shopping for my dress. Mom was too busy with three kids at home to get away. We called her to tell her what we found. "I love the thought of you two shopping!" she howled.

My date should have gone shopping as well.

He wore a brown leisure suit.

* * *

In the spring of my freshman year, I began looking for jobs in journalism in Toledo for the summer, but found none, so I became a summer replacement bank teller, moving from branch to branch as needed. Dad always asked where I was going to be each day, and, at least once a week, he came into that branch and wrote a check that apparently could be cashed only at my window.

One day, I filled in for a teller at a branch in a northern section of town called Point Place. There, I came upon a saying she had tacked into her teller's cage: "What you do today is important because you are exchanging a day of your life for it."

I couldn't take my eyes off that phrase. I had never been one to waste a day; nonetheless, from that moment on, I vowed to fill up every page of my diary. I was a busy girl already, but I decided I needed to get busier, to do more, to make a difference with each day, if I could. It all made sense. The first syllable of the word *journalism*, after all, meant "day" in French.

That same summer, I wrote a letter to *Sports Illustrated* in response to a July story titled "Chi, Oh My," about the division-leading Chicago White Sox and Cubs. (That didn't last.) As I read the article, I thought about the World Series, and the rotation of home and away, day and night games that was to occur for the 1977 Series.

Less than two weeks later, Jim called me at the bank with some news: "Your letter's in *Sports Illustrated*!"

They had edited out my first paragraph but the point remained intact:

Sir:

   You failed to mention one important fact about an intracity World Series. This year the three National League Series games are scheduled to be night games. But if the Cubs win the pennant, those games will have to be played in the afternoon, as Wrigley Field has no lights.

   If, as some say, part of baseball's problem is its submission to television's commercialism, then the Cubs will have pulled the greatest upset of all.

                                        Christine Brennan
                                        Toledo

In my diary that day, August 5, 1977, I wrote: "They cut it a little but I did it. I'm very proud to be in *Sports Illustrated*!"

In less than a month, I found myself sending a second letter to the magazine. I read the college football preview issue and was surprised to see that in the Big Ten report, nine teams were mentioned, but not Northwestern. I knew we were lousy, but weren't we worth a sentence? A phrase? Buoyed by my recent publishing success, I pulled out my electric typewriter and wrote once again to *SI*.

Two weeks later, Jim called me again:

"It's in!"

Sir:

I expected to see Northwestern mentioned in the Big Ten report in six words or less. (Something like "The Wildcats will finish last again.") However, those words were nowhere to be found. You excluded Northwestern and reported on only nine of the Big Ten schools.

You have forgotten the team that holds up the entire league. You have forgotten the brains (surely not the brawn) of the Big Ten. You have forgotten the last school other than Ohio State or Michigan to finish second in the conference since 1967. NU did it in 1971.

Christine Brennan
Toledo

They edited my letter a little again, but that was fine with me. I was ecstatic. As I wrote in my diary, "I'm 2 for 2."

The next summer, 1978, after my sophomore year, I found a job in journalism. I was hired by the *Blade* to be a city-desk intern. I wrote a lot of obituaries in those three months. No matter how short they were, no matter how ordinary the person's life, I have never been more serious about a task. I knew it probably would be the last story ever written about the person, so it had to be perfect. The pressure was on: the "Medill *F*" times ten. I checked my facts, rechecked them, then checked the story a third time. It certainly brought home the old journalism adage: "It's my story, but it's their life." I wanted to be respectful and understanding of the people on the other end of the phone, and I learned that people really do want to talk to reporters, even at times like that. I enjoyed writing the obits. There was nothing morbid about them. As he opened the *Blade* each night, Dad, the obit reader, asked me which ones I had written so he could read those first.

I soon was sprung from the obit desk to write my first full-length story for the *Blade,* the first professional byline of my career. I was assigned to interview a thirty-year veteran mail carrier, a fellow named Don Busdieker, as he went through the final day on his route before he retired. I went door-to-door with him all morning, taking notes as he said his good-byes and people told their favorite stories about their longtime mailman.

My story appeared June 26, 1978, prominently displayed in the local news section. Mom and Dad were as excited as I was when the paper arrived. Dad bought a few extra copies and some of their friends even came by and dropped off their copy of the section.

Dad took me aside that night. "This is a great start to your career. Why don't you have the article mounted on a piece of cardboard, signed by you, and give that to Mr. Busdieker? That way, when you're a famous journalist, he'll be very proud to have such a special copy of your first professional article."

A famous journalist? I thought Dad was being silly. Instead, I simply sent Mr. Busdieker a handwritten thank-you note along with another copy of the article.

The bylines picked up. I covered a mushroom foray, an expedition by about forty members of the Ohio Mushroom Society into the woods of northwestern Ohio. "A lot of people think it's a lot of foolishness," the foray chairman told me. I didn't. The story made the front page of the Sunday *Blade.* I reported on the strike of migrant laborers against the tomato growers in the area. I wrote about an Alcoholics Anonymous conference, the benefits of a mosquito-eating fish, a day in the life of a suburban barbershop, and county fairs in Bowling Green, Ohio, and Monroe, Michigan.

The variety extended to sports only once that summer. I covered the national Quarter Midgets of America auto races and interviewed one twelve-year-old participant from San Francisco. The kid's name was Jimmy Vasser. "It's serious. It's not a game," Jimmy said. By dumb luck, I picked the right kid to interview; Vasser would grow up to become one of the nation's top Indy car drivers.

I was being pulled in two directions within journalism at that time, not that I minded. There was my interest in sports, and then there was general news. "I feel like a *real* reporter," I wrote in a letter home while covering the early developments in the 1978 U.S. Congressional race in the district that included Northwestern for the *Daily.*

There was one very good reason why politics so interested me. Dad had become the Republican party chair of Lucas County, and as the 1980 presidential race heated up, candidates started making their way to Ohio, some of them even to our house. Dad brought Illinois Congressman Phil Crane, who happened to go to the same high school at the same time as Mom, in for dinner one summer evening in 1978. Most people would be thrilled to have a presidential candidate in their home. I cared far more about who was accompanying him: *Chicago Tribune* reporter Jack Fuller, who years later would become the paper's publisher.

As soon as they came through the door of our house, Dad introduced me as a journalism student at Northwestern, which was where Fuller had gone to school, and I asked if he would have a few moments to talk to me while he took notes on Crane's visit. A few moments? He spent more time talking with me than he did jotting down notes for his story. Not surprisingly, he still came up with a solid front-page piece.

At the time, I was entertaining the dream of becoming a political reporter, of following politics the way Fuller was that evening at our home. I had no idea how this could happen to me, how I could ever get that kind of a job. Sports journalism was about to enter my life in a big way, but political journalism was always there, lurking. That summer in Toledo, then, for that one night, I couldn't believe my good fortune.

Back and forth I went that summer. In the *Blade* newsroom, I wrote my news briefs and obits by the handfuls. Yet almost every day I was in the office, I made a pass through the sports department to talk with the sportswriters I read all the time: Dave Woolford, Dave Hackenberg, John Bergener. I spent so much time hanging out with them that they finally asked, "Why don't you go for a sports internship next summer?" I shrugged. Sure, I thought, why not?

That was the momentous way I officially became a sportswriter. A kind, soft-spoken *Blade* executive named William Day ran the internship program, so, near the end of the summer, I wandered by his office and mentioned it to him. Within a few months, Mr. Day was writing me at Northwestern to offer the paper's sports internship for the summer of 1979. I called and took the job. "You'll be our first full-time woman sportswriter," he told me.

I called Dad at his office to tell him. I felt confident he would be thrilled, and he was. Whether it was as substantial as politics or not, he knew I wanted to give sports a try, and he was entirely supportive of that effort.

Before that job, though, I had another internship. Dad drove with me to Lexington, Kentucky, to get me settled in as a general assignment reporter for the city and state desks of the *Lexington Herald* as part of Northwestern's Teaching Newspaper Program in the fall of 1978. One of my first stories was covering the visit of Lady Bird Johnson to the University of Kentucky. Another day, I drove to Appalachia and wrote about women mine workers. Even in such a bleak place, I was thrilled to be out of the office, on assignment, gathering quotes, then reporting back to the paper.

But just like at the *Blade,* I felt the tug of the sports department and soon was volunteering all my free time, at nights and on weekends, to cover sports. The characters in the sports department were larger than life—not Oscar Madison, but almost—and always seemed to be having a good time. I pushed away my feelings about games and scores all being so inconsequential and just started to smile at their jokes, their pranks, their childlike humor. I asked if I could go to University of Kentucky football games, and soon I was running quotes and sending pages of the sportswriters' copy via telecopier back to the newsroom. I did this as my excuse to see what was going on inside the press box. Being in the sports department was like being a little kid again. I felt like I was home.

My education as a sportswriter continued the next summer back at the *Blade.* Toledo turned into the center of the sports universe the week that Inverness Club hosted the 1979 U.S. Open golf tournament. I wasn't assigned there, but my editors lent me a press pass for one day so I could peek at the course and into the press tent. Such a simple thing, but something I really wanted to do. It was mostly empty when I stepped inside. I walked each row slowly, looking at the cards with the names of the writers at their seats, legends such as Dan Jenkins of *Sports Illustrated,* Thomas Boswell of the *Washington Post,* and Dave Anderson of the *New York Times.* I was hoping I might bump into one of them, but I was content just to see where they sat.

The *Blade* kept me busy covering local golf tournaments, the Glass City Marathon, the NASCAR event at Michigan International Speedway, and the Toledo Mud Hens. My heroes from the late 1960s were long gone, but I was thrilled to be in the tiny press box at the Lucas County Recreation Center, covering one of my girlhood teams.

I also worked nights writing headlines and editing wire copy. I would stay late, whatever it took to get the job done. But even then, even as I was in the office well past midnight, I was entranced by the work. Only it *wasn't* work. No matter what the assignment, I realized I was getting paid to do what most people pay to do—go to sporting events. I enjoyed this, and Dad did too. He told me he got a kick out of reading my stories in the sports section, which, after the obituaries and the comics, was his favorite part of the paper.

This all was part of my journalism education, part classroom, mostly real life. I realized I wasn't the most talented kid in my class back at Northwestern, not the most gifted writer, not the best-read. But I made sure to be one of the best-prepared. I was quick on my feet and loved flying by the seat of my pants when something out of the ordinary happened. I was willing to work as hard or harder than anyone else. In journalism, I already had learned that was crucial. It was all about digging a little further, thinking a bit differently, taking a different path than your competition, and having the stick-to-it-tiveness to make ten phone calls when one or two might suffice. "If your mother says she loves you," several professors said, "check it out."

As the years went by in college, I was caring more about my looks, not that by female standards I was really *caring* about how I looked. I was beginning to wear minimal makeup—blush, lipstick, eyeliner—and I even bought clip-on earrings for special occasions.

I still was a goody-two-shoes, almost laughably so. I'd have a beer or a mixed drink at formals and fraternity parties, but I never smoked a cigarette and never touched marijuana. There was no way on earth I was going to try that. The thought of disappointing Mom and Dad was deterrent enough if I had been intrigued, which I wasn't.

I started having plenty of dates. Sometimes too many. One night, I went out with a fraternity boy for an early dinner, then was back at the sorority house by 8 P.M. As I was studying, the phone rang. It was another guy from a different fraternity asking if I wanted to go to one of the local hangouts. I said sure, and he came to get me at 10:30. We were having a nice time when I looked across the room and saw my first date of the evening. Unlike me, he did not have a second date. I smiled a faint smile, waved, and shrugged. That was a short relationship.

Early in my senior year, I met a gorgeous freshman named Thad—we called him "Thad the Lad." I went out with Thad the Lad a few times. He met some of my Chi Omega friends and spent some time over at the sorority house.

One evening, the house phone rang. It was Thad the Lad calling for me.

"I just wanted to let you know that I went to the doctor and I might have mono," he said. "I'm not sure yet, but I wanted you to know it's possible, and it might affect you since we . . . you know . . . kissed those few times."

I wasn't too rattled. We hadn't kissed that much. I wished him a speedy recovery.

"Thanks," he replied. "Now, could you put Sherry on the phone?"

Sherry Krsticevic was one of my best friends in the sorority house.

"What?"

"Well, yeah, I kissed Sherry too."

I really didn't want that much information.

"I'm not going to find Sherry to give her the phone," I replied sternly. "Call back and ask for her."

As the phone rang and I heard Sherry being paged, then the phone rang again and I heard another woman being paged, I smiled. Thad the Lad clearly was a popular guy in the sorority.

One of the big social surprises for me, the ugly duckling just a few years earlier, was becoming a member of the homecoming court at Northwestern my senior year. I was nominated, the campus voted, and I made the top five. It seemed absurd to me that I was waving from the top of a float in the homecoming parade. But when the pictures appeared in the *Daily*, I wrote in my diary: "I think I really looked pretty. Amazing." It had to be the first time I ever used the word to describe myself.

Amy, Dad, and Mom join me in the
Northwestern stands for homecoming in 1979.

My days as homecoming royalty definitely were over when I took the field by Lake Michigan for Chi Omega's flag football game against Delta Zeta the next afternoon. I was our quarterback, but during practice, my passes were off. Sherry Krsticevic was one of our "linemen." She grabbed me by the shoulders and shook me.

"Listen, your days of being feminine are over! You have to play like a man!"

We still lost, 12–6.

My senior year, there were U.S. hostages in Iran and Soviets in Afghanistan, which led to President Jimmy Carter calling for draft registration and the U.S. boycott of the 1980 Moscow Summer Olympics. At the *Daily,* where I was managing editor, we surveyed the campus on the prospect of an Olympic boycott and a war in the Middle East. Eighty-two percent of the students said the United States should not boycott the Games, and 68 percent believed the events in Iran and Afghanistan could lead to war. If there was a draft, 46 percent of men and 67 percent of women said they wouldn't go.

Soon, Northwestern was becoming a national sounding board on the issue. Reporters were calling the *Daily* and asking to speak to some of us. The *Wall Street Journal* was one of the publications that phoned, and on January 31, 1980, I was one of several students featured in a front-page article.

"We've all had it pretty easy," I said. "[A return to the draft isn't anything anyone wants], but it seems to be the only alternative we have to show the Soviets that we will protect our interests and fight for what we believe. I don't want to go to war, but we have to back President Carter. In a democracy, you have to go with what the elected leader of that democracy believes."

Dad, a subscriber to the *Journal* since the early 1950s, bought four extra copies that day.

Less than two weeks later, an editor at the *Chicago Tribune* called and asked me to write an op-ed piece for the Feburary 11, 1980, Perspective section. I defended the right to resume the draft.

A Northwestern professor drew an interesting anal-
ogy about the events in Iran and Afghanistan. "The
crisis in the Middle East," he told me, "is your generation's Pearl Harbor. The public outrage expressed at
these events is like that of 1941. . . ."

We have lived in luxury, based on a predominantly
stable world, since our early teen-age years. Viet
Nam is but a memory tinted with thoughts of braces
and first dates. The Cuban missile crisis occurred
before many of us entered school. My generation has
had, for the most part, a lifetime in a bubble, with
thoughts of college, careers, and money always fore-
most in our minds. Our sacrifices, on the whole, have
been small and insignificant, not deeply personal or
long-term. . . .

Many of my fellow students fear registration and
the draft. They fear losing their families, friends,
careers, and lives. I'm afraid of war; a lot of people
are. But if the world situation continues to follow its
present course and if the USSR continues to trample
the rights of our friends across the world, we cannot
sit idly by and watch as we would watch a football
game. We have to be ready to blunt the Russian
sword. . . .

This was the first time I had ever carved out an unpopular position in print. I wasn't a columnist for the *Daily*. I had never
given my opinion in public forums such as these, and certainly
not with such a wide audience. I was a Republican, and out of
step with almost all of my friends. But they always tolerated me,
joking that everyone needed one token Republican friend.

But now I was putting my opinions out there for more people
to see, opening myself to criticism in all kinds of new ways, from
people I knew and from people I didn't know. To my surprise, I
found that I rather liked it.

* * *

The only Olympic Games held while I was at Northwestern, the 1980 Winter Games in Lake Placid, New York, were inextricably linked with Carter's decision on the Summer Olympics. The friction that always occurred between the United States and Soviet Union only seemed heightened that winter. If it was possible, we despised each other even more.

The U.S. hockey team had become the darlings of the Games and was heading for a showdown with the Soviets in the medal round on the afternoon of Friday, February 22, 1980. It was a grand mismatch; the popular comparison at the time was that it was like a high school football team taking on the Super Bowl champion Pittsburgh Steelers. The Americans had been trounced by the Soviets, 10–3, in an exhibition three days before the Games began. As U.S. coach Herb Brooks told his team, "You don't have enough talent to win on talent alone."

The game would be shown on ABC on tape delay Friday night. Most people were willing to wait. Of course I wasn't.

I went to my room on the fourth floor of the sorority house, turned on my clock radio, and started fiddling with the dial. Miraculously, I found the game on a Minneapolis radio station. It faded in and out; every time I lost it, I jiggled the antenna, held my breath, and gently turned the dial until I found the broadcast again. I couldn't believe my ears when the first period ended, 2–2. *We're tied with the Soviets?* I started pacing around my bedroom.

I had trouble with the signal most of the second period, but did catch the score at the end of the period: 3–2, Soviets. *Oh no. Here they come.* I had the feeling that they would pour it on in the third period.

Then I completely lost the signal. I fiddled with the radio frantically, to no avail. I pointed the antenna toward the window. Still nothing.

When I figured the game was over, I dashed downstairs to the TV room. The set was off. One of my sorority sisters was sitting on the couch, knitting. I told her I was dying to find out who won the game, so I turned on the local news and sat on the edge of my seat when the sportscast came on.

The announcer said he was going to give the score of the U.S.–Soviet game. But first, he asked viewers to turn down the volume on their TV sets and look away if they wanted to wait until the taped broadcast to find out what happened. Of course I did neither.

"Great news!" he said. He gave the score: the U.S. 4, the Soviet Union 3.

My mouth fell open. I looked at my sorority sister, who had glanced up, but only for a second, so as not to miss a stitch.

"Did I hear that correctly?" I gasped. "We won?"

"Yes, that's what he said."

She kept knitting. I leaped into the living room: "We beat the Soviets!"

That night, I missed half of ABC's broadcast of the game for a friend's violin recital. But I made it back to Chi Omega for the final ten minutes. Knowing the result made those last few minutes seem far less frantic, but no less exhilarating. Over the din, I heard the now immortal call of ABC's Al Michaels: "Do you believe in miracles? Yesss!"

Not wanting the evening to end, a group of friends and I piled onto the el and ended up hopping from club to club on Chicago's Lincoln Avenue. We celebrated as the rest of the country did that night. The chant that had been initiated in the rink in Lake Placid rang out on street corners across the nation. We shouted it as we danced in the streets till 4 A.M. "U-S-A! U-S-A!"

"Beautiful," I wrote in my diary. "Twenty of my peers set the country, and the world, on its ear. It was better than winning a war."

6

WELCOME TO THE
LOCKER ROOM

All week long at the *Miami Herald,* there had been a tremendous buildup to the big event. There had been meetings, phone calls, and more meetings.

The occasion?

I was to go into my first men's locker room that Saturday night.

The Miami Dolphins were playing the Minnesota Vikings in a 1980 preseason football game at the Orange Bowl. I was a summer intern at the *Herald,* between my undergraduate and master's years at Northwestern, and sports editor Paul Anger assigned me to write a sidebar on the visiting team. That required going into the locker room to interview the players after the game. The NFL still had no policy about women reporters being allowed to go into men's locker rooms; some were open, some were not, based on the whim of the team. The Vikings' locker room was going to be open that night.

The significance of the night was twofold: it was not only going to be the first time I had ever been in a men's locker room, it also was to be the first time a woman had ever been in the Vikings' locker room.

Four years earlier, my moving into a coed dorm in college had been a bit of an issue in our household. Now I was telling Mom and Dad about this new development over the phone.

"Oh my, really?" Mom asked with a chuckle. She quickly added, "You can handle it."

Dad had a smile in his voice too. "Just keep eye contact at all times, honey."

The game was Saturday night, August 23, 1980. I dressed conservatively in a simple skirt and blouse. I purposely wore the skirt. It was the closest I could come to a neon sign: *Warning! Here comes a woman!*

The Vikings beat the Dolphins, 17–10. As soon as the game ended, a group of reporters was allowed into a room adjacent to the Vikings' locker room to interview their venerable coach, Bud Grant. As he spoke, reporters peeled away, one by one, to walk into the locker room. Soon, I was alone with Grant. I asked him a few questions about the game. From watching him on TV for years, I expected him to be gruff. I couldn't have been more wrong. When we were finished, I turned toward the locker room.

"Are you going in there?" Grant asked. He sounded sincere, and not at all menacing.

"Yes."

"You really want to go in there?"

"Well, I don't want to go in, but I have to go in there to do my job."

"All right then," Grant said with a smile and a shrug. "Do whatever you have to do."

And with that, I turned around and walked into a room full of naked men.

It was worse than I thought. Not the naked men. Actually, there were very few naked bodies. The players were in various stages of undress, many still wearing their football pants.

No, I could never have anticipated the problem I was about to confront. It was a preseason game, so there were many extra players on the roster, but no names above the lockers. And even though I was carrying a flip card, the sheet given out in the press box containing all the players' names and numbers, most of the players had taken off their jerseys, so I couldn't tell who anyone was.

To further complicate matters, I also couldn't look around. If I did that, the players could accuse me of being in the locker room for the wrong reason. And that was the one thing I had to avoid.

As it was, as soon as I walked into the steamy, overcrowded room, I heard whoops and hollers from distant corners, from players I couldn't see.

"We don't go in the women's bathroom!" someone yelled. "What are you doing in here?"

"Here for some cheap thrills?" screamed another.

I took a few tentative steps into the room, then stopped, not knowing what to do. I was stuck. It seemed like a lifetime standing there, but really was only twenty to thirty seconds when, out of the noise and confusion, a player in uniform walked up to me. It was Tom Hannon, the Vikings' fourth-year safety out of Michigan State.

"Who do you need?"

I smiled.

"Tommy Kramer," I said.

Hannon pointed. "He's right there, putting on his necktie." I looked, and immediately recognized Kramer, the quarterback.

"Mark Mullaney," I said.

Hannon pointed out the defensive lineman.

I mentioned another lineman; Hannon helped identify him as well.

"That's all you need?" he asked.

"And, well, you."

"You bet."

After interviewing Hannon, who had intercepted two Miami passes, I thanked him for his help and beelined to Kramer, then the others. Every one of them was dressed but the one lineman who obviously desperately wanted to be interviewed buck naked. He didn't even bother to reach for a towel. As I moved toward him, he walked the rest of the way to me with a smirk on his face, enjoying the discomfort he brought with every step he took. I found this awkward, but not awkward enough not to do my job. I was determined to get the quotes, so I interviewed the naked guy. As luck would have it, the notebook I had brought was not the stenographer size, but an eight-and-a-half-by-eleven. With my height, looking the lineman right in the eye, when I looked down as I was writing, I saw only the notebook.

Forevermore when going into locker rooms, I carried an eight-and-a-half-by-eleven notebook, perfectly positioned.

All this interviewing, which seemed like an eternity to me, took about ten minutes. When I burst out of the locker room, I had just thirty minutes until my deadline, so I ran across the field in the now empty Orange Bowl to catch the elevator back up to the press box. I sat down next to Henry Seiden, a colleague at the *Herald,* who was already writing furiously.

He stopped for a second. "Everything go okay in there?" he asked.

"Yes, thanks, everything's fine."

I pulled out my bulky Texas Instruments computer, with its scroll of paper coming out the top. There was no time to think about what I had been through. I wrote as quickly as I ever had:

"Minnesota Viking defensive end Mark Mullaney says he wants to be part of a legend in the making. Saturday's game against the Dolphins, he said, may have been the start. . . ."

After finishing and sending my story, I sat back and looked at Henry.

"Oh boy," I said, exhaling and forcing a big smile.

"Good job," he said, patting me on the back. "I'm sure that wasn't easy."

Finally, I could think about what I had just been through. I wanted to talk. Henry wanted to listen. I pieced the past hour together slowly, reliving the locker room scene. "I just focused on the interviews and tried to ignore all the things that were being said."

Henry asked if anything had gone wrong.

I shook my head no. "It went okay. It went fine, actually." I didn't even think to tell him about the taunts and jeers, or the naked guy. The end result was the important thing for me.

I didn't dwell on the locker room at all—I barely gave it an extra thought—as I went out with a few of the writers after the game. Then, before going to sleep, I pulled out my diary: "It was tough—not embarrassing though," I wrote. "Just did my job and got out of the locker room and wrote the story."

I finally made up my mind to become a sportswriter. The persistent tug of sports had just been too great for me to ignore. The two summer internships in Toledo and Miami—even with my first locker room visit—had convinced me that this was the way to at least start my career. I could always move to news or political coverage later, I thought, but if I wanted to get out of the blocks quickly and have an opportunity to travel and cover big events, sports was it.

After completing my master's degree back at Northwestern, I became the *Herald*'s first full-time female sportswriter in April 1981. I was given a big job: to be the beat writer covering the University of Florida football team, one of the most important assignments in the sports department. Back then, there was just one professional sports team in Miami, the Dolphins. Major League Baseball, the NBA, and the NHL hadn't yet arrived in South Florida. So there really were just two major sports in Miami: pro football and college football.

The Florida beat was a coveted assignment. I was not quite twenty-three, fresh out of college, never having covered football in my life—and now assigned to a major college football team by one of the top-ten newspapers in the nation.

This didn't sit well with everyone at the *Herald*. On my first day on the job, Paul Anger welcomed me into his office, then let me in on a little sports department secret.

"There are some people who are a little upset that we've hired you to come right in and cover the Gators," he said. "I don't want you to worry about that, but I do want you to know it."

I thanked him for telling me. I knew the main reason I had been hired was that the *Herald* wanted a woman sportswriter. It also didn't hurt that I was from Northwestern. The *Herald* had a reputation for hiring Northwestern alums. My good friend Chris Spolar was one. She had not been there long when she called me at Northwestern, where I was a senior.

"They're salivating for a woman sportswriter," Chris told me.

If I had been a white male with the same résumé, coming out of Northwestern with four internships, including one at the *Herald* eight months earlier, I still probably would not have gotten this job. I was hired as a token, and I knew it from day one. There was no need to apologize for it, or dwell on it. It was my reality.

I was unfazed because I knew I was ready for this job. I had had an extremely productive internship at the *Herald* the previous summer. I was assigned to cover an American Soccer League team named the Miami Americans and threw myself into the beat, a journalistic gold mine of stories about a financially strapped team and league. There were outrageous, amusing stories about players not being paid and games being canceled at the last minute, stories that often made their way to the front page of the sports section. I covered some horse racing (my previous experience in that area had been watching the Triple Crown races on TV every spring), wrote a feature on a Dolphins rookie, and had a top-of-the-sports-front news story comparing NFL coaches' salaries when Don Shula signed another contract with the Dolphins.

The *Herald* even sent me on the road, which was almost unheard of for a summer intern, flying me to Tampa to write some features on the Tampa Bay Buccaneers. When I returned from the trip, I had to fill out my expense report. Veteran writer Michael Janofsky, one of the stars of the sports section, stopped by my desk to take a look.

I had put down breakfast at McDonald's: $1.25. Lunch wasn't much more. Nor was dinner.

"Let me see this," Jano said, grabbing the expense form. He took a pen and started to put 1's in front of all of my meals, turning my $1.25 breakfast into $11.25.

"You're making us all look bad," he said, half serious, half not.

"But that's what I spent," I apologetically told him, grabbing the sheet back and returning my expenses to their original amount. "I'm an intern. Blame it on that."

I'm not sure my little stand endeared me to the veteran sports staffers, but I still did it.

Soon, it was the spring of 1981 and I was back in Miami full-time. I've been asked many times over the past quarter century by students and strangers how difficult it must have been to be the first full-time woman sportswriter at the *Herald*. And each time I'm asked, I try to think of how petrified I was, or daunted, or concerned, and I can think of only one example.

I was very worried that first day on the job about finding a parking space for my car, then locating my desk. What twenty-two-year-old thinks of anything else on her first day at work? In hindsight, I realize this sounds a little flip. I certainly came to understand fairly quickly that had I failed, it would have been bad not only for me, but for other women coming up in the business. But I was not thinking of failing.

This is not to say that I didn't face some issues with the men in the sports department. The writers were always coming and going on road trips, but it didn't take long for a veteran curmudgeon named Gary Long to introduce himself to me.

"Ah-ha," Long said in his down-home Hoosier twang, "it's the skirt thing."

"What?" I asked, smiling and oblivious, wanting to be nice to a coworker.

"The skirt thing. Why you were hired. You know, because you're a woman."

"Oh, yeah, right." I laughed and waved my hand, as if to say I understood he was just teasing, even if he wasn't. I truly didn't know. I was too naive and too confident—naivete and confidence, a perfect combination in my new line of work—to be insulted. I didn't for a moment take what he said personally. I had stories to write and deadlines to meet and nothing, absolutely nothing, was going to get in my way.

In his next breath, Gary told me that he and some of the other writers got together to play tennis every week, and he had heard I played tennis and wondered if I wanted to be part of the group. I said yes, absolutely.

It was the beginning of a wonderful friendship, Gary the lovable, needling male chauvinist and me, the Skirt. He mentioned "the skirt thing" probably twenty-five times in the three and a half years I was at the *Herald*. I laughed every single time. This wasn't brain surgery we were talking about, nor rocket science. If I couldn't laugh a little at myself and my situation, I wasn't going to last very long in this men's world into which I had crash-landed.

Gary had covered the Florida beat in 1980 and now was moving to Florida State while I replaced him on the Gators. He knew the Florida team inside and out. I, on the other hand, had never covered a football game from a press box as a beat writer. I was going to have to do that every Saturday that fall, with hundreds of thousands of readers judging my every word.

Gary told me he took copious notes at every football game. So, one day, I wandered over to his desk and asked if he had a moment to show me how he kept score of a game. He looked up from his desk as if he were wondering why it had taken me so long to come by. He pulled out a stack of file folders from a cabinet and suggested I pull up a chair. For the next hour, he showed me how he used different-color pens for each team, how he wrote down every play and all his little symbols for various offensive formations, passes, and rushes, as well as defensive plays.

"Now you're ready to go," he said as he closed the last file.

I mentioned this to Dad on the phone, that the man who had been teasing me now not only had become a good friend, he also was showing me the ropes. Dad didn't say much then, except that he was glad to hear it.

Later in my career, Dad asked if I realized what had happened that day.

"Here's a guy who's giving you the business and you understood that and never gave it a second thought. And then it turns out he becomes your mentor. That's just great."

Covering the Gators on those warm fall Saturdays in Gainesville, Florida, was a refreshing, even exhilarating change of pace for a Big Ten native like me. Becoming immersed in the football culture of the little towns of the South was so different from the more urban existence of Ann Arbor and Evanston, with their close ties to Detroit and Chicago, and I reveled in the change. I was thrilled to be covering Southeastern Conference football; how many Auburn-Alabama games had I watched on television as a girl? And all those Crimson Tide Sugar Bowls, some on New Year's Eve. I could hum the fight song by heart. Now, to cover the Gators when they went on the road, I was traipsing around Alabama, Mississippi, Louisiana. I always loved to travel, always asked for a window seat on planes. Now I was getting to see places I had never been.

I had a fellow traveler on my maiden voyage through the SEC. Back in those days, newspapers cut costs by sharing a telephone in the press box, and Paul Anger had told me the *Herald* would be sharing with the *St. Petersburg Times,* its journalistic equal on the west coast of Florida. When I got to Gainesville, I was to look up Shelby Strother, my counterpart at the *Times.* We would be competitors, but we also would sit next to each other all season and share that phone.

Shelby and I were almost inseparable on game days that season on the Gator beat. He was thirty-five, a shaggy-haired air force veteran, the first Vietnam vet I knew, the first child of the sixties who became a friend of mine as an adult. He reminded me of Dad in that he was larger than life, the center of attention in every room, and always on the verge of cracking everyone up with a sly joke or story. He also had some unusual endearing qualities. At dinner in a fine restaurant the night before a game, he could be seen buttering his nose. And in the press box the next day, he might start chirping like a cricket.

Shelby became a dear friend, an adviser, and a protector of sorts. Most women sportswriters of that era, especially the pioneers who came five to ten years before me, didn't have many supporters in the male sportswriting corps, but lucky me, I did. I had my *Herald* editors back in Miami, and Shelby, on site.

Shelby made his presence known the first game we worked together, the Florida-Miami game of 1981 at the Orange Bowl. Interviews of the Florida players after the game would be conducted in the visiting locker room, the same place I interviewed the Minnesota Vikings in the summer of 1980. Only this time, I couldn't get into the locker room. Florida had a policy of not allowing female reporters in its locker room. This was not unusual in 1981. Only a few years earlier, some teams actually issued press box credentials that said: No women or children allowed.

Paul had called ahead early in the week to make sure I would be allowed to go through the doorway and down a hallway into the coach's press conference, passing by the locker room as I went. But after the game, two state troopers were at the main door telling me I was going to do no such thing. I stood my ground. A few of the male sportswriters stood there with me. Shelby said he wasn't going in if I wasn't going in. Then he started to plot how he and a few others might sneak me past the guards by surrounding me as we walked in, but I was too tall to be that easy to hide. Shelby was six-three, but a few of the other men were my height or a bit shorter.

Shelby was trying to think of another plan—"I'll divert their attention, then you guys rush in"—when Florida's assistant sports information director showed up and waved us all in, me and the men who kindly waited with me.

After meeting Shelby, I decided to read every story of his that I could get my hands on, so I started buying the *St. Pete Times* and found myself reading the kind of writing I rarely had seen in newspapers. It was lyrical, it was long, and it told a story in the way the very best sportswriting does. Shelby's brilliant work made me realize I had a lot to learn. My years at Northwestern had taught me how to write news and features with a no-nonsense, get-out-of-the-way, let-the-story-tell-itself style. Flair was not my forte. But it was Shelby's. I wanted to learn from him, so I grabbed every second of his time that I could. We would talk about writing while sharing a ride to a game, or walking out to the parking lot. I would grill him about leads, about features, about poetry, about anything to do with writing. I wanted his opinion on everything because he was so different from anyone I had ever met in journalism.

One day, I spent fifteen minutes at my computer trying to come up with a lead on a story on Georgia running back Herschel Walker that would be worthy of Shelby. We were on the road covering a game and I knew I would see him for lunch. That was when I would try it out on him.

I prepped him as best I could, then blurted it out.

"The day started early and ended late."

Shelby stared at me.

"Doesn't that happen every day?" he asked.

"Good point," I said.

I changed my lead.

But for every criticism Shelby offered, he had a compliment ready as well, not that I deserved any of them at the ripe old age of twenty-three. During the middle of that first season, he pulled me aside in the press box. "I've been reading all your stories, and I have to tell you something. If I didn't know you were writing them and if I didn't look at your byline, I'd think a man was writing them."

In 1981, that was about as fine a compliment as a woman in sports journalism could receive. But that didn't mean the beat was coming easily to me. Never having covered a football team before, I was struggling. It was one thing to be filled with football knowledge while watching games as a fan next to my father for more than a decade in Toledo and Ann Arbor. It was quite another to synthesize what had happened in three hours on the field into a thousand-word story on a tight deadline for the biggest newspaper in the state of Florida.

There were times I looked at my computer in the press box

and sat there, stuck, unable to come up with a start for my story. Although I had notebooks full of clips from the *Daily Northwestern* and my internships, I hadn't written many game stories. In a rookie reporter's panic after every game, I interviewed every Florida player I could find, massively overreporting every week, then coming back to the press box to rifle through my notebook for inspiration.

"There are a million ways to write any story," I said back at my seat in the press box, more a lamentation than an observation at that particular moment, with the clock ticking toward my evening deadline back in Miami.

"I know," said Shelby, sitting next to me, practically elbow to elbow. "Just pick one and go with it."

Eventually I became unstuck, but not before I pushed my patient editors to the brink of using wire copy several times for the first edition. I soon learned that quotes were overrated, that one or two good ones worked better than ten mediocre ones. But there were other issues. After I returned to Miami from writing my first game story, Paul walked with me to the back of the sports department where we kept stacks of the past weeks' papers. He took out a red marker and circled a spot in my story where, referring to the second quarter, I used the term "second stanza."

"Don't do that again, okay?"

I nodded, realizing that in a pinch, trying to say something other than "quarter" or "period," I threw in "stanza" because that was a word sports announcers sometimes used. My inexperience was showing, but I was determined not to let that last.

Shelby and I crossed paths at events other than Florida football games over the next few years. We both found ourselves at the Washington Redskins–Miami Dolphins Super Bowl at the Rose Bowl in January 1983. Gary Long and I were sent out in the last wave of reporters on the Saturday before the game. It was the longest trip I had made as a *Herald* reporter; I was so excited to be at my first Super Bowl that I could barely sleep the night before. It was just my second trip to California. I can even remember where I sat on the plane.

One of the first people I ran into in the press hotel was Shelby, who felt the same sense of excitement. I marveled at his childlike wonder over sports, and told myself to try to be like that myself when I reached my thirties.

That trip, I was in L.A. only about thirty-six hours, and I wanted to take advantage of every minute of it. So, after I wrote my stories following the Redskins' victory, Shelby and a few other writers and I embarked on an all-night tour of Hollywood and Beverly Hills in a rental car. The guys dropped me back at my hotel room by 4 A.M., enough time for me to get ready and head to the airport for my early-morning flight back to Miami.

The *Herald* really was just an extension of college for a young reporter like me. At times it was comfortable and nurturing; at others, a brazen baptism by fire. The latter meant dealing with the great Don Shula.

During my 1980 summer internship, I had my first opportunity to ask Shula a question. I was dispatched to training camp with a specific assignment: to ask about problems with Miami's running game. It hadn't been as productive as expected. A knot of reporters and cameramen were gathered around, and there I was, not all that many years removed from being a young Dolphin fan. Snapping to attention, I told myself I no longer was the poem-writing fanatic who adored Shula's team. I was a journalist, and this was no time to waver.

I eventually summoned the courage to jump in: "Coach, what's wrong with the running game?"

Shula, who was sitting on a bench, slowly looked up to see who had asked the question. He clearly didn't like it. He glared at me. Uh-oh, I thought, here it comes.

"Well, you know, we ran the ball pretty well the other day," Shula started out, looking utterly disgusted with me. He proceeded to list a few positive statistics about his running backs.

I somehow stood my ground and followed up by asking if he planned any changes.

No, he didn't.

And then, silence. His stare told me there would be no more

questions from me on this day. I had my notebook out and my pen poised, but no news to write. And Shula was still scowling at me.

I was painfully aware that everyone in the scrum of reporters and cameras was looking right at me. But—and here was a surprise to me at that moment—I didn't crumble. I didn't even feel like crumbling. Your mind races to those mental common denominators of the past at times like this: crusty Northwestern professors, tough city editors, and, of course, my father. I could hear Dad's voice in my head: "Stand up straight, shoulders back!"

Even though I felt I was handling this rebuke well, I must have looked a little shell-shocked because Chuck Dowdle, the town's best-known TV sportscaster, came up after the interview to tell me not to worry about it, that everyone got dressed down by Shula at one time or another. Without my knowing it, Dowdle then tracked down Shula and told him that wasn't the nicest way to treat the new kid on the block.

The next time I was at the Dolphins' camp, Shula made a point of smiling and saying hello. It was the beginning of one of the most interesting coach-reporter relationships I have ever had. I came around on the days beat writer Larry Dorman was off and got to know Shula and the team fairly well. The Dolphins were one of the first NFL teams to allow equal access for female reporters to their locker room by issuing robes to their players in 1981. Leave it to Shula to find a way to solve that problem a few years before the NFL finally made equal access mandatory in every locker room in 1985.

After one game, I was in the Dolphins' locker room conducting an interview for a sidebar I was writing when I felt a slight tug on my elbow. I really didn't want to be interrupted. I kept on working. The tug came again. I swung around impatiently.

It was Shula.

"Everything going okay in here?"

The question startled me. "Ah, you bet, Coach," I said, hoping I didn't look as perturbed as I felt a moment earlier. "Everything's great, thanks."

"Good," he said, smiling kindly. "Keep up the good work."

I believed from that moment on that Shula looked at me a bit like one of his own kids. I knew his children, who were about my age, from seeing them at games and other events around town. And, of course, I, like them, grew up with a strong male presence in my life. Dad and Shula, Shula and Dad. There were some uncanny similarities, not the least of which was they were two tough son of a guns who really were just old softies at heart. Whenever I could, I talked to Shula about Dad, just little things, about how he had played football and gotten me into sports. Shula always seemed interested. For most people, he had two seconds for small talk. For me, sometimes there was a whole minute.

I often chuckled when people at a cocktail party or on a plane found out what I did. Their eyes grew wide when they asked what it was like to go into the men's locker room. The first five hundred times I heard the question, I smiled and said it was no big deal. It wasn't sexy or exciting, I said. It was hot and cramped and steamy. I sometimes was wearing a coat coming in out of a cold outdoor press box at a game up north and soon I would be perspiring in the sweltering locker room, while all I wanted to do was get the quotes I needed and get back to the press box to write on deadline.

The 501st time I was asked, I got a little sick of it. Here I was, trained at a top journalism school for a career I had been preparing for my whole life, and all people wanted to know was if I saw football players in various stages of undress.

All women sportswriters walked a fine line dealing with the public on this R-rated issue. On one hand, this was serious business for the hundred or so women in sports journalism back then. It was about having the right to equal access in locker rooms, which translated to having the right to do our jobs the same way male sportswriters did. *Sports Illustrated* reporter Melissa Ludtke and Time, Inc., sued baseball commissioner Bowie Kuhn and the New York Yankees in U.S. district court for this right after the 1977 World Series—and won the following year. It was a watershed moment.

On the other hand, a serious reply wasn't going to work with the stranger at the cocktail party or on the plane. I asked Dad what he thought I should say, what he would want to hear from someone like me. He said, "Make a point, but do it with a smile. Make them laugh. Have a little fun at your own expense."

I started getting invited to give speeches in Miami to football fan clubs, schools, business luncheons. I often would open my talk like this:

"I ask a lot of questions in my line of work, but I get asked two in particular: (1) Do you get into the locker room? And (2) What do you see?

"The answers are yes and not a whole lot."

I then went on to say, "All I see is the whites of their eyes. Eye contact is very important in my line of work."

But while the Dolphins allowed women into their locker room, the situation was not at all resolved on the college football beat to which I was assigned. And it was no laughing matter.

Florida's official policy was not to allow women in the locker room. We were told before the season that I would stand outside the locker room door and the sports information director would bring players and coaches out to me. Upon hearing this, the *Miami Herald*—specifically Paul Anger and I—had two choices. We could bring a lawsuit against the school three years after the 1978 Ludtke ruling. Or we could play by Florida's rules, meaning I would try to do my job in a hallway, while Paul and I monitored the stories in other newspapers around the state to see if I was losing information or insightful quotes by not being with the other reporters in the locker room.

We chose the latter, at least for the time being. Today I can't imagine a scenario in which you wouldn't threaten a lawsuit, but 1981, in the South, was a very different time.

As it turned out, the decision to bar me from the locker room had little effect on my work. Shelby and a few others made sure I missed nothing; if anything extraordinary was said in the locker room, they filled me in. Meanwhile, as I stood outside the locker room door talking to players by myself, I often could pursue a line of questioning that no one else considered, and get an answer no one else had.

Then, depending on the layout of the locker room area at Florida's away games, something truly bizarre occurred. Even though I was barred from the locker room, I sometimes ended up *in the locker room*. Charley Pell, Florida's head coach, who made the policy of not allowing women in (he said he didn't want women around college players while they were dressing), sometimes actually waved me in when he saw me standing alone at the doorway, waiting for a player to come to me.

"Go ahead," he called once or twice, smiling. "Come on in." All the players were wearing towels anyway.

The Florida sports information office, led by Norm Carlson and John Humenik, always kept an eye out for me, whether I ended up in the locker room or not. Norm walked players to me, and one time, John grabbed my hand and trooped me right through the locker room to get to the coach's interview room.

"Keep your eyes closed," he said with a laugh, as if we were playing a game of blindman's bluff.

"Oh, my eyes are closed, John, my eyes are closed."

A sense of humor was required at moments like this. I was under a microscope. I knew people were watching the new "girl" on the beat. Dad said it best: "You're like Caesar's wife. You must be above reproach." I learned that my attitude, my demeanor, and my attire all were crucial. I always dressed conservatively, on the sporty, jocky side, so there was no danger of my wearing a miniskirt or an inappropriate top.

Inappropriate? Most days, what I was wearing wouldn't have been considered inappropriate in a convent.

Other issues bubbled to the surface when a young woman was working in a man's world. In my first year of covering the Gators, one of the assistant coaches, a married man, insisted on walking me back to my room in the team hotel on a road trip the night before a game. Then, at my door, out of the blue, he kissed me. I pushed him away.

The next day, I had to interview him.

A couple of years later, on the road one weekend, I attended a party for school officials the evening before another college game. Back in my hotel room, asleep at 2 A.M., I heard a knock at my door. It was one of the team's former star players, now in the pros, still single, who was living in the city we were visiting that weekend. He had been at the party and we had chatted briefly. Now he was at my door.

"Can I come in?" he yelled.

"I'm asleep," I replied.

"You sound awake to me."

I laughed.

The door remained closed.

Some things were more serious than others. A married editor at the *Herald* started to show interest in me. It shocked me, but thankfully it ended nearly as quickly as it began. However, for the first time, it occurred to me that I might have been treated well at the *Herald* because someone in the hierarchy of the paper liked me, not because of my ability.

I quickly pushed those thoughts out of my mind. I was confident enough to ignore the doubts that had suddenly crept in. But I wondered about women who were confronted with more persistent sexual harassment, or weren't quite so confident. What happened to their self-esteem? What happened to them?

Even though I adored college football, I had something else I wanted to cover even more when I set foot in the *Herald* sports department in 1981. I was looking ahead three years to the 1984 Olympic Games. I mentioned to Paul that I'd love to cover the Winter Games in Sarajevo and the Summer Games in Los Angeles. I said this within a month of my arrival in Miami, and then brought it up a few more times the next year or so. Soon, Paul had heard enough and I was the *Herald*'s Olympic and international sports beat writer when I wasn't covering football games.

One of the first stories I wrote was about track and field, not that anyone I interviewed was heading to the Olympics. The coach of a track club for Miami's inner-city kids was running such a low-budget operation that he didn't even have a stopwatch to time the children. As soon as my story was published, the phone on my desk started ringing. People wanted to donate. I gave them the coach's number. That summer, the children received all the running equipment they needed, and the coach finally bought himself a stopwatch.

On my new beat, I was envisioning going to Sarajevo, covering figure skating, skiing, speed skating. Paul reminded me I worked for a paper in South Florida that had limited interest in winter sports. I didn't go to Yugoslavia.

But there still was L.A. I soon began keeping files on every summer sport, just in case Paul would send me. I did end up at those Games, my first, a dream come true, but even before that experience, I actually was leaving the country for other destinations along the Olympic beat. First stop: Havana, Cuba.

In 1983, ABC Sports chartered a jet to take a few writers to Havana to cover a U.S.-Cuba boxing match being televised by *Wide World of Sports*. Paul asked me if I wanted to go.

"Cuba?" I replied.

"Cuba?" Mom said when I told her.

Yes, Cuba.

I had never been to a communist nation, and if I had harbored any lingering doubts about my decision to become a sportswriter—and I really did not—they would have been assuaged on that trip. There was nothing frivolous, nothing "Oscar Madison," about reporting from communist Cuba in 1983.

My press pass from the U.S.-Cuba boxing match.

"Cuba still seems locked in the 1950s," I wrote in a story that ran on the front page of the *Herald* sports section on April 11, 1983. "When Fidel Castro came to power in 1959, the clock stopped. The revolution trapped the cars, the popular music, the hotels, the mansions, the paint jobs—and the people. Almost everything came to a halt. But not sports."

That four-day trip was the first of five I would make to Cuba in the next decade, most related to the Pan American Games. It's strange where sports take you. I have never been to Kansas City to cover a sports event, but I've been to Havana five times. I met Fidel Castro a few times, always in a group of other journalists, usually after midnight, which was the time that he almost always welcomed visitors. Our interviews with Cuba's president followed a similar pattern. We usually were enjoying a late group dinner laden with anticipation, knowing we probably would never get to dessert because Castro would be calling. All of a sudden, one of our guides would tell us it was time to go and in a flash we were whisked in the darkness in a waiting van to Castro's office.

We were not kept at bay when we were with him; on the contrary, we usually were gathered quite close to him. Once I was so close, I was inadvertently pressing my notebook against his back, writing away, as he held an impromptu news conference with us. That sometimes happened in locker rooms, in the crush of a media horde around an all-star linebacker. Now it was happening with one of the most notorious dictators on earth. Castro always greeted us in full military dress, with shined boots and immaculate fingernails. His hands were his most remarkable feature; for a man of such military might, they were smooth, beautiful even. His nails were nicer than mine.

One time, at the end of one of our press gatherings, Castro looked directly at me and wanted to know, through an interpreter, why I had not asked a question. I was stunned. I couldn't believe he had kept track. I had a bad cold and lost my voice, I whispered. He nodded and smiled.

On another visit, in January 1991, I listened to him tell us, always through that omnipresent interpreter, that he had heard on

CNN that the Gulf War had just begun. How strange this was, to be in a small room of journalists with one of the great enemies of your nation, hearing him tell you that your country was at war. Our group of Olympic journalists left the country soon afterward as previously planned. As we were driven through the dark streets of Havana in a van, we listened to the BBC's broadcast of President George H. W. Bush's speech via shortwave radio. We never felt threatened or in danger because we were convinced that Castro himself wanted nothing but our safe return home. Yet when our small jet landed in Miami an hour and a half later, I phoned home right away and spoke to two very relieved parents.

Miami was the perfect place to start my career, but it was tough being so far from home. There were times I couldn't believe I had taken such a leap. But my thinking was simple: anything for journalism. I would go almost anywhere for this adventurous career, even if it meant being a three-hour plane ride away from the people I loved the most.

When I departed for Miami, it was Mom who said she knew I would have to leave Toledo to find my way in journalism. Dad was a bit more emotional. While he always was the one to drive me to my next destination, to help me find an apartment to rent, to make sure there was a double lock on the door, and to drive around the neighborhood to help me find the drugstore, the post office, and the nearest McDonald's, he also was the one tugging on me, just a little, to find a way to stay close to home.

"I always wanted what's best for my kids, but it's tough when to be the best, you have to go far away from home," he said. "I wish I could put all of you in a bubble and protect you forever."

Dad even came up with a suggestion after I finished my master's degree: Why not stay at home and write books?

"On what?" I asked. "I haven't lived yet."

Dad didn't have an answer. But even as I sounded exasperated with my father at that moment, I also knew what he was doing and I loved him for it.

While I was in Miami, Kate graduated from Indiana University and was on her own working as a buyer for the LS Ayres department store chain headquartered in Indianapolis. Jim was at Indiana University himself and Amy was still at home. Sunday seemed to be the day that everyone was calling home to talk to Mom and Dad, so to keep things organized, I started calling home every Sunday at noon. Usually, though, I called several times a week, and I always checked in when I landed after a flight.

I made sure to go back to Toledo, the only place I have ever called home, every chance I could. I vowed to never miss a Thanksgiving or Christmas with my family, and to this day, I never have. Perhaps this sounds strange, but it seems perfectly normal to me.

I had a full life in Miami too, anchored around the *Herald,* where about a dozen of my Northwestern friends were working. My social life was predictably unpredictable. I met my first Miami boyfriend not in Miami, but in the Auburn University press box when I inadvertently set my briefcase on his foot. Gene Wojciechowski was a sportswriter for the *Fort Lauderdale News* covering the Florida-Auburn game and happened to be assigned the seat next to me.

In 1983, the *Herald* switched me from the Gators to the Miami Hurricanes. This was officially a promotion, although I was not entirely sure about that. Florida was supposed to have a good team, while Miami was going to start a freshman quarterback. Experts were predicting a .500 season for the Hurricanes.

But almost everything about the Miami assignment became a pleasant surprise. The freshman quarterback, it turned out, was Bernie Kosar. And, as soon as I got onto the Miami beat, I found out access to the locker room would not be an issue. Miami coach Howard Schnellenberger believed strongly that female reporters should not be denied any of the rights afforded their male colleagues. This was unusual for a college coach, extremely commendable, and a huge relief to me. I could focus solely on my job.

But just because that issue was resolved didn't mean there would be no conflict between the coach and the beat writer.

Miami did lose its first game, to Florida, 28–3. But then the Hurricanes reeled off easy victories over marginal opponents, including Houston, Purdue, and Notre Dame. Later in the season, Miami defeated Cincinnati, 17–7, in a downpour at Riverfront Stadium. Dad drove down for the game to see me, but he and I never forgot that trip for another reason: it was there that I found out for the first time just how much trouble a beat writer could get into for doing her job.

In the locker room after the game, a Miami running back told me that the Cincinnati defense was stealing Kosar's offensive signals. It was embarrassing for an offense, especially one as intricate as Miami's pro-style passing game, to have its signals decoded. I asked Schnellenberger about it and he vigorously denied that it happened. The Cincinnati coach said it did. Kosar told me Cincinnati was only guessing. I quoted them all in a sidebar that ran inside the Sunday *Herald*.

Two days later, I received a call that Schnellenberger wanted to see me. Anytime you walked into his office, you felt like you were being called in to see the principal. This was an imposing man with a voice deeper than Dad's. He took a puff on his pipe and leaned forward over his desk.

"Bernie Kosar isn't going to talk to you anymore," he said. "You misinterpreted what he said, and he can't trust you anymore."

I could feel my mouth dropping open, my face turning red. I was caught completely off guard. I fumbled around, starting to defend myself, saying that I had quoted Kosar accurately.

Schnellenberger continued. "You know, everyone here, from the top down, doesn't trust you. We all think you're here trying to get all the stories you can."

I wanted to say that was my job description, but I was so surprised that I wasn't able to think clearly. Our conversation, such as it was, soon ended. I left Schnellenberger's office, composed myself, wrote a feature story I'd been working on, then drove downtown to the *Herald* to meet with Paul Anger and his boss, Ed Storin, the assistant managing editor in charge of sports.

"We'll defend you, don't worry about that," Paul told me.

They decided to send Edwin Pope, the highly respected *Herald* sports columnist, to see Schnellenberger the next day.

When Edwin returned, he called me into his office.

"I told Howard that if you're doing your job correctly, and he's doing his job correctly, you're not necessarily going to get along," Edwin began. "There's going to be some antagonism. I said that his team needs the *Herald* more than the *Herald* needs it, and Kosar needs the *Herald* more than the *Herald* needs him. I told them to get used to having a tough reporter who is going to ask tough questions."

Edwin told me that Schnellenberger listened intently and acknowledged I was doing a good job, perhaps too good a job. "She's too businesslike and brusque," Edwin told me Schnellenberger had said.

Edwin said he responded with one word: "So?"

I couldn't help but smile. At a time when lesser sports editors might have avoided putting a woman reporter on the beat to placate a coach, especially in the South, Paul sent Edwin to the university to defend me. I thanked them both profusely. I was very fortunate to have them on my side.

Edwin's visit improved my relationship with Schnellenberger. He still shot me looks if I asked tough questions, but he always answered them.

Kosar, however, remained a problem. Schnellenberger wasn't kidding. His quarterback was giving me the cold shoulder. I figured this would go on for a few games, perhaps even the rest of the season.

It lasted a little longer than that. Twenty-one years, to be exact.

In the two decades that followed, bizarre things happened: Kosar hung up when he heard my voice on a conference call when he was with the Cleveland Browns and I was at the *Washington Post*. He worked very hard to avoid me at a small reception at a black-tie dinner in Washington. Over the years, reporters in other cities would ask me why Kosar was angry with me, and I said I really wasn't sure. Could it be that one Cincinnati story, all these years later?

Kosar was back in Washington for another black-tie event in

2004 to which I also had been invited. To my complete surprise, I was told he wanted to see me. "I have to apologize," he said. "I've acted like a jerk for all these years. I should have told you this sooner, but I was just too immature. I'm really sorry for the way I treated you."

I immediately accepted his apology and we spent the next thirty minutes catching up on the past two decades. He was delightful. I was never angry with Kosar. How could I be, considering what his team had meant to me?

That 1983 season, Kosar might not have been talking, but Miami kept winning. When the regular season was over, the Hurricanes were 10–1, ranked fifth in the country and bound for the Orange Bowl to play undefeated, top-ranked, and almighty Nebraska. The Cornhuskers were being called one of the great teams of the century. Few gave Miami any chance in the game.

In a meeting with my editors at the beginning of Orange Bowl week, I wondered aloud what would happen if Miami upset the Cornhuskers.

"Then Texas [ranked second] would be number one," an editor said.

"Okay, but what if Texas also lost, what then?" I replied.

"Auburn?" someone said.

"Illinois?" said another.

"But they're ranked number three and number four," I said. "I'll bet the AP poll voters would leapfrog Miami over them."

"Well, we'll never know," one of my editors told me.

"Why?" I shot back. "Why can't we know? What if we could find out how the Associated Press poll voters were going to vote *before they voted*? What if we could call all the AP voters before the game and give them the various scenarios and scoop AP on its own poll?"

My editors stared at me, dumbfounded.

"You can't do it," one said. "It'll take too long to find them all."

That was just the challenge I needed. I called the AP and asked for the list of their sixty poll voters. They were happy to oblige; it soon came to me over the wire. Across the next three days, as the

Orange Bowl neared, I made more than 250 phone calls. I fever-
ishly tracked down phone numbers for all the voters and called
them in hotel rooms at other bowl games, at home, on vacation,
wherever I could find them. I asked each person the same set of
five questions to determine how he or she would vote in certain
scenarios. The big question was: If Miami beats Nebraska and
Georgia beats Texas, who would you vote No. 1?

I did this in whatever spare hours I could find Orange Bowl
week, usually late into the evening, when the time difference
worked with me for calling the West Coast. I already had had a
full day covering practices and news conferences for the *Herald,*
but I didn't mind the extra work. I was running on adrenaline,
and, as Dad said over the phone several times, "This is your
week."

I had never had more fun working on a story. It was like working the phone bank of a telethon for a few days. With help from
two part-time *Herald* staffers who made some calls when time
grew short, I found and interviewed all but six AP voters. Thirty-
one of the fifty-four voters—a majority of the sixty-member
board—said they would pick Miami if it won and Texas lost. It
didn't matter if I found the final six. I had my story.

In a piece stripped across the top of the Sunday sports section
January 1, 1984, under the headline A UM WIN CAN WIN IT
ALL, I wrote:

> University of Miami Coach Howard Schnellen-
> berger has been talking about winning the national
> championship since he arrived in Coral Gables in
> 1979. Now, five seasons later, on the eve of the
> Orange Bowl, his team is close.
>
> It may be even closer than he realizes.
>
> Miami will become the Associated Press national
> champion if it upsets top-ranked Nebraska Monday
> night in the Orange Bowl and if No. 2 Texas loses to
> Georgia in the Cotton Bowl that afternoon, accord-
> ing to a *Herald* survey of 54 out of the 60 voters in
> the AP college football poll. . . .

My favorite quote in the story came from Douglas Looney of *Sports Illustrated,* who had written an article proclaiming Nebraska the greatest team of all time. "For me to say Miami would beat Nebraska . . . the words choke in my throat," he said. "I live in Connecticut and I have a better chance of sunbathing on the beach January third than Miami has of being number one."

I'm guessing Looney didn't work on his tan that day, but he should have, because in one of the greatest upsets in college football history, Miami defeated Nebraska, 31–30. The game ranks with the 1969 Michigan upset of Ohio State as the two most memorable I've seen in person. It was the kind of game that takes your breath away, Miami jumping to a big lead, then Nebraska storming back, then Miami surging again, then Nebraska losing when a last-minute two-point conversion pass is tipped away by a defender's fingertip. Earlier in the day, as if it were scripted, Georgia upset Texas, 10-9. I knew from doing the poll story that Miami would be No. 1 if those two games turned out as they did. The *Herald* editors knew it too. They ran my game story under a banner headline: UM IS NO. 1.

> They've been dreaming about the national championship at the University of Miami since Coach Howard Schnellenberger arrived five years ago.
>
> Now they can stop dreaming.
>
> And pinch themselves.
>
> Miami 31, Nebraska 30.
>
> Going into Monday night's 50th Orange Bowl Classic, Nebraska was considered one of the greatest college football teams ever.
>
> Miami was not.
>
> But, by barely surviving a furious two-touchdown rally in the final five minutes and stopping a two-point conversion attempt with 48 seconds to go, the Hurricanes almost certainly won the national title all but conceded to Nebraska.
>
> Because No. 1 Nebraska (12–1) lost for the first

time in 16 months and because No. 2 Texas lost . . .
No. 5 Miami (11–1) is expected to be voted Associated Press national champion Tuesday night. . . .

I left the press box well past midnight, giving the field one final
look out the window before I turned to go. I shook my head and
smiled. I had just covered a national championship season—from
the first practice in August to the final seconds of the final game in
January. I drove to the hotel that served as Miami's Orange Bowl
headquarters to stop in briefly at the Hurricanes' post-game party
before calling it a night and heading back to my apartment.

I searched for Schnellenberger as soon as I entered the party.
When I saw him, I walked swiftly to him, putting my right hand
out as I approached for what I expected would be the heartiest
of handshakes.

But Schnellenberger would have none of that. Flush with victory, he said, "Christine Brennan, I'm going to kiss you." And
then he did.

The next day, the polls did indeed rank Miami No. 1. The city
held a parade, the college sports world was still in shock, and
the story didn't end. Within a few days, I was writing a book
that the *Herald* wanted to publish. *The Miracle of Miami*, written in one sleep-deprived week, is just 116 pages. It's so thin you
can't see it on the shelf unless you put two or three copies together. But it was a book, my first book.

Dad wrote me a letter that I received a few days after I had
finished.

"I want to congratulate you," he said. "I have to say that I
would have hoped your first book would have been on a more
substantial topic, but it's a great start and I'm proud of you."

I looked at the letter. *A more substantial topic?* I read it again.
And again. I felt Dad was being a little rough on me.

Through the night, I thought about what Dad had written,
and I decided that he was giving me one of his not-so-gentle
nudges to never rest on any success. Dad was just being Dad. I
smiled. I could deal with that.

When the books arrived at the *Herald,* Dad asked me to order a box for him. The next time I was home, I personalized more than a dozen copies so he could hand them to his friends. I think by that point he was prouder of what I had done than I was.

Luck is such a big part of everything we do. Had the Hurricanes been the .500 team I was expecting them to be, I never would have had the opportunity that presented itself during Orange Bowl week, getting such wonderful exposure because I was writing for the one paper being read by everyone who had come into town for the game. One of the out-of-town reporters happened to be my Northwestern classmate Michael Wilbon, the college-football writer for the *Washington Post*.

Unbeknownst to me, Mike left Miami with a batch of newspapers in his luggage. They contained all the stories I had written that week. Somehow those papers found their way to the desk of *Post* sports editor George Solomon, and eight months later, I was walking in the door of the *Washington Post* as its newest sportswriter.

7

THE BIG LEAGUES

Sonny Jurgensen puffed on a cigar at Redskin Park as we watched practice together from a bench on the sideline.

"You know, you don't have many friends out here," the great Hall of Fame quarterback said.

He was right. I was still in my first season on the Redskins beat for the *Washington Post,* and I had worn out my welcome quickly. Coach Joe Gibbs was worked up about my being in the locker room. Dave Butz, the six-seven, three-hundred-pound defensive tackle, was too. Veteran quarterback Joe Theismann was snarling about something or other, running back John Riggins was wary of me, and some of the other players had no idea how to react when I walked into the locker room, including veteran kicker Mark Moseley, who suggested I wear a cow bell after I happened to walk in as he was pulling on his blue jeans at his locker near the door.

"Yes," I said to Jurgensen, "I know."

"Does that bother you?" he replied, launching a plume of smoke into the still air.

"No, not really. I'm not here to find friends. I'm here to do my job."

Jurgensen nodded his head, looked at me, grew quiet, took another puff, looked at me again.

"Smoke bothering you?"

"No, not at all, thanks. Actually, I don't mind it. My Dad smokes cigars, so the smell reminds me of him."

Jurgensen nodded once again. As I looked at him, I thought I detected a smile.

I left the *Miami Herald* and went to work for the *Washington Post* in September 1984. The *Washington Post*! When I stepped off the elevator into the fifth-floor newsroom, I felt as if I were walking into the pages of a journalism textbook. I felt that way on my first day at the *Post,* and I still felt that way on my last. Ben Bradlee was the executive editor when I came to the paper, my ultimate boss. He would come by the sports department and slap me on the back, shouting, "Brennan, what have you got for us today?" You always wanted to find something, if only because it was Ben.

Most of the personalities from the Watergate era were still at the paper. Bob Woodward was an editor whose advice I sought a few times. Carl Bernstein had left the *Post* by the time I got there, but I met him at several *Post*-related functions and parties. Katharine Graham, who was chairman of the board and chief executive officer, once asked me to speak to a group of visiting schoolchildren, including one of her grandchildren, at a *Post* luncheon. I was delighted to accept. There was no more glorious place to work, I believed, than the newspaper of Watergate fame.

Some of Dad's political friends back in Ohio, however, weren't quite so sure. Dad was teased that his daughter had gone to work for the "liberal *Washington Post.*" He laughed and made sure to mention I was working in the sports department.

Within four months, I was assigned to the Redskins. Friends at the *Post* told me it was one of the two most important beats on the paper. The White House was the other. This made me laugh. They responded to my laughter with grim looks, and then amended the statement: if the Redskins went to the Super Bowl, the White House would become number two for the week.

There was a running joke in the sports department that went something like this: if Ronald Reagan and Mikhail Gorbachev were going to have a summit and the Redskins defeated Dallas, the *Post*'s front page would declare REAGAN, GORBACHEV TO MEET—but only below the screaming banner headline: REDSKINS BEAT COWBOYS.

I charged into this world of skewed perspective with my eyes wide open. In July 1985, I drove two hours from Washington into the hills of southern Pennsylvania to cover my first Redskins training camp in Carlisle. I arrived prepared to ask the tough questions and report the significant stories on the most important beat I most likely would ever cover. I had had three and a half years at the *Herald* to prepare me for almost anything.

The only thing that I wasn't ready for was the media's interest in me.

Within days of my arrival, all four of Washington's TV stations asked me for interviews. I asked the first producer who approached me why he wanted to talk to me.

"Because you're a big story during this training camp."

At an NFL owners' meeting that May, Commissioner Pete Rozelle had told all the teams that they must open their locker rooms to both male and female reporters for the 1985 season. Prior to his decision, the Redskins were one of nine NFL teams that still barred women from entering the locker room. I covered some NFL games when I first arrived at the *Post* in the fall of 1984, and I discovered a mosaic of rules and regulations, depending on the team and sometimes even the week you were covering them. That fall, I stood outside the Redskins' locker room whenever I needed a quote, waiting for players to come out to find me. All the male reporters went right inside. I also stood outside the Dallas Cowboys' locker room as everyone else streamed in. After a Cowboys game against the St. Louis Cardinals in Busch Memorial Stadium—there I was, working in the press box that we had toured when I was in eighth grade—I was promised that I'd get all the players I wanted. What I didn't realize was they all would come out at the same time. Tony Dorsett, Danny White, and Gary Hogeboom all left the locker room on their way to the team bus within three minutes of one another. Dorsett wouldn't even stop to talk; he made me walk with him to the bus. Those interviews turned out terribly. I had to scramble to find any usable quotes. This was no way to work.

Another weekend that 1984 season, Lesley Visser of the *Boston Globe* and I were covering a New York Giants game. On that day, we two representatives of Eastern media behemoths were told to stand in the Giants' weight room—or was it the *wait* room? Lesley asked—and be ready for interviews. We had asked to speak with Phil Simms and Lawrence Taylor. We waited. And we waited. Finally, we heard a door open. In lumbered an offensive lineman, still wearing his uniform. It was spotless. I carried a flip card with the rosters and starting lineups. I quickly looked up his name.

Our first interviewee had not played in the game.

By the spring of 1985, this kind of nonsense was no longer acceptable to George Solomon and the *Washington Post*. After assigning me to the Redskins beat, George visited Rozelle and NFL Director of Public Relations Joe Browne in New York to discuss the locker room issue. Not long afterward, Rozelle informed the owners of the new rule. Over the years, I've been asked if I believed Rozelle did this because the *Post* was putting a woman on the Redskins, one of the highest-profile beats in the league. I didn't know then and I still don't know now if that was the reason. Whether it was coincidence or not, the important news was that it was done. Equal access was the rule in the NFL.

The only problem was, at least one NFL coach didn't like what Rozelle had done. And that coach was Joe Gibbs. He gave an interview to the Washington CBS affiliate saying, quite stridently, that he didn't believe I should be in the locker room while his players were changing clothes. He said he wrote a letter to Rozelle complaining about the new policy but was told that the rules were the rules and I would have to be allowed in.

Gibbs finished his TV interview by saying that he would abide by those rules, even if he didn't agree with them.

I didn't see the interview when it aired live because I was at the team's training camp in Carlisle, but I certainly heard about it. My answering machine was filled with messages from friends telling me what Gibbs had said. Most were irate.

When I saw the interview, I wondered what the fuss was. What Gibbs said at the end was most important to me. He would abide by the rules. I didn't mind at all that he personally disagreed with them. I only cared that he would implement the league's policy.

True to his word, Gibbs allowed women—usually just me—equal access to the Redskins' locker room Monday through Friday at practice, and Sunday afternoons or Monday nights after every game. When the Redskins' locker room was open to men, it was open to women. Gibbs and I never once talked about the issue. We didn't need to; there was nothing to discuss.

We gather for a Joe Gibbs press conference at Redskin Park.

*　*　*

Gibbs set the tone for the team by obeying NFL rules, but his classy attitude was matched by that of the team's owner, the indomitable Jack Kent Cooke, one of the richest, most pompous, and most entertaining men on earth. As in any other business, the attitude of the entire organization was set from the top down. What the owner and coach said would happen did happen. It also didn't hurt that I was sent to Redskin Park by a huge newspaper, a formidable presence in the community. There was no chance the Redskins were going to mistreat the beat writer for the *Post*. If there was an entity grander in scale than the Redskins in Washington, it was the *Post*.

That doesn't mean, however, that I didn't have my awkward moments.

On one of my first few days in the locker room during the 1985 regular season, hulking defensive lineman Dave Butz called me over to his locker.

"Are you going to be in here when I'm naked?" he asked.

"Well, yes," I said.

"Then I think you should be naked too."

I laughed. He didn't.

"No, Dave," I said, "that's not how it works."

Butz, a wily veteran, clearly enjoyed playing mind games. He once gave me a multiple-page psychological test to take home so, as he said, he could try to figure me out.

"No women in the locker room!" he yelled at least one hundred times during my three seasons when he saw me in the locker room. One time I approached him, expecting to conduct an interview, figuring this was just playful banter.

"I'm not talking to you," he said sternly.

"What do you mean?"

"I don't like that you're in here, and I'm not going to talk to you when you're in here. I'll talk to you outside the locker room, but I won't talk to you in here."

I nodded. Okay, I said. This was workable. I didn't need to talk to a defensive tackle very much anyway. It wasn't as if he was the starting quarterback.

But one day, I did need Butz.

In 1987, he was hospitalized with a bad case of the flu the week before a game with the New York Jets. But Butz checked himself out of the hospital the morning of the game and played, performing admirably considering he had lost twenty pounds that week, according to Gibbs.

After the game, I wanted to check that figure with Butz—the twenty pounds—to make sure it was correct, so despite his rule, I walked to his locker, looked him in the eye, and asked my question.

"Dave, did you lose twenty pounds this week?"

"I don't talk to you in the locker room," he reminded me.

I smiled. "Well, I'd like to get this right, Dave, with your help."

He shook his head.

This fellow was just so incredibly challenging. But two could play this game. I wasn't about to leave and let him win.

I looked around and spotted Frank Herzog, the radio voice of the Redskins and the sportscaster from the local ABC affiliate. He was approaching Butz and me.

"Frank, will you do me a favor and ask Dave if he lost twenty pounds this week?"

Herzog: "Dave, did you lose twenty pounds this week?"

Butz: "I lost about twenty-one."

I thanked Frank, nodded at Butz, and walked away with my answer.

I never could get mad at Butz. He intrigued me the way a perplexing big brother confounds his sister. And it was a good thing I didn't get angry over any of his antics because it turned out that he actually fashioned himself as my locker room defender.

In my first year on the beat, the immature yet talented defensive end Dexter Manley was wearing only a towel when he beckoned me over to his locker, yelling, "Come over here, Chris, I've got something to show you."

I was twenty feet away. I gave him a dismissive wave. "Yeah, right, Dexter," I said, and kept on walking. I never gave it a second thought. It was Dexter being Dexter, pure silliness, nothing more.

But word got around among the players that Manley had hassled me. So, a few days later, after a Redskins victory, Butz called me to his locker for an unprecedented conversation.

I walked toward him wondering what he was up to.

"Is anyone bothering you in here?"

"No," I said, stifling an inclination to say, "Yes, you."

"You're sure?"

"Yes, I'm sure."

Butz stared at me, wanting to give me time to tell him what he thought I had to say. But I said nothing because no one was bothering me. Certainly not Dexter, who was a humorous, harmless man-child.

"Well," Butz finally said, "if anyone ever gives you a hard time in here, you just let me know and I'll take care of him."

I looked at Butz in disbelief. He was serious. I thanked him. That was nice, I thought to myself. Weird, but nice.

It was more than a year later, over the phone, that I finally asked him why he said what he said.

"Because, even if I don't like it that you're in there, you should be treated right when you're there."

A few years later, TV personality Geraldo Rivera made the topic of women in the locker room the subject of one of his hour-long shows. Several of us were invited to attend, including two esteemed veterans, Lesley Visser, who now was with CBS, and Suzyn Waldman, of New York's WFAN radio. None of us wanted to go on a tabloid show, but we felt that if Geraldo really was going to put on such a show, we needed our side of the story presented as professionally as possible. I was glad we said yes when the show's producers asked me if I could come up with a foil for us. I suggested Butz, who I knew would be a classy opponent, and a known quantity. He agreed to do it.

They sat us next to each other on the set, Butz and I, and of course, we argued. As we went around and around on the issue of women in the locker room, Geraldo interrupted us.

"You two are like an old married couple."

While the Redskins did their part to make sure things went smoothly in the locker room, I also did my part. There was a strategy to surviving in the locker room. Lesley once told me, "You have to be a little deaf and a little blind," and she was right. What you didn't hear or see would be crucial to your survival.

Peripheral vision was critical too. I had several go-to guys, players I wanted to check in with after every game. I always talked to a few of the offensive linemen—the Hogs, as they were nicknamed—usually Mark May, Jeff Bostic, and Russ Grimm. I knew where their lockers were at RFK Stadium and I would make sure to see if they were around. I usually did this as I leaned into the pack of journalists to listen to what one of the game's stars was saying; quarterback Doug Williams or running back George Rogers were two of the big names when I was there. I would try to get to the high-profile players first, before they grew tired of answering the same question over and over.

If one of the players I needed wasn't at his locker, it usually meant he was in the shower. This was when peripheral vision became useful. I knew these players so well and respected most of them so much that the last thing I wanted to do was see them naked.

As I stood at another player's locker, jotting down notes about what he was saying, I would notice that, say, Mark May was returning to his locker with a towel wrapped around him. A few of the male sportswriters beelined for him immediately. But not me. I waited for another minute or two until I was sure he had pulled on his pants, then I walked over to him. I tried to do this for every player I was planning to interview. I wanted them to feel as comfortable as possible.

During those three intense years covering the Redskins, I worked hard to be accepted as a serious, legitimate reporter doing my job. I wasn't there to date the players. I wasn't there to look around. I wasn't there to cheer for them. If they went 16–0 or 0–16, it didn't matter to me. I was there to cover the team and report the story.

But I knew I had to fit in, so it didn't hurt that Dad taught me to throw a spiral when I was ten.

Before practice one day at Redskin Park, Assistant Coach Dan Henning fired a football my way. "Hey, Christine!" he yelled. I snapped to attention and caught it, no problem.

"Wooooo," a few of the players yelled.

I returned the favor. I tossed a fifteen-yard spiral, a pretty tight one, back to Henning. He dropped it.

Being athletic had its advantages. Being tall did too. One day, all-pro cornerback Darrell Green didn't like the way I portrayed him in a story about his being named the NFL's fastest man. Somehow, God got involved in the middle of this. Green is religious, and soon he was lecturing me that my God couldn't possibly be his God.

Try as he might, Green could not get me to agree. We both were standing as we spoke. I was taller than six feet in my slight heels. He was five-eight in his street shoes. I'm not sure that made a difference as we went back and forth, with no declared winner in an argument he desperately wanted to win—but I'm also not sure that it didn't.

I was taller than six Redskins the final season I covered the team and saw eye-to-eye with nine others. That was about one-third of the team. And many more players were just an inch or two taller than I. There is no doubt that my height was a great advantage in being able to survive on the beat.

So too was the sense of humor Mom and Dad had instilled in us. There were some funny things that happened on the beat, none more bizarre than what occurred during one lunch hour on a practice day in 1987.

The Redskins' locker room was open to the media for an hour every day at lunch. The players came and went, often with a plate of food, sitting by their lockers, talking to reporters and camera crews, shooting the breeze with teammates. This day, I was planning a small feature on a backup running back the Redskins had just signed. He and I were sitting side by side on a bench, looking at each other as I asked him a few questions.

All of a sudden, someone shouted my name. I swung my head to see who it was.

It wasn't one person. It was a half dozen players, all standing fully clothed with smiles on their faces. As I stared at them for a split second, they parted—like Moses and the Red Sea—to reveal the team's strength coach, Dan Riley, standing there before me, completely naked.

I did the only thing I could think to do. I nodded, smiled

slightly, and turned back to the running back, whose eyes were popping out of his head.

"Let's pay no attention to them," I said, continuing the interview as best as I could.

I heard some rustling behind me, some grumbling, the sounds of people moving away. I never looked back over my shoulder. I didn't want them to think for a moment that I cared in the least what they were doing.

Did I really care? Of course. I instantly wondered if I had handled the situation properly. I actually thought their stunt was pretty funny. Was it proper behavior in the locker room in the presence of a woman reporter? Of course not. But no matter how long I had been on the beat, this still was their turf and I had to play by at least some of their rules. And I had to be able to laugh. The situation had not been threatening. I knew every one of those guys, and I liked them all. Riley, especially. He was one of my favorites, a gung-ho kind of fellow who had shaved his head when his young son lost his hair while undergoing chemotherapy, which thankfully was successful.

An hour later, I was outside by the practice field, waiting for drills to start. The players began their long, slow march out of the locker room in uniforms, pads, and cleats, ready for another day of practice. One of them came up behind me.

"Hey, you've got to tell me something."

It was Clint Didier, the Redskins' starting tight end and one of the pranksters who had stood in front of Riley.

"Did we get to you, even a little bit?"

I smiled. Now that we were outside the locker room and not in the heat of the moment, I felt I could let my guard down.

"Sure you did, but you didn't think I was going to let you know that in there, did you?"

I was in the Redskins' locker room for only about four hours out of my sixty-hour workweek. (Male reporters had the same time limits, of course.) Yet it sounds as if I spent my whole life there.

One day in the locker room, a little-used reserve player beckoned to me.

"If [So-and-so's] wife asks if you called his house, just say you did, okay?"

"What?"

"Just say it."

"What's going on?"

"You see, his mistress called one night at the house and his wife answered and [So-and-so] told his wife it was you."

"Oh, great."

Another time, a player told me the word was out in the locker room that I was having an affair with a local sportscaster who was married. I wasn't, but that didn't stop the players from giggling every time they saw the unsuspecting announcer talking to me.

Another player asked me to stop talking to him as I passed his locker. "The players are gossiping," he said.

"About what?" I asked.

"About us."

I was incredulous. There was no us.

"Yep," he said. "Remember, we're talking about football players. They have nothing better to talk about."

During my three years on the beat, I probably had a dozen Redskins ask me out. Some were married, some weren't. One in particular, one of the stars of the team, called me at home to ask me to have dinner with him. He called more than once. At least he was single.

I probably should have expected this, but I didn't, not at first. Just call me naive. Politely, I always said no when they asked. I explained that it wasn't right for a journalist to be involved socially with players she covers. That would create conflicts of interest that I just couldn't tolerate. My work was too important to me. And I did have a life away from Redskin Park. Well, sometimes. I was on a date at a D.C. restaurant when I excused myself to go to a pay phone and check in with the office. I said I'd be back in no more than five minutes. But I got word that one of my Redskins sources was trying to reach me. News was breaking, so I stayed on the phone and worked the story. Forty-five minutes later, I returned to the table. Miraculously, my date was still there.

As for the Redskins who were interested in me, I'll stop

being a journalist just for a moment and admit I was always a little flattered. It's hard not to feel that way after you never went out in high school. I had to smile; NFL players were asking out the formerly dateless Christine Brennan. But those married men were something else again. I would have told them to get lost under normal circumstances, but I couldn't. I was around them five or six days a week for six to seven months out of the year.

One night, right on deadline, I was writing a story on my computer in my Redskin Park cubicle when I looked up and saw a married member of the coaching staff staring down at me, smiling. I usually worked late into the evening, often all alone. On this night, all the other reporters were already gone.

"Do you stay at the same hotel as the team when we're on the road?" he asked.

"Yes."

"Would you like to get together this weekend?"

Yikes, I thought.

"No thanks," I said.

He pressed the issue, but I firmly declined. I thought we were finished, that the issue was settled. Within a few seconds, he turned to go, then swung back toward me.

"Would it be okay if I kissed you?"

"No!"

He walked away. I looked back at my computer screen. By this point, in my third year on the beat and seventh year of sportswriting, I had become pretty good at blocking out the strange and the bizarre, but this was just too strange and too bizarre. I stared at the screen. I couldn't focus. I had trouble concentrating for a few minutes.

The phone rang. It was one of my editors.

"What's taking you so long?"

It was a strange working life I was leading. I was employed, of course, by the *Post,* but during the three years I covered the Redskins, for six to seven months out of the year, I rarely saw my colleagues. I went to the office once a week to pick up my mail.

While I was there, I saw what I was missing by being at Redskin Park. The banter in the sports department was fast and funny. George Solomon had assembled a staff of young, hungry writers who not only competed for space in the paper but also for airtime above our desks. Two of those all-league talkers were Michael Wilbon and Tony Kornheiser. Later on, they would take the chatter elsewhere and give it a name: ESPN's *Pardon the Interruption.*

Mostly, though, my only contact with the editors and reporters at the paper was over the phone. Often I was talking to them in a whisper. In the era before cell phones, I never wanted the beat writers for the *Washington Times, Baltimore Sun,* and other papers to know what I was working on, but that was a problem because we all were gathered in one big room, where we easily could be heard from our cubicles. So I learned to hunch over, put my hand over my mouth, and talk as quietly as possible into the receiver. Or, better yet, make sure my conversations occurred when the other reporters were out of the room. Or sometimes, better still, drive to a nearby hotel and use a pay phone in the lobby.

Ironically, the people I worked with, answered to, and was edited by were the people I rarely saw, while the Redskins were the ones I was around every day. If I wrote a negative story about a player, odds were I would see him the next day and have to deal with his anger while it was still fresh. Of all the lessons I've learned in journalism, this was one of the most meaningful. It's easy to practice hit-and-run journalism—show up, write about someone, never see him again. In sportswriting, with all the travel, it happens a lot.

I had to practice hit-and-stay journalism. The experience of facing the people I wrote about, of standing up for myself and being able to argue on my feet with the most popular sports stars in town, was invaluable. The way I looked at it, if I could handle Jack Kent Cooke screaming at me from a foot away, I could handle anything.

Cooke was a self-made billionaire who used the phrase "if I die," not "when I die." That meant the most surprised person on the planet April 6, 1997, was Jack Kent Cooke. That was the day he died. But he was very much alive when I covered the team. When he visited the lush practice fields at training camp in Carlisle, Pennsylvania, or dropped by Redskin Park near Dulles Airport in Virginia, and the beat writers would gather around him, he would single me out. "Miss Brennan," or "My deeeear girl," he would say. He complimented me. He asked where I bought my clothes. (No place special, that's for sure.) He touched my hair. When he doled out handshakes to the guys, he gave a kiss on the cheek to me.

I was uncomfortable with this. I smiled and tried to ignore it. I shifted my feet. I swallowed hard and charged right in and asked my questions. Cooke laughed heartily and answered half of them.

Cooke told me to call him anytime, at home or at the office, and I took him up on his offer. I picked his brain on personnel decisions, contract negotiations, whatever was in the news. The give-and-take was invaluable to me and allowed me to present the most informed and complete picture I could of what was going on inside Redskin Park to the readers of the *Washington Post*.

But all good things must come to an end. On a mild late-December day in 1986, the Redskins were playing their first play-off game in two years, against the Los Angeles Rams. I had received a tip that General Manager Bobby Beathard had said the team might be interested in trading Dexter Manley. That certainly was plausible, considering the big defensive end had just pulled one of his infamous stunts and gone AWOL the day after Christmas, missing practice and meetings. (We later learned his absences and bizarre behavior were caused, sadly, by drug and alcohol problems.)

I had a standing invitation to visit Cooke at his A-list pregame parties or in his box overhanging the field. I told George Solomon about the tip, so he and I walked into Cooke's box to see what we could find out.

"Are you considering trading Dexter?" I asked when we got Cooke away from his guests.

Cooke's eyes bulged. "Where did you get such an idea?"

I told him word was out that Beathard was saying it. I would have checked with Beathard himself but he had stopped speaking to me in a snit in March.

Cooke told us he would check it out and let me know. George and I left. In the second quarter, with the Redskins on their way to victory, we were summoned by a security guard to return to the owner's box at halftime. As we walked in, Cooke's guests walked out: George Will, Lesley Stahl, Bobby Beathard.

Alone with us, Cooke exploded. "You lied to me! You said we're trading Dexter, and you said Bobby is saying it. That's not true. Miss Brennan, I'm not sure I can ever trust you again."

I managed a "What?" before Cooke turned toward George to continue the tirade. Outside the open-air box, the band was playing a happy halftime tune. Fans were cheering. Christmas still was in the air. And I couldn't believe what we were hearing.

When Cooke took a breath, I jumped in, setting him straight on what I had asked. He wasn't in the mood for listening. I laughed to myself, or so I thought, shaking my head and rolling my eyes.

Cooke noticed. He pointed his finger and shook it in anger.

"I'm thinking less and less of you every minute, young lady," he said. "And don't ever come back to any parties I have in here."

I probably should have been shaking as George and I walked out the door, but Cooke's five-minute rant had been so absurd that I just could not take it seriously. We went back to our seats in the press box for the second half and went on with business as usual. I kept my play-by-play of the game, took my notes, and wrote my game story, and while Cooke's outburst was on my mind all evening, I knew I had done the right thing, asking a question that needed to be asked.

The next day, that was confirmed in a story in the *Washington Times,* our local competition. The story included references to team management wanting to possibly shop Manley to other teams. We hadn't written the story because Cooke had denied it. So even though I asked the right questions, I got beat.

* * *

Cooke didn't speak to me again after that incident. When I called, he never called back. He was never available to help me with a story. If he acknowledged me at all, it was only in groups. This was becoming contagious at Redskin Park because by this point, Beathard was nearing the first anniversary of his self-imposed silence with me. He got angry when I wrote in March 1986 that he was close to signing a new contract with the Redskins.

He signed the new contract in April.

The day in March that my story appeared, we both were in Palm Springs, California, at the NFL owners' meetings. Beathard, dressed in his typical attire of T-shirt, shorts, and running shoes, walked out of a meeting room and caught my eye.

"I'm never speaking to you again!" he blurted out. "I told you not to write about my contract!"

"No, you didn't," I shot back quickly, "and even if you did, since when do you make decisions for the *Washington Post*?"

"Get your information on the Redskins from someone else," he said as he stormed down the hallway.

Beathard was a control freak masquerading as a California surfer. He didn't seem to be bothered by anything—except me. A month or so after I started covering the team, he and I were sitting in his office when, out of the blue, he said, "It messes up everything that they're sending you out here."

He was concerned about the locker room. I said I had no problems with it.

"I know you're a nice girl and I know you don't really want to go in there," he said.

I reiterated that it wasn't an issue. I don't think he heard me.

Why did these problems flare up with Cooke and Beathard? I refused to believe it was solely because I was a woman. I never let myself use that as an excuse. I always wanted to believe there was another reason, perhaps my reporting, perhaps a particular story they didn't like. But the fact was the Redskins had never had a woman reporter in their midst before, and they obviously didn't know whether to open the door for me or slam it in my face.

Sometimes it was a little bit of both. At training camp one summer day, rookie quarterback Mark Rypien and I were walking in an alley together on our way to the practice field. As we turned onto a sidewalk, I kept talking to Rypien but when I turned my head, I realized he was no longer there. He had moved to my other side, to the outside of the walk, by the street, as some men do when they walk with women. Dad always did this. I thanked Rypien for his etiquette and have never forgotten about it. But when there was news to report about him, positive or negative, I wrote it, and he understood that I would.

While Cooke and Beathard were giving me the deep freeze, my relationship with Joe Gibbs never changed. He has always been one of the fairest men I've met in sports. We did, however, have quite a few disagreements, as any beat writer and coach do when they see each other almost every day of the season. But they all were resolved in record time, thanks to Gibbs.

Although what happens at NFL practices can be as secretive as what used to be going on behind the walls of the Kremlin, I was allowed to watch the Redskins practice every day—with one rule. I couldn't write about plays the team was working on. No strategy was allowed in the newspaper. I could report injuries and position changes, just not the game plan. Journalists don't like any rules limiting our reporting, but this was a reasonable request we easily could live with at the *Post*.

One day, I watched the Redskins perform a trick play, the flea flicker, at the very end of practice. The players were whooping and hollering as they ran the play, throwing the ball back and forth, with the receiver running so fast he nearly slammed into a brick wall twenty yards past the end zone. As soon as the pass was completed, the players ran off the field like a bunch of kids getting out of school early.

I thought they were just clowning around, so I ended my story that evening with a note about the fun the players were having with this trick play as practice ended.

The next day, Gibbs waved me over as he walked out to practice. He wasn't smiling.

"Why did you write about the flea flicker? We were planning to use that play this week, and now we can't because it won't be a surprise anymore."

My jaw dropped.

"I didn't realize that was a real play." I felt awful. "I'm sorry, Coach. I blew it."

Gibbs nodded. "Well, it was a play, but we can't use it now. Anyway, don't do that again. Now let's move on."

Another time, Gibbs was angry with my reporting about running back Kelvin Bryant, who was in the hospital with bruised ribs—or so we thought. The Redskins were not being forthcoming about what was wrong with Bryant. While they were pumping out a press release or two with little or no information, I called Bryant's room in the hospital, and to my surprise, he answered the phone. I knew Bryant well and got along with him, so I asked him what was wrong. He told me without hesitation that he had blood in his urine, which was more serious than what the Redskins were letting on. I called the team's public relations director to see if he wanted to tell me what was going on, but he never called back, so I wrote a news story quoting Bryant that appeared in the paper the next day.

After practice, Gibbs called me over and accused me of "taking the low road, trying to pull us down." I disagreed, asking why he was blaming me for problems he and the Redskins staff had created. Gibbs told me I shouldn't have called Bryant. I said it was my job to pick up the phone to try to get information. He told me he thought I was focusing on insignificant details. I told him I didn't have the luxury of sitting back and watching a story develop for a week, that I wrote for a newspaper that must present a daily, if changeable, picture.

"Well, I said what I think," Gibbs said. "Now we'll go on. And make sure to let me know if you disagree with anything I do."

It wasn't always so serious on the beat, even when it seemed as if it should be. Veteran quarterback Joe Theismann suffered a gruesome broken leg in a Monday night game eleven weeks into the 1985 season. As terrible as that was, the ensuing quarterback soap opera the next few years was a story any journalist craves. One piece of the puzzle was Theismann himself. In the summer of 1986, I broke the news that he had a $1.4-million Lloyd's of London insurance policy for a career-ending injury. I received a tip from a highly placed source within the Redskins organization, made some calls, and had a story. When I called Theismann to ask him about it, he declined to comment.

However, after the story ran, Theismann definitely wanted to comment. He called me at the office and he was furious. He told me his insurance policy was private and none of my business. I told him it *was* my business, because fans and readers were wondering if he would come back, and if he didn't, it certainly was reasonable to guess that one of the reasons might be that he could collect all that money, far more than his annual salary. (As it turned out, his career was finished.) He argued, but he never said my story was wrong. He was just angry that I had found out.

As was Theismann's way, we talked and talked and talked about it. For a half hour, we talked. Joe was known as such a world-class talker that the old joke was you could leave your tape recorder with him and come back in an hour and he would have filled it up. But he always wanted to talk on his terms— and definitely not at home. I occasionally called players at home and most had no problem with that. But when I obtained Theismann's home number and called him there for a story, he immediately had the number changed. I eventually obtained the new number, then called that the next time I needed to talk to him. He got angry and changed to another number. The third time this happened, he changed it back to the first number. I kept all three numbers in my book so I could always find him.

After the conversation about his insurance policy, Joe assured me he was not going to speak to me again. I must admit I didn't mind, because I didn't think I could have taken much more talking. I shrugged it off as another typical spat between a beat writer and a star player and figured that Joe would eventually come around, as he always did. Plus, I was going on vacation and told myself to worry about it when I returned to Washington.

A few days later, I flew into the tiny Traverse City, Michigan, airport. I walked into the terminal. I looked to my right. I saw my parents. I looked to my left. I saw Joe Theismann.

He had played in a golf tournament and was headed home. He looked at me in disbelief.

I was just as shocked.

"No," I told him, "I'm not following you."

Joe said a curt hello. I introduced Mom and Dad to him. At least he didn't yell at them.

Dad so enjoyed the years I covered the Redskins. He was a Chicago Bears fan from way back, but he followed the Redskins closely during my tenure on the beat. Once, he even stopped to see me at training camp in Carlisle on his way to Gettysburg for one of his many visits to the battlefield. I took him to a night-time scrimmage and had him come on the field with me afterward to meet Joe Gibbs.

"Hey!" Gibbs said when I introduced him to my father, brightening in a way I had not seen before. The two men, not all that dissimilar in build, talked for a few minutes about football. I simply stood back and watched.

"Thanks, Dad," I said as we walked away. "At least he now knows I actually have parents."

I was always calling home to tell Mom and Dad about my experiences on the beat, some more entertaining than others. Driving back from training camp at about eleven one summer night in 1987, I wound around a bend near Gettysburg and came upon four police cars, lights flashing, and a collection of five expensive foreign cars and sports trucks. I drove by and recognized a Redskins wide receiver standing by the side of the road.

I turned my car around and stopped. I walked up to not one, not two, but six Washington Redskins. I looked at them. They looked at me. Of all the people on earth they wanted to see at that moment, I had to be at the bottom of the list.

"You're not going to write about this, are you?" one pleaded.

"I don't know," I replied.

I spoke with a policewoman, who told me they'd been speeding. I asked a policeman if the players were going to be cited.

No, he said.

Then he high-fived one of them.

"You guys gonna beat Dallas?" he asked.

The players and the police hopped back into their cars and went to the station. I tried to follow but was too far behind and lost them. Or they lost me. I stopped at a pay phone and phoned the station and got the runaround. By then it was 1 A.M. There was nothing more I could do that night, so I continued back to Washington.

When I awoke that morning, I called home and mentioned the incident to Mom. "I have to pursue this, even though I don't really want to," I said. "I feel sorry for the players, but news is news and I can't unlearn what I already know."

"Honey, that's why people dislike reporters," dear old Mom told me.

We did end up running a short story the next day because it turned out that two players were charged with speeding.

Asking questions wasn't always heavy lifting. After Kelvin Bryant left the hospital, he was back at practice and trying to avoid reporters. As he dashed toward the locker room door, Michael Janofsky, my old expense-account adviser at the *Herald,* was standing beside me at Redskin Park. He had become the NFL writer for the *New York Times.*

"Kelvin, are you a hundred percent okay?" I asked as he ran by us.

"No."

Mike and I followed him.

"Ninety percent?" Mike asked.

"No."

I bid low as most of Kelvin disappeared from view. "Seventy percent?"

Mike: "Eighty?"

Me: "Seventy-five?"

Mike: "Seventy-seven?"

The door slammed shut. Mike and I looked at each other. This wasn't journalism. This was *The Price Is Right.*

* * *

The 1987 season was my third and final year on the beat. Most of the *Post*'s Redskins beat writers of that era covered the team for two or three years, then graduated to another assignment. That was the perfect amount of time, I figured. You learned a lot, you got kicked around a little, and you lived to tell about it.

By that last season, the owner and general manager were not talking to me, but I actually found covering the team more rewarding that season than either of the previous two. It was the year the NFL brought in replacement players during the strike by the regular players. There were picket lines to cover and a whole team of new players for three games that actually counted in the NFL standings. These were men who never quite made it to the big leagues, misfits, you might call them—even a commercial real estate broker. News was breaking out everywhere.

The replacement Redskins were being housed at the Marriott next to Dulles Airport, and one day I received a call from one of them telling me that some of the striking Redskins had just shown up at their hotel. This spelled trouble, so I drove over from Redskin Park to see what was happening.

As soon as I walked into the lobby, a security guard asked me to leave and escorted me to the revolving door. I went all the way around and came right back into the lobby. The guard grimaced. "Get out," he said.

"What do I need to do to be in this lobby?" I asked him.

"You need to be a guest at the hotel."

I thought for a moment, then started walking past the guard.

"Hey, where are you going?"

"I'm going to check in."

It turned out that some angry words were exchanged between the players, nothing more. But I certainly was glad I was there to see it, even if I never made it to my hotel room. Preventative journalism, it's called. You're there just in case something happens.

That night, I called home to tell Mom and Dad about the incident and couldn't help but chuckle when I told them about registering at the front desk.

"Would you have done that, Dad?"

"What do you think, honey?" he said. Then he laughed approvingly.

My experience on the Redskins beat and exposure from writing about the most popular team in town brought an unexpected change into my life: television. Local stations were asking me to be part of their weekly half-hour shows on the team. I would race out of Redskin Park some nights just in time to get miked and go live on a set in northwest Washington. *Post* sports columnist Tony Kornheiser teased me that I never saw a TV camera I didn't like. That was particularly funny coming from a man you now see all over television, but he was right. I immediately felt at home on TV. I soon was flying to New York to be an occasional guest on ESPN's *The Sports Reporters* with Tony and one of my heroes, the host of the show, the legendary Dick Schaap.

I enjoyed doing TV work because it was such a departure from print journalism. When I'd write a feature on the Redskins, I could delete my lead, start over, move paragraphs, flip-flop ideas and thoughts. I could take a few hours to make it just so. But on live television, you fly by the seat of your pants. Once you say something, there's no taking it back. You can't reel it back in. It's out there. That immediacy is exhilarating.

But I will always be a print person first, and I realized this on my first ESPN assignment in January 1989. I was asked to do a feature on the Baltimore Orioles and the new stadium they were building at Camden Yards. To get some perspective for the piece, I visited political pundit George Will, one of the first journalists to cross over from print to television and a well-known baseball aficionado. He gave me some good sound bites for my story, but he gave me even better information regarding my career.

"Are you going into television full-time?" he asked me.

"No, I don't think so."

"Good," he replied. "Don't ever give up your writing. Do TV on the side, but don't leave print entirely. Newspapers will always be your foundation."

This advice flew in the face of almost everyone else's. "Don't you want to be on TV?" I was asked by friends and strangers alike. I always said that I didn't know, that although TV was alluring, I was happy in newspapers and I loved writing. Now I had an expert I could quote on the subject.

Covering the Redskins brought all kinds of new experiences into my life. I had not taken the assignment to become well known, but that's what happened. There were offers of speeches. People came up to me in the grocery store to discuss the team's running game. I was written up in the gossip column of *Washingtonian* magazine, where rumor had it that actress Sigourney Weaver might be interested in playing a female beat writer covering the Redskins. And I received lots of mail.

"I am a born-again, world-class, 68-year-old male chauvinist pig," Harvey K. LeSure Jr. of Bethesda, Maryland, wrote in my third season on the beat. "Imagine my consternation a couple of years ago when I picked up the *Post* and discovered that a *woman* was covering the Redskins! However, I had to read your articles if I wanted to know about the Redskins, so I was stuck. After a couple of weeks of this, I suddenly realized that I was actually *enjoying* your column. I came to the conclusion that this lady knows her football. . . . If you can win me over, and you have, you can win anyone over."

But as soon as I'd get a vote of confidence like that, other precincts would begin reporting in. Several angry letter writers had this advice for me: "Go back to the kitchen where you belong."

Clearly, they didn't understand the ramifications of their suggestion. Before a dinner party I was throwing in Washington, I called home in a panic to ask somebody—I couldn't find Mom, so I called Kate—how to brown meat.

Bewildered to that day by my ineptitude in the kitchen, Kate helped me through my crisis, then called Mom later and asked, "What was she doing all those years?"

Mom reminded Kate exactly what I was doing: "When we were cooking, she was in the backyard throwing the baseball with Dad."

Another type of letter bypassed advice and went right to a declaration: "Your an idiot."

I didn't get back to that writer, but now I wish I had, with a simple reply: "Your write."

8

LET THE GAMES BEGIN

My transition from covering the Washington Redskins to taking over the *Post*'s Olympic beat was symbolized by two suitcases. I flew back to D.C. from the Redskins' Super Bowl victory in San Diego in the winter of 1988 with a suitcase full of warm-weather clothes. I left Washington a few days later with a suitcase full of sweaters. I was headed to Calgary and the Winter Olympic Games.

People looked at me like I was crazy when I said I wanted off the Redskins beat. They couldn't imagine that there would be a better job in sports. But while I felt a great sense of accomplishment in covering the Redskins for three seasons, there was nothing I wanted to cover more than the Olympic Games.

One day about a year after leaving the Redskins, I hopped in a cab at Union Station in D.C.

The driver looked at me in his rearview mirror.

"You're the sportswriter! Where have you been?"

"I just came in from New York," I said.

"No, I mean, where are you working now that you left the *Post*?"

"I didn't leave the *Post*."

"Yes, you did."

"No, I'm still here. I just left the Redskins beat."

"Oh, I assumed you were gone."

By the time I became the *Post*'s Olympics writer, I had covered one Olympics, the 1984 Los Angeles Games that I had lobbied so hard for in Miami. It was then that I realized the story of the Olympics was much more than the sixteen days you see on television. Starting in the spring, I reported on all the major U.S. Olympic trials: men's basketball, track and field, swimming, gymnastics. There was a quickening pace to those months as the teams were selected. I watched swimmers fail to make the U.S. team by the slimmest of margins, sometimes just the length of a fingernail. Runners won or lost an Olympic berth by a fraction of a second. The stories of those who made the team and those who did not were far more compelling than an NFL game story. I hadn't realized that the run-up to the Olympics would be almost as fascinating as the Games themselves.

The gymnastics trials were held in June 1984 in Jacksonville. The morning after the competition, I scheduled an interview with the new women's champion. Mary Lou Retton was sitting by the motel pool with her family. I struck up a conversation with her mother.

"I worry about her," Lois Retton said. "I worry when she travels, about the security when she performs. She's sixteen. She should be going to proms and ball games. I feel like I've lost her to the world. Will she ever come back?"

She did, just a little more famous. Mary Lou became the darling of those Games, of course, and more than twenty years later, she still is someone I seek for perspective when I'm writing about issues involving little girls in big-time sports. She has one of my favorite quotes on the subject: "While other kids were reading about the Great Wall, I was walking on it."

On Saturday, July 28, 1984, I was sitting in the sunshine in the press section in the L.A. Coliseum with a laminated press credential around my neck, waiting for the opening ceremonies to begin. This was it. My first Olympics. Edwin Pope, the *Herald* sports columnist who had gone to bat for me with Coach Howard Schnellenberger, was next to me.

"There are very few times in your life when you can say that you're in the place where everyone on the planet would want to be," he said above the crowd. "This is one of those times."

Soon, I picked up our phone in press row and called home. I just had to talk to Dad and Mom from this place at this moment.

"How much are you enjoying this?" Dad yelled into the phone over the crowd noise.

"Can you believe I'm here?" I shouted back.

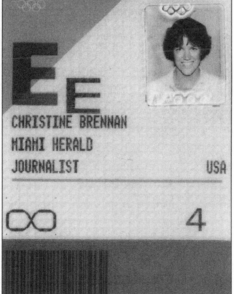

My 1984 Olympics press credential.

Those sixteen days could not have been better, one storybook day after another. Great weather, no smog, no gridlock. Was this really L.A.? The whole scene would have been perfect had the Soviet Union not boycotted, returning the favor for the U.S. boycott in 1980. (The reason the Soviets gave for not coming to Los Angeles was that they feared for the safety of their athletes.) The absence of the strong Soviet team robbed the Olympics of the fierce Cold War rivalries that gave the Games their competitive fire. There were times a gold medal went around an athlete's neck in gymnastics, in track, in swimming, that would have been silver or bronze if the Soviets and East Germans had been there. That was disappointing. Without the Eastern Bloc countries, the U.S. dominance gave rise to an over-the-top boosterism manifested in the omnipresent chants of "U-S-A! U-S-A!" The cheering that had been so spontaneous and meaningful in Lake Placid in 1980 rang hollow at times four years later as the Americans cleaned up against weaker competition. This grand international event occasionally had the feel of an all-American birthday party. Nonetheless, U.S. fans were generally hospitable, showering applause and cheers on most visiting athletes, particularly those from Romania, who defied the Soviets to come to L.A.

Dad was so caught up in the whole thing that he decided to fly out for a few days. He stopped in Denver, where Kate, newly married, and her husband, Tom, were living at the time, and they all came together and camped out in my hotel room for two days. Just like so many times before, sports had brought us together.

I bought them tickets through a newspaper ad for an evening of track and field so they could spend a few hours in the Coliseum, but Dad spent most of his time in Los Angeles trading pins. He brought bags full of Ohio flag pins, cheap little things, and somehow convinced fellow traders from numerous nations to give him all kinds of wonderful international pins in return. He giggled a mischievous laugh as he came back into the hotel room and dumped the pins he had acquired fair and square on one of the beds.

One of the most compelling stories of the L.A. Games was the failure of distance runner Mary Decker to win a gold medal. Decker was one of the most celebrated members of the U.S. track and field team, and she had been named *Sports Illustrated*'s Sportswoman of the Year in 1983. The night she raced in the 3,000 meters, Decker got into one of the most memorable entanglements in Olympic history. Running closely in a pack near Zola Budd, the barefoot South African representing Great Britain, the two of them bumped into each other, and with most of the sports world watching, Decker tumbled to the ground. She cried out in frustration when she looked up and saw the race going on without her.

I was among the several dozen reporters who followed Decker, in the arms of her fiancé, discus thrower Richard Slaney, out of the stadium and into the night. We tried to get close to ask a few questions as she was taken away for medical attention. I caught a word or two of what she said, nothing more. She was in tears, eight years of waiting for the Games (due to the 1980 U.S. boycott) now down the drain. Decker's misfortune was magnified by the fact that she wouldn't get another chance for four more years. As ever, it was this characteristic—the long wait—that attracted me to the Olympics above every other sporting event. It made it all so incredibly meaningful, every event a Super Bowl of its own: ten, twenty little Super Bowls a day, all over the landscape. The athletes who chose to compete in this world, to roll the dice once every four years, were, to me, among the most fascinating people in all of sports.

Soon after my first Olympics ended, I told Dad that I would never miss another if I could help it. If a newspaper wouldn't send me, I'd pay my own way. I had found the very best event in sports and I wasn't going to let it go.

Four years later came the Calgary Games. I was not yet covering figure skating, the sport that would become my signature; Sally Jenkins had the "sequin beat" for the *Post*. I was driving into the Rocky Mountains west of Calgary every day to cover the Alpine skiing events. I soon realized the allure of covering skiing. It certainly wasn't the nicotine-crazed European press corps. It was the perks. You also got to ski. *Sports Illustrated* photographer Heinz Kluetmeier pointed out that my press credential also was a lift ticket. This wasn't a boondoggle; it was a necessity for photographers and some writers to position themselves at different spots on the slope. I quickly came to understand there wasn't much to see on the face of the mountain except a blur going by every few minutes, so I positioned myself in the pressroom, where the entire race was shown on TV monitors.

Alas, skiing was a sport that could best be covered indoors. Golf was another, especially on deadline. This disheartened me because it certainly was hard to "smell it," as Dad would say, from the tables in the media room. But sometimes you had no choice.

Six months later, I went to Seoul, South Korea, site of the 1988 Summer Games and my first great trip around the globe. I was jet-lagged for a week. For the first time I had to get used to reporting from halfway around the world, which meant I was living in two time zones at the same time. When I was waking up at 7 A.M. in South Korea, it was 5 P.M. the day before in Washington and I was on deadline. Some reporters wore two watches. I just did the math and grew comfortable living on one time and working on another. For the first time in my career, I felt like a foreign correspondent.

Michael Wilbon and I at the opening ceremonies
of the 1988 Summer Olympics in Seoul.

I wrote in my diary that these Games were "the salad bar of sports," and I kept going back for more.

Gymnastics gave us the larger-than-life Bela Karolyi, the often ruthless, always comical, bear-hugging, grammar-mangling Romanian kingmaker of the little girls' sport. Karolyi, who had coached Nadia Comaneci and Mary Lou Retton to Olympic gold medals, said before the Games that because he was passed over for the 1988 Olympic head coaching job, he wasn't interested in taking a lesser job just to get to Seoul. "This is not a slumber party," he roared. "Nobody can ask me to come and sleep like a dog under a bridge."

In the end, after making just enough noise, he was named the head coach—and got his own room.

Karolyi has been a quote machine for two decades, and I've gladly been there to record more than a few gems. He once talked about the competition among his little gymnasts. "The girls, they must be little tigers," he said, his words dripping with a deep Transylvanian accent. "Kicking, biting, roaring to the top."

Another time, he was furious to see gymnasts yawning during an Olympic event. "This is the Olympics, good Lord. You'd better eat your shoes, eat someone alive, ignite something." He then decried their "laziness and lousiness."

Karolyi was at his best in 1988 when the U.S. team lost the bronze medal by a fraction of a point to the East Germans on a controversial penalty called by a top official, Ellen Berger, who happened to be East German. Karolyi went into overdrive. He stomped down a hallway at the gymnastics venue late one night with a parade of journalists following behind him. I was one of them. At each closed door, Karolyi stopped and threw the door open, seeing if he could find the villainous Berger.

On his futile march, he screamed, "I want to see Ellen Berger as a hamburger!"

It was a serious story, but I couldn't keep a straight face. None of us could.

If you cover the Games for a U.S. newspaper, you have to become an expert on certain sports. For the Winter Games, that's figure skating. There can be no doubt about that; the television ratings dictate that it's the nation's favorite Olympic sport. For the Summer Games, it's track and field, swimming, gymnastics, and, once upon a time, diving.

The time difference between Seoul and Washington meant that an event held in the late afternoon or early evening in South Korea would be in the middle of the night back on the East Coast. Why I decided to stop in at the diving venue for the qualifying rounds of the men's three-meter springboard competition in the early evening, I do not know. I had already covered the day's swimming events and was planning to go to a party with friends, but then I joked with my *Post* colleagues at our office in the Main Press Center that I would swing by the diving "just in case someone hits their head."

Dad always told me it was better to be lucky than smart. I wandered into the diving venue not knowing how long the qualifying had been going on or even where I was headed in the building. I ran into Peter Finney Jr. of the *New York Post,* who also didn't know where he was going, and, together, we decided to try to figure it out. We went up the first staircase we came upon, turned into an empty section of stands—and to our surprise, found ourselves no more than fifty feet from the greatest diver of all time, Greg Louganis, who was preparing to take his turn off the board at that moment. Our view of Louganis was unparalleled. Looking straight at him from the side, I watched him leap into a reverse somersault and immediately thought, *He hasn't jumped far enough away from the board.* But my next thought was, *It's Greg Louganis, don't worry.*

My brain had that conversation for a split second—*He's too close. . . . But it's Louganis*—before it was interrupted by the awful thudding sound of Louganis's head hitting the board.

For a moment I thought he was dead as he folded like an accordion into the pool. I expected to see blood, to watch rescuers diving in to save him. But what happened next was stunning. Louganis popped to the surface rubbing the top of his head and pulled himself up the ladder with an embarrassed grin and a shrug as his coach, Ron O'Brien, rushed to him.

At that moment we knew Louganis wasn't seriously injured, so the question became: Could he continue to compete? If not, he wouldn't qualify for the next day's finals. That would have been quite a story in itself. For thirty minutes, we reporters tried to get an answer, but guards wouldn't let us get close to Louganis or his coach or anyone from the U.S. team.

In that half hour, I watched waves of sportswriters stream into the venue, alerted by their editors to Louganis's accident. Soon, it was Louganis's turn again in the rotation, and he did in fact show up—with four temporary sutures in his head. He climbed onto the board and patted his heart, which made us all smile, and once again leaped for a dive that was eerily similar to the previous one.

I could feel my heart pounding. Standing in the journalists' pen on the pool deck beside the diving well, I held my breath. Louganis twisted in the air, cleared the board with room to spare, and sliced into the water without a splash. He nailed the dive. It was perfect. He easily qualified that day, and went on to win the gold medal the next day wearing a patch over his four stitches. Whenever I'm asked about the heroic moments I remember most in sports, that's usually the one I mention first. Louganis went from that gruesome accident to winning the Olympic gold medal in twenty-four hours.

The next big story of those Games began for me when I got a phone call in the middle of the night from Bruce Schoenfeld, a good friend who was working as a writer for NBC. Bruce woke me up to say Canadian sprinter and 100-meter gold medalist Ben Johnson had tested positive for a banned substance and was going to be stripped of his medal later that morning. By the time the news conference was held a few hours later in the Main Press Center, we were right on deadline the previous evening back in the United States.

My boss, George Solomon, went to the press conference and I stayed in our press center office, watching the proceedings on a TV monitor while furiously writing my story.

As soon as the news conference ended, George came running

back to the office only minutes before I had to push the button to send the story, which was going to be on the front page of the paper. I don't think I had ever felt more tension on a big story on deadline.

I needed a press-conference quote from George—and fast. He was rifling through his notebook. I was getting nervous. My colleagues Tony Kornheiser and Bill Gildea were also in the room, at their computers, with a bit more time to spare, now watching George and me.

George found a quote from the chairman of the International Olympic Committee's medical commission, Prince Alexandre de Merode of Belgium, and read it to me. But in his haste, George didn't give me de Merode's full name.

In my haste, I started typing the last name, then frantically asked George, "What's his first name?"

George didn't miss a beat: "Prince!"

Kornheiser laughed so hard he had to walk out of the room. I quickly came to my senses. I knew de Merode's first name. It was Alexandre, of course. I typed it in, pushed the button, and sent the story.

I sat back. George sat back. We looked at each other, exhaled, and laughed.

The fallout from the Ben Johnson saga was far more meaningful than the silliness in our press center office might have implied. Although there had been other positive drug tests in international sports, and other scandals, this time it happened in the marquee event of the Olympics. If you couldn't trust a footrace among eight men at the Olympic Games, what could you trust? This was a watershed moment in sports, the kind from which historians and journalists mark time.

As much as I loved the Olympics and hated seeing the Games sullied, I embraced this sordid story. We were on the cutting edge of one of the great issues of our day in sports. Random, knock-on-the-door, out-of-competition drug testing began in earnest in the Olympic world after the Johnson scandal, and the spotlight eventually turned on the U.S. major leagues. That Johnson passed numerous drug tests while cheating didn't affect only athletes. Sportswriters on the Olympic beat and later on the major-league beats in the United States were forced to report with a heightened degree of skepticism. For the first time, we knew we couldn't necessarily believe everything we saw on the field in front of us.

Steroids became one of the major topics of my career from that moment forward. Johnson's positive drug test and subsequent expulsion made the use of performance-enhancing drugs the single biggest issue on the Olympic beat from 1988 to the present day, and I continued to write about the issue as a columnist for *USA Today* as it exploded in Major League Baseball.

My years covering steroids in the Olympics were instrumental in helping me understand the magnitude of the problem in baseball. On May 20, 1999, while many reporters were still writing glowingly about the Mark McGwire–Sammy Sosa home-run race a year earlier, I wondered in a column about McGwire's use of a substance—the steroidlike androstenedione—that was banned almost everywhere but baseball:

"[McGwire's] squeaky-clean image might be changing, and his sport could be on the verge of a public-relations nightmare for which it can blame only itself."

It didn't surprise me when Barry Bonds was caught in this web of suspicion a few years later. It was only a matter of time for the mighty to start falling in baseball as they had in the Olympics. Major League Baseball finally started testing its players for steroid use in 2004, thirty-two years after the Olympics initiated full-scale testing.

"For baseball," I wrote in 1999, "this is a system that works like a dream. When you have no steroid tests, you can say you have no steroid users."

After those grueling Seoul Games, I took a weeklong vacation to Hong Kong and China with Kornheiser and several of his sportswriting buddies. On my Chinese visa, my occupation was listed as "housewife." The guys were all "merchants." I was about to complain when Kornheiser told me China didn't like aggressive women. I happily became a housewife for one week out of my life.

But then I blew my cover, with Kornheiser's help, on our second night in Beijing. We were wandering around a neighborhood when we saw a strange sight: a pool table sitting outside on a street corner, with a group of men gathered around.

We walked up and started watching. Soon, a new game was forming. Tony and Mike Littwin, a sports columnist for the *Baltimore Sun,* were pushing me toward the table.

"She's Minnesota Slim," they loudly told the crowd.

I rolled my eyes. Pretty soon I had a pool cue in my hand, an awestruck male opponent, and the luckiest run I've ever had on a pool table. Everything I touched went in. Tony and Mike and our traveling gang were cheering me on. For a few minutes, I *was* Minnesota Slim. I looked around. The crowd had swelled to at least a hundred men, pressing close to the table to see what was happening.

Inevitably, my luck ran out and I started playing pool as I usually do. I couldn't make a shot. My opponent won. I was happy for him. Who knows what humiliation he would have faced had he lost to a woman?

At that time, athletic Western women were a novelty in Asia. Even in Seoul, with the place teeming with female athletes during the Olympics, women reporters covering the Games drew stares when we traveled around town. I was in the subway with Kristin Huckshorn of the *San Jose Mercury News* when a girl approached us. She touched Kristin's blonde hair. Then the girl looked at me and made a basketball dribbling motion. With my credential hanging around my neck, and my height, she must have thought I was an Olympic basketball player.

One of the most fulfilling aspects of the Olympic beat was the relationship a reporter could have with the athletes she covered. While confrontation was becoming the norm on many professional sports beats, fomented by shock jocks on sports talk radio, the Olympics became a refuge for solid, old-fashioned reporting—and solid, old-fashioned reporter-source relationships.

The difference between my old world—the NFL—and the Olympic world became apparent to me when I went to Southern

California to write a feature on Edwin Moses, the outstanding 400-meter hurdler, before the Seoul Olympics. I had met him a few times over the years, but we didn't know each other well. Nonetheless, he gave me more time than I needed to watch him train and then to talk over dinner. As we said good-bye in the restaurant parking lot, I offered to send my story to him when it ran. To do that, I needed his address. In the darkness, Moses took my notebook and wrote on an empty page.

When I got back to my hotel room, I looked at the notebook. Not only had Moses given me his home address, he also had given me his home phone number, unsolicited. When people asked me why I had left the Redskins to cover the Olympics, I always told that story. Joe Theismann got angry and changed his number whenever I obtained it; Moses willingly gave me his number even though I never asked for it. A small story, but a metaphor for the difference between the typical professional athlete and the typical Olympian.

Jackie Joyner-Kersee was an athlete cut from the same cloth. At the 1992 Barcelona Games, she was attempting to become the first woman in Olympic history to complete a double-double—winning the same two events in consecutive Summer Games—but lost to Germany's Heike Drechsler, her good friend and rival, in the long jump. It was the first time Drechsler had ever beaten Joyner-Kersee, who settled for the bronze medal.

Joyner-Kersee hugged and congratulated Drechsler a half dozen times and looked very happy in defeat. So happy, in fact, that I asked her about it in the press conference after the event.

"I feel I gave it my best shot and today my best wasn't good enough," she said. "I feel I'm a strong person and I'm able to deal with it. It's part of athletics. You're not going to win all the time. In my first competition, when I was nine years old, I finished last."

She continued. "It does hurt when, in the Olympic Games, the day is not your day. Then I look and see that the person in front of me has been trailing me all these years, and it kind of eases the disappointment."

Mike Barrowman was that same kind of Olympic athlete: polite, humble, unassuming. He was a swimmer from Potomac, Maryland, a Washington suburb, who was expected to win a medal in the 200-meter breaststroke at the 1988 Seoul Olympics.

He finished fourth.

I watched from the press section as he hung on to the lane rope, catching his breath, staring at the scoreboard in shock that day in South Korea.

At that moment, still in the water, Barrowman decided that he never wanted to feel so awful again. He instantly dedicated himself to winning the gold medal four years later in Barcelona.

Because he was the Washington area's top Olympic hopeful, I reported on him periodically over those four years, even traveling to the University of Michigan, where he went to college, to write about his life there. It was rather two-dimensional: studying and swimming. As the 1992 Games neared, he swore off parties and even left school for six months of intense training.

In the sweltering early evening in Barcelona on July 29, 1992, at the outdoor Olympic pool, I watched from the press section as Barrowman swam four laps of the breaststroke faster than anyone ever had. He smashed his own world record by nearly half a second, a wide margin in swimming. He had done it. He had won the Olympic gold medal.

Later that evening, I caught up with Barrowman in a parking lot outside the swimming venue as he was heading off for an ESPN interview. I had been in his press conference but I wanted to ask a few more questions, so I waited for him in the warm Barcelona night.

I asked if he had his gold medal. He said no, that he had put it around the neck of his coach, Jozsef Nagy.

"You've already given it away?"

No, he said, smiling. He planned to get it back from him the next day.

Barrowman had given up a lot for that gold medal. But, I wondered, what had it given him? He knew he wasn't going to make much money from it. There wasn't a great demand on Madison Avenue for a 200-meter breaststroker. So, was it worth it?

He didn't miss a beat.

"Yes," he said emphatically. "I have done what I wanted to do. I have done everything now."

Our *Washington Post* team at the 1992 Barcelona Olympics, including Christine Spolar next to me, George Solomon with an arm on Tony Kornheiser, and Michael Wilbon, seated.

—

Barrowman represented one kind of Olympian; Tonya Harding, another. She was in a class all by herself.

Harding had established herself as one of the best figure skaters in the world even before 1994, when the infamous Whack Heard Round the World propelled her name into cultural lore and legend. I was in the press section in Minneapolis when she landed the first triple axel ever by a U.S. woman at the 1991 national championships. I wrote a front-page story in the sports section on that.

Tonya Harding was a different kind of skater, a chain-smoking asthmatic who spent her time working under the hood of the truck she owned. She qualified for the 1992 Olympic team in Albertville but purposely arrived late in France, saying she would not be jet-lagged. Then she skated badly and her coach admitted that yes, she probably was jet-lagged. That was vintage Tonya, frittering away what should have been a certain Olympic medal, just to be different.

By the 1994 U.S. national championships in Detroit, which also were the Olympic trials, I had been covering figure skating for the *Post* for four years and was captivated by both the athletes and all of the eccentricities surrounding the sport. At an NFL play-off game a few years earlier, Michael Janofsky, who had moved on to the Olympic beat for the *New York Times,* leaned over my shoulder and whispered in my ear, "Figure skating is the best sport."

He was right. There was a richness, a texture to skating that other sports simply did not have: the judging controversies, the costumes, the personalities, the pushy parents, the great East-West battles (Katarina Witt versus Debi Thomas, for instance), the amazing Russians, and, of course, the perilous nature of trying to land triple jumps on a quarter-inch blade of steel on the slippery ice.

Figure skating was made for journalists. Because the judging is so confusing, the sport requires explanation. If a golfer makes a par, you can count the strokes while watching on TV and realize it's a par. You don't necessarily need anyone to tell you what happened. But when one skater defeats another skater despite the general feeling that the loser should have been the winner, it is up to the journalist to tell you why. I once wrote that there are two parts to covering a skating competition: you watch the event, then you go to the hotel bar or the judges' hospitality suite to find out what really happened.

We Olympic journalists brought an irreverence to the sport that we occasionally unleashed at events. Because it increasingly was becoming a sport full of little girls, the *Chicago Tribune*'s Philip Hersh dubbed it "The Young and the Breastless." We joked that we often were writing about plunging necklines and lace and earrings and velvet costumes—and then, of course, there were the women. Jere Longman, then of the *Philadelphia Inquirer,* described one ice dance team as being dressed as "after-dinner mints." And when Canadian Kurt Browning showed up at the 1992 Albertville Olympics wearing an orange jeweled gladiator outfit, we said that he looked like "the *USA Today* weather map on a hot day."

On January 6, 1994, a group of us Olympic writers were watching the pairs short program at Joe Louis Arena in downtown Detroit when we heard the news that something had happened to defending national champion Nancy Kerrigan. What, we didn't know, so we immediately went to the pressroom, where details were emerging about an attack that injured Kerrigan's knee.

Within half an hour, someone in the pressroom yelled, in jest, "Where was Tonya?"—proving that a group of cynical journalists could crack the case days before the authorities did. At the beginning, though, most of us viewed the Kerrigan knee-clubbing in the same vein as the stabbing of tennis star Monica Seles the year before: another vicious attack on a top female athlete by a male assailant.

Back in Washington the next week, I awoke to the all-news station on my clock radio announcing that the FBI was investigating whether Tonya Harding's live-in ex-husband was involved in the attack on Kerrigan. I sat straight up in bed. From that moment, we were off and running on a sports story like no other, a story that built day by day with stunning new revelations until it spilled over to the grandest stage in sports, the Olympic Games, this time being held in beautiful Lillehammer, Norway. The dear, sweet Norwegians were preparing a quaint Games in their Currier & Ives winter wonderland. So much for that. The good old U.S. of A. dumped its dirty laundry right on top of them, with Tonya Harding crash-landing into the pristine Scandinavian landscape.

Early in the controversy, as Harding and Jeff Gillooly, the live-in ex-husband, were being questioned by the FBI and we were beginning to hear details of their alleged involvement in the plot to attack Kerrigan, I was driving to the *Post* thinking about where this story might be headed. It seemed logical that the U.S. Olympic Committee wouldn't want Harding on the team.

Isn't the best question always the most obvious one? When I got to my desk, I called USOC executive director Harvey Schiller in his Colorado Springs office.

"Are you trying to figure out how to keep Tonya from going to the Olympics?" I asked.

"We are," Schiller said. His bluntness surprised me.

"We're hoping she withdraws for the good of the team. Her presence could be a logistical nightmare. There could be camera crews on every floor of every hotel."

This was big news. I wanted to use Schiller's name and his quotes, but he said he preferred to be anonymous because of the sensitive nature of the issue. I talked to others during the day who offered the same sentiments but also didn't want to be named, so Schiller and the others became "informed sources" in my story. This was not an unusual arrangement; it allowed Schiller to deny that he had spoken to me if he needed to, but the quote allowed me to show readers exactly what was going on inside the USOC during this most unusual time. (Schiller agreed to go on the record for this book.)

The next morning, my story led the sports section, but I already was thinking ahead, trying to figure out what might come next in this most bizarre of stories. I was doing sit-ups on my living room floor while watching CNN Headline News when, at the top of the hour, the anchor led with news that the USOC didn't want Tonya Harding to represent the country at the Games.

The report sounded a bit different from my story, so I listened closely to hear the source of the news. When the piece concluded, the anchor said, "According to today's *Washington Post*."

I had my answer. I was the source.

And so it went for the craziest, most interesting, and most entertaining seven weeks of my career. I wrote almost every day for the *Post*, traveling to Boston for Kerrigan's first practice after the attack, then to Portland to report on Harding for a week. While in Portland, I met *Nightline* producer Sara Just on the steps of the Benson Hotel as we waited for the valet to bring our cars so we could join the media circus watching Tonya skate on a rink in the middle of a suburban shopping mall. As Sara and I spoke, she mentioned that she was looking for someone who could discuss the Tonya-Nancy story on an upcoming broadcast.

Less than a week later, back in Washington, I made my first appearance on *Nightline*, thanks to Tonya Harding.

Talk about a story made for television in the mid-1990s. As the cable news networks were coming of age, five months before the O. J. Simpson saga, the Tonya-Nancy story became their first round-the-clock soap opera. It also became mine.

My phone began ringing and didn't stop. After *Nightline*, it became alphabet soup: CNN, NBC, NPR, ESPN. By the time the story made its inevitable move to Norway, it seemed the whole world was talking about it. In addition to covering the fastest-moving story of my career for the *Post*, I unwittingly became a Tonya-Nancy expert on-air. I went on *Meet the Press, Nightline* again, the *Today* show, Larry King, and, for several days in a row, both the ABC and NBC evening news.

With all this TV time, my family was seeing more of me than they had when I was back in the States. Mom called my brother, Jim, to tell him about one of my upcoming TV appearances to talk about Tonya.

"I'm getting sick of her," Jim said.

"Tonya?" Mom replied.

"No, Chris."

In Norway, I was on the clock eighteen hours a day. I told myself I would sleep when the Olympics were over. Dad offered another option: "You can sleep when you're dead."

"At the rate I'm going, that might be soon," I replied.

Tonya's story only became stranger as the Olympics moved along. After filing a $25-million lawsuit to pressure the USOC to allow her to compete in the Games, Tonya performed poorly in the women's short program and nearly didn't skate two days later in the long program after her skate lace broke. Watching at home on tape delay on CBS, a huge TV audience knew what was happening backstage due to a well-placed, behind-the-scenes camera.

But live in the arena, we had no idea why Tonya wasn't appearing when her name was called. I thought we were living out the scene from the music festival in *The Sound of Music* when the von Trapps escape from the Nazis. I half expected a military officer to come running out shouting, "She's gone!"

In the end, Kerrigan won the silver medal and Harding finished eighth. Tonya later pleaded guilty to hindering the prosecution in the Kerrigan case and was kicked out of the U.S. Figure Skating Association. Her going-away gift to the sport was the TV rating she left behind: nearly half the nation—a 48.5 rating—watched the women's short program. It was the sixth-highest-rated TV show in history. Not just sports. All TV shows. Number one on the list is the last episode of *M*A*S*H*, followed by *Dallas*'s "Who Shot J.R.?", an episode of *Roots*, two Super Bowls, and Tonya and Nancy. With all the cable channels and choices available to viewers in the twenty-first century, no show will ever come close to replacing those six at the top.

After I heard about those TV ratings, I started to wonder: With the overwhelming popularity of figure skating, why had no one ever written a book taking a journalistic look at the sport? You'd walk into a bookstore and see dozens of books on baseball, golf, football, tennis, but nothing on skating, which polls and TV ratings were showing was the most popular televised sport for women and girls—even before it was visited by Tonya and her friends.

It's not often that a serious journalist will say something like this, but here goes:

Tonya Harding changed my life.

Within six months of the Tonya-Nancy affair, in the summer of 1994, ESPN executive editor John Walsh offered me a job as an on-air reporter in the sports network's Chicago bureau. I was torn; I had been at the *Post* for nearly ten years and still loved my job. I also didn't want to leave Washington. I was happy writing about the Olympics and doing the occasional column and did not miss the day-in, day-out work of an intense local beat, which is what the TV job would be. It would be very much like reliving my Redskins days. I would be back to the daily grind. On the other hand, I enjoyed doing TV work, and this would be my chance to do it full-time, and at a high level, on *SportsCenter.*

Back and forth I went, until I spoke seriously with my family. What they all said, in one way or another, independent of one another, was simple: the job at ESPN wouldn't be nearly as gratifying as covering international sports and the Olympics for the *Post.* So, if I took the job, it would have to be about the thrill of being on TV. If that was tugging at me hard enough, then I should leave the *Post.* If not, I should stay.

Jim put the finest point on it: "If it matters to you if a bunch of guys in a bar in Omaha know who you are, then take the job."

I turned down ESPN.

At about the same time, I floated my figure-skating-book idea to editor Lisa Drew at Scribner and soon was signing a contract to write the first-ever serious look at a season in the sport. I took an eight-month leave of absence from the *Post* to write *Inside Edge,* which became a national bestseller. It turned out the market was there, and the timing was right.

But my book wasn't only about riding the crest of the Tonya-Nancy wave. It also became a vehicle to tell the very serious story of the impact AIDS was having on the sport.

When I started the project, I hadn't planned to write about AIDS. But then I went to interview a figure-skating judge in his home in suburban Washington. I saw some pictures of the judge and his friends. I asked him who they were.

He pointed to one young, handsome man.

"He's dead."

He pointed to another. "That's his lover. He's still okay."

Then, on a trip to California, I visited a hard-luck skater named Rudy Galindo. I knew that he had lost two coaches and his only brother to AIDS-related illnesses. He was a man in his twenties who was attending funerals like someone in his seventies. I included his story in a chapter called "Skating's Tragic Secret."

During my interview with Galindo, with my tape recorder running, he said that he was gay. This wasn't necessarily surprising news, but never before had a competitive figure skater acknowledged this on the record.

The importance of Galindo's statement would not come to light until a year later, when out of nowhere, he won the 1996 national championship with a riveting performance in his hometown of San Jose and was thrust into the public eye.

Inside Edge came out in January 1996 to coincide with those national championships. At the press conference after his victory, Galindo was asked about his sexuality by a reporter who made reference to my book. Galindo, emotionally spent, said he didn't want to talk about the subject.

But people wanted to hear his story, so they turned to *Inside Edge*. I was on tour for the book, and interviewers kept asking me about Galindo, so I told his story. Officials of the U.S. Figure Skating Association didn't like this. They took exception to the publicity that was being generated about Galindo, AIDS, and homosexuality in their sport. More specifically, they took exception to me.

They grew so angry that, in April 1996, they took the extraordinary step of banning me from covering the sport. My editor at the *Post*, George Solomon, got the matter resolved in six weeks, but it remains one of the most oddly amusing developments of my career. Because the ban occurred when no skating events were held, I missed nothing.

But the news did raise a ruckus. A couple of days after word got out that I had been banned, sports anchor Keith Olbermann summed it all up on ESPN's *SportsCenter*: "In practical terms, this means she is no longer permitted to eat the pretzels and potato chips in the pressroom."

There's a refrain those of us who cover skating use often, and it applies here as well: "Only in figure skating . . ."

9

SPORTS AND THE
SINGLE WOMAN

It didn't matter how old I was, I always listened to Dad. Sometimes I disagreed with him vehemently, but as I was moving through my late thirties toward my forties, I still listened. We were two self-assured Tauruses butting heads, arguing over anything from the latest Republican turn to the far right (which both of us couldn't stand, but Dad often tried to explain the way loyal party men do) to the vitally important fact that we were five minutes late leaving our Ottawa Hills driveway for another trip to the airport. From the big to the small, most of it forgotten the next day, if not the next hour, it was as if a mirror were arguing with itself.

I never stayed angry with Dad for long. When we argued over the phone, if I didn't call to apologize within a few hours, he did. I couldn't stay mad at Dad. I didn't want to miss anything he said. By now, his sales pitch about life was ingrained in me.

Though I had been out on my own for a long time, when I needed his rules for life, I knew I could summon them in a moment and use them as my road map.

With his trapdoor memory and love of history, he painted a big picture of life that could not be dismantled. Everything—the economy, crime, wars, you name it—could be explained through history, and every explanation ended with the following words: "How lucky we are to have been born in the United States of America at this point in history."

Dad's sayings popped up when we spoke on the phone, during my numerous visits to Toledo, even during an argument. "To whom much is given, much is expected. . . . How are you going to make a difference? . . . Get up early and get going. . . . You're lucky to have this day. . . . You're tough enough to handle anything. . . . Your name is Brennan. You are different. Do more."

And one that I try to remember at press conferences: "Put your brain in gear before you put your mouth in motion."

But the one saying that continued to ring in my ears was his all-time best: "This ain't no dress rehearsal."

When *Inside Edge* became a bestseller, I was back at the *Post* and gearing up to cover the 1996 Atlanta Olympics. But I also was already envisioning a second book on figure skating, following the skaters through the 1998 Nagano Winter Games. If I got a contract from Scribner for that book, I knew I would be able to leave the *Post* and go off on my own. As wonderful as the *Post* was, this had been my goal for several years. I wanted to be independent. I wanted to be my own boss. I wanted to do more TV work, more radio work, and more public speaking, but none of it full time. I also wanted to spend more time talking to students. I knew the only way I could do all of this was on my terms, free of an attachment to a newspaper that hired me to be a full-time staff writer and reasonably expected me to be in the office or on assignment five or six days a week.

But those plans stayed on the back burner until after I covered the Atlanta Olympics for the *Post,* a Games that were both exhilarating and disappointing. Every Olympics is the sum of its many parts, and Atlanta had too many outside influences fighting against the magnificent competition that occurred within its venues. The Games began marvelously, with Muhammad Ali lighting the cauldron, but the overwhelming corporate presence of the Games' sponsors—you couldn't miss Bud World and Coca-Cola City—dominated the Georgia landscape and the Olympic ideal.

Dad had driven in for the Games, to go to events and trade some pins, and he came by to watch us tape ESPN's *The Sports Reporters* on a special set in Centennial Olympic Park, the Games' meeting place. After the show, we walked around, looking at the booths, the displays, the corporate logos.

"It looks like a county fair," I said.

"A bad county fair," Dad replied.

But those cosmetic problems, as large as they seemed in the Games' first few days, were overshadowed the night a bomb exploded in Centennial Park, across the street from the press hotel.

In the early morning of Saturday, July 27, 1996, I returned to my room after covering the last swimming events of the Games. I was putting my swimming notes away and gathering my track and field files when a loud, powerful explosion went off right outside my second-floor window. I opened the drapery and saw a puff of smoke in the brightly colored spotlights near the stage where a band was playing. I wondered if the explosion was part of the act. I watched for a moment, saw nothing more, and turned away to go back to work. But less than thirty seconds later, I turned back to the window and had my worst fears confirmed when I saw a column of police cars and rescue vehicles moving toward the scene. It was one long line of flashing lights. I turned on CNN. I looked out the window again. I was looking at the same scene, just from the opposite side. For the first time ever, an international news event had literally come to CNN's doorstep, and to mine.

I made two calls: First to Dad in his suburban hotel room. I was worried that he might have been in the park and was relieved when he answered the phone.

Then I called George Solomon in his room down our second-floor hallway. George had heard the blast, too. I asked what he wanted me to do. "Keep looking out the window," he said, "and call back to the office in Washington with anything you see."

I had one hour of sleep that night. (That was one hour more than some of my colleagues had.) The *Post* actually stopped its presses while we dug for information and dictated updates to our editors in the chaotic aftermath of the homemade pipe bomb blast that killed one woman and led to the death of a cameraman. One of my jobs into the morning hours was to work the phones to find out if any U.S. athlete was injured in the blast. None was.

It was the oddest feeling to be sitting in the Olympic Stadium the next evening, no more than twenty hours later, covering the men's and women's 100-meter finals. Throughout the rest of the Games, news about the bombing and security ruled the day, and I became a regular on ABC's *Good Morning America* from a rooftop overlooking the bombing site. Although it was NBC's Olympics to broadcast, ABC had a strong presence there, an eerie reminder of the night all those years ago in Toledo when I watched Jim McKay talk about the saddest Olympic day of all.

After the Games, I left the *Post*. I quit not because anything was wrong, not at all. I walked out the door of the most exciting place I had ever worked because everything, in fact, was right.

I resigned when Scribner offered me a contract to write my second figure-skating book, *Edge of Glory*. It was September 1996. I was thirty-eight. Some people thought this was a risk; I thought it was a natural progression. It was time for me to go off on my own, to try new things, to speak out more.

In addition to the book deal, I signed a contract with CBS Sports to report several figure-skating features and do interviews on a made-for-TV skating event; I signed with a national speakers' bureau; and I kept up my work with National Public Radio's "Morning Edition." I had no master plan; I was delighted to see what would come next.

In early 1997, out of the blue, I received a letter from Monte Lorell, the sports editor of *USA Today*. He asked me to have lunch. By August, I was writing my first column for the paper. It was on figure skating for the monthly Olympic section, preceding the Winter Games in Nagano, Japan. *USA Today* wanted me to go to the Games to write columns for them, and I also went to finish my book. I was busy over there. I wrote for the paper every day from Nagano, e-mailed the final book chapters back to New York, and worked as an analyst on skating for ABC News and ESPN.

At lunch one day in Nagano, Monte asked me to become a general sports columnist. A few months later, I took him up on the offer, but for only one column a week. I chose Thursday, a good day to reflect on the issues in the news. I have been on contract with the paper ever since. *USA Today* is the largest-circulation newspaper in the United States, with the nation's best-known sports section. I never thought my words would reach so many people on a regular basis.

I also didn't think they'd anger so many people on a regular basis. I never would have guessed it when Monte asked, but I soon became known to some as "The Issue Woman," and one friend jokingly nicknamed me "Crusades and Hand Grenades."

Things had changed in sports departments since the days of Oscar Madison. The sports section no longer was the escape it once had been, but a mirror of what our society had become. Someone once said that a columnist's job was to stir the pot. That sounded right to me.

For example, my first column from the 2004 Athens Olympics wasn't on sports, but on my own personal test of the Greeks' security system little more than a week before the opening ceremonies. Within hours of landing in Athens, I decided to walk from my media dorm room toward the Olympic Stadium to see how far I could go. I got right in. I never walked through a metal detector. Nobody bothered to do more than glance at my purse or check my pockets, and I reported it.

I heard from a lot of people about that column and did a few radio interviews. But I'm happy to report that security tightened quickly. A week later, I had to go through three security checkpoints just to do my laundry.

Another example: When *USA Today* sent me to South Africa to cover the President's Cup golf matches in 2003, I didn't devote my first column to golf, but rather to apartheid and the work of Arthur Ashe.

And while I have written quite a few columns on Tiger Woods's greatness on the golf course, I've also taken him to task off it.

Once, I was critical of Woods for not taking a stand on the South Carolina Confederate flag issue. The next day, I received a call from a friend saying that radio host Rush Limbaugh, of all people, actually read a portion of my column on his show, then angrily dismissed me as a "liberal Democrat."

While I was streamlining my newspaper work, my television existence became nomadic. I wandered among the cameras of CBS, NBC, ABC, ESPN, and CNN for several years after I left the *Post*. (There were no hard feelings at ESPN, where I continued to take part-time assignments after turning down that full-time

A TV interview with former Yale quarterback
Brian Dowling (BD of "Doonesbury" fame) at the
Harvard-Yale game in 1999. *(Courtesy Steven Conn)*

job.) But things became more structured with an ABC News deal that began in 1999 at the outset of the Salt Lake City Olympic-bid scandal. That ten-week contract to be an on-air consultant has led to a series of longer contracts with ABC News and ESPN that have covered the 2000 Olympics in Sydney, the 2002 Olympics in Salt Lake City, the 2004 Games in Athens, the 2006 Olympics in Torino, and all kinds of events and issues, ranging from steroids in baseball to violence in the NBA stands.

I was so pleased to have *USA Today* in my life because I never could have gone cold turkey into TV. Frankly, my eyelashes couldn't stand all the mascara. The amount of makeup you have to cake on when in front of the camera to counteract the bright television lights is extraordinary. But if you don't put it all on, people start calling with one specific comment: "You looked so pale."

Your appearance becomes paramount on TV. In print, the only thing that matters is what you write. You can sit in your sweats all day and no one cares what you look like. But on TV, even in the news divisions for which I often work, how you look does matter. The last thing you want to do is distract viewers from hearing what you have to say, and bad makeup can be a major distraction.

I've needed quite a bit of help over the years to get the hang of this. I even took a lesson from ABC News' top makeup man in which he drew the cosmetics onto the outline of a face on a piece of white paper so I could "paint by the numbers" later.

Sometimes, no matter how hard you tried, it didn't matter. At the 1998 Nagano Olympics, I was working with ESPN giving daily figure-skating reports. One night after I quickly piled on the makeup and fixed my hair, coating it in hair spray, ESPN reporter Steve Cyphers and I went outside the venue to find that we were in the midst of a driving rainstorm. We had no choice but to do our stand-up right then, without cover, in the monsoon.

When I came back to the pressroom, drenched and disheveled, a friend stared at me in horror.

"You went on TV looking like that?"

At the Salt Lake City Olympics, I taped ESPN's *Pardon the Interruption* in the early afternoon on the rooftop being used by ESPN and ABC for our various live shots during the pairs figure-skating scandal.

Invariably, a strong breeze would kick up at the exact moment we went on the air, and my hair would go horizontal when it should have been vertical.

"That's okay," cohost Tony Kornheiser said on the air. "At least you *have* hair."

All this TV work gave Mom and Dad a new hobby, which they attacked with relish: taping my appearances at the Olympics and elsewhere. They also taped most of the Games themselves, knowing I was able to be at only one or two events each day. When I would go home to Toledo for a visit after each Olympics, a dozen VHS tapes would be waiting there for me, with my parents' meticulous notes about what was on each one. For Christmas after each Olympics, one of my gifts to Mom and Dad was a large package of blank videotapes to replenish their stash.

When my schedule allowed it, I still always talked to Mom and Dad Sundays at noon. That was my time, and creatures of habit that all of us were, we stuck to our appointed hour. On one particular Sunday when I was still in my early thirties, we were discussing a few dates I had had with a man I definitely was not going to marry. I expressed my disappointment that once again, I was bored in a relationship, even though this one had barely gotten off the ground.

Mom spoke up.

"You know, if your life were a movie, and after covering the Redskins and Super Bowls and traveling around the world to cover the Olympics, if the movie ended with you deciding to get married to some nice man and have two children and a nice house with a picket fence and a dog, do you know what the audience would do?"

"No."

"They would cry," Mom continued, "and it wouldn't be tears of joy. It would be tears of sadness. The people in the theater would be sad that you gave up all the excitement in your life to do what people are supposed to do and get married."

I was silent when Mom finished. I couldn't believe what she had just said.

When I told other single women friends about the conversation, they first thought I was making it up. Most of them were living with constant pressure from their mothers to get married, especially if they were the oldest daughter in the family. And here I had a mother who was encouraging me to do the opposite.

When Dad and I discussed men, he gave me similar advice, typically rooted in demographics and statistics.

"As more people get divorced," Dad said, "there will always be men for you to date. In fact, as you go from your thirties into your forties and beyond, with your job as a woman in a man's world and your interests and your personality, you'll never lack for companionship."

I smiled and told him I would get married in my fifties, if I ever got married at all—and everything became so much simpler in my dating life.

Dad's reassurance also came in the form of a compliment: "As you get older, you just keep getting prettier," he said to me several times as I approached forty. I laughed and told Dad he was extremely biased. I did know, however, that as a teenager I had left myself with lots of room for improvement.

Mom and Dad were very logical with us four children, and undemanding in a social sense. They had always sought achievement and honesty and dedication and politeness from us—but not necessarily a spouse. If they minded that three of the four of us were single in our thirties, I never knew. Of course, it didn't hurt that by 1992, Kate and her husband, Tom Backoff, had three children—and that Mom and Dad were a mile away from them, living on the very same street.

Jim married Angela Sciarappa in 1996 and started his family of three children in 1999. Amy married Derrick Swaak in 1999, and they have two children. By the fall of 2003, with the birth of the last of the eight kids, I had four nieces and four nephews, and enough birthday parties, ball games, choir concerts, and school musicals to fill up all the free days in my schedule. I can't count how many times I've flown to Toledo to watch a junior high girls' basketball game or a high school hockey game. I've always felt grounded in Toledo.

Amy *(on left)*, Jim, and I, with Kate in our grasp,
at the church after Jim's wedding in 1996.
(Courtesy Garry Weber, photographer)

I joke about my single life, yet the truth is, you always think you're going to get married. It was going to happen this year, or the next. But then it just didn't. I met interesting men, had wonderful dates, kept meeting interesting men, kept having wonderful dates, but always got, well, bored in the end. Or the ones I liked and didn't get bored with got scared off by me or my job or my height—or maybe they just didn't like me.

I met one of my first boyfriends in D.C. when he called and left a message after seeing me on a local TV show talking about the Redskins. My college pal Chris Spolar, then at the *Post,* said I shouldn't call back. "What if he's an ax murderer?"

"He sounds nice," I replied.

"Ted Bundy sounded nice."

It turned out Joe Gallaher wasn't an ax murderer, but a very successful businessman who worked from his Potomac, Maryland, home. He and I joked that if we ever got married, he would stay home with the kids and point to a map of the United States to say, "This is where Mommy is today."

You don't choose to be single. At least I didn't. It just slowly starts happening to you over time. The fact that each day has come and gone, thousands of them now, and I'm not married—that surprises me too. Although then you hear that the census data says one out of four U.S. households consists of a person living alone, and you don't feel so different. In fact, you feel pretty normal.

During my twelve years at the *Post*, I met many people who felt the same way. Washington is the kind of town where arriving at a dinner party without a date is hardly embarrassing. In fact, it can be quite liberating. I prefer to accentuate the freedom that comes with being single, which is not an insignificant issue. I'm also part of a gang of girlfriends that celebrates birthdays and holds dinner parties and knows how to deftly signal in a quiet moment in the kitchen whether it's a thumbs-up or thumbs-down for the latest guy you've brought to the party.

In our family, as we kids grew into our thirties and forties, there was the same sense of being all-for-one-and-one-for-all. Kate is a stay-at-home mom and volunteer who has become my alter ego. In speeches, especially those I have given to women's groups, I often joke about my out-of-the-suitcase existence, and Kate's stable, traditional, three-kids-and-a-husband life.

"You can have it all as a woman of today," I say. "It just takes two women to do it."

I now use Amy as an example as well. She was a national sales manager for Fairmont Hotels and Resorts in Chicago before marrying and moving to New Jersey to become a full-time mother and community leader. The same goes for Jim's wife, Angela, who was a private banker before she started having children.

We're a family of traditionalists in that way. I often tell Kate, Amy, and Angela that their job is far more important than mine, and I mean it.

But as I've become older and realized that Mom knew what she was talking about with her "movie" story—that I would suffocate in the traditional American family setting—I also know that at some point in my life, I won't be running to the Olympics and TV appearances and speeches as much as I am now, and perhaps I will want to get married. Someday, perhaps, I will get tired of meeting new people and the wonderful uncertainty of having almost no routine and the delight of looking out airplane windows like a little kid. Perhaps someday I will not want to be so independent. Perhaps someday I will no longer love the excitement of a first date. Perhaps.

Everyone's a critic: Kate and Tom's kids with my books and a *USA Today* in my 1999 Christmas card picture.

—

Being a single woman in the sports world, I have come to realize there is some interest in my social life. It took me a while to understand why anyone cared, but as my profile grew, it happened, and I accepted it. People at speeches or on radio shows seemed to be interested in hearing me tell the story of one D.C. boyfriend calling the trunk of my car "the Mobile Locker Room," with good reason. To this day, I keep golf clubs, golf shoes, Rollerblades, a tennis racket, tennis balls, a baseball glove, a basketball, and a football in my trunk. You never know when a game—any kind of game—will break out.

A woman who leads this kind of life is a curiosity to many people. If you're the one living it, you not only have to understand that, you also have to be able to laugh at it. Larry King and I both were guests on a Fox Sports Radio show from the 2004 men's Final Four one morning when host Tony Bruno told Larry that I had been covering the World Figure Skating Championships in Dortmund, Germany, then taken two days off in France, then returned to the United States. "In the past five days, Christine has been in Germany, Paris, London, Washington, and San Antonio," Tony said.

"That's why she's still single," Larry replied.

Another day I was a guest in the studio on Washington's WTEM Sports Radio. Host Steve Czaban plays the Neanderthal quite well to my women's libber, and we've gone round and round over the years on Billie Jean King and Title IX and women's soccer and the like. Mostly, we do this good-naturedly, especially when I remind Steve he might not be enjoying those private, men-only golf courses he occasionally plays when his daughters get old enough to want to go with him and he has to explain why they can't.

"You'll become Mr. Title IX someday," I say with a smile, "and I can't wait."

On this particular day, as we went back and forth like this, the subject of my not being married came up, and Steve blurted out, "The man who can handle you hasn't been invented yet."

Steve's cohost, Andy Pollin, a good friend of mine, gasped. But he didn't have to be concerned. I was laughing.

"Why, thank you, Steve, I'll take that as a compliment."

Steve smiled, Andy took a deep breath, I winked at Andy— and we went to a commercial.

Being single and untethered to a full-time job has had its great advantages. If I wasn't at a sports event, or in D.C., the odds are I would be in Toledo. I always tried to get home every six to eight weeks, including, of course, all those holidays. When I was there, I'd sleep in the same bed in the same room I shared with Kate all through high school. Mom would call up the stairs to me as she did thirty years earlier, and when she did, her voice would sound so rich and strong that for a moment she was no longer in her sixties or seventies, but young again.

Even as they were growing older, Mom and Dad never acted old. They would joke about "playing nursing home" in the evenings by falling asleep in front of the TV or at their desk, but they couldn't have been living a more vibrant life. They went to Europe or on other grand adventures several times a year. Dad never stopped going to the office, even as Jim became company president and Kate's husband, Tom, became vice president. Dad was repelled by the thought of retirement. Mom, meanwhile, was volunteering at Christ Presbyterian Church or at the Sunset House, a retirement community down the street.

Mom's was a familiar face at all kinds of volunteer events, but one day, as the church was getting ready for its annual bazaar, she dashed in early and started rooting through the clothes being put out for sale. When someone asked what she was doing, she said she was looking for Dad's sweatsuit. She had mistakenly given it away and needed to get it back, pronto.

Dad was serious about his workout gear because he was serious about his walking. For months on end, through all kinds of weather, he walked four miles a day under the big maples and oaks of our neighborhood, or amid the untouched acres in a park just down the street. Dad often was in the headlines for his political work, but he also made news for walking twelve hundred consecutive days in the mid-1990s. 4800 Miles and Going Strong, wrote the *Village Voice* of Ottawa Hills. The *Blade* wrote about his streak as well. Snow could have been falling all day and night, the schools closed, the streets impassable—and Dad still would have been out walking in the dark, before sunrise.

Later on, Dad would proclaim, "I walked right down the middle of the street."

To which Mom added, "That's because no one else on earth was out."

Mom was more sensible. She would pedal on a stationary bicycle in front of the television in the family room, lifting soup cans to work on her biceps.

Occasionally when I was home, we would launch into more

serious issues. I asked Dad on one of our trips to the airport if he was at all afraid of death. "No," he said. "Not at all. You live on through your children."

I loved that thought.

"So," Dad added with a wink, "keep doing interesting things, okay?"

I so enjoyed their take on life, the notion that you greeted the day with delight, even if it was raining and miserable and your knees ached and you were getting old and gray, as Mom sometimes said. On her seventy-first birthday, I called from the British Open golf tournament in Scotland to sing "Happy Birthday." I asked Mom how she was doing.

"Well, I'm still here in the kitchen, hanging on to the counter," she said with a sarcastic laugh, referring to her bad knees.

"It sure beats the alternative," Dad chimed in from another phone in the house.

That was their outlook on everything, a Depression-era perspective that was so worthy of imitation.

Mom, Dad, and I at a dinner in Washington in the mid-1990s.

No matter how far apart we might be, we were an integral part of each other's lives. When I was a guest on the national Jim Bohannon radio show on my book tour in 1996, and the next caller was "Jim from Toledo," I perked up.

"Happy Birthday tomorrow, honey," Dad said. Bohannon then signaled his producer and we came back from a commercial with "Happy Birthday" playing.

At the 2000 Sydney Olympic Games, I was on a live chat for usatoday.com, answering questions about women's soccer and gymnastics, when this one popped up: "toledo, ohio: your mother wants to know if you are getting enough sleep."

Fifteen time zones away, I laughed and typed, "Is this you, Dad? Yes, I'm getting enough sleep. Just barely enough!"

For all these years, I was living a charmed life as a professional daughter. I wanted to call home to hear my parents' laughter, their delightful banter, Mom's light dismissals of Dad's latest pronouncements. As always, I called or e-mailed with my flight information before I boarded a plane, and I called to let them know I had arrived. Mom and Dad enjoyed knowing that I was safe, and I enjoyed letting them know. No matter how old I was, I still was very much theirs.

10

"BABE CITY"

It was Saturday, July 10, 1999, a sun-splashed day in Southern California. I had never seen so many dads with their daughters gathered in the same place. It was like Dad with us at Michigan Stadium in 1969, but this time, it was an entire stadium full of dads and kids. A crowd of 90,185, the largest to ever witness a women's athletic event anywhere in the world, filled the Rose Bowl for the Women's World Cup soccer final. Forty million more watched on television. For the first time, a women's sports event had become *the* place to be. Any die-hard sports fan would have loved a ticket to that game.

Women's sports had attracted large audiences before, in the Olympics and professional tennis, especially, but there was something different about the women these fans had come to see, the members of the U.S. Women's World Cup soccer team. They weren't wearing dresses, like tennis players or figure skaters. They weren't in leotards like gymnasts, or bathing suits like Olympic swimmers. They were the first female superstar athletes to be dressed like men, in baggy shirts and shorts.

How far had women's sports come in the twenty-seven years since Title IX? People around the country fell in love with these women not as sex symbols, but purely as athletes and role models. Delightful TV commercials surrounded the event, including Gatorade's "Anything You Can Do, I Can Do Better" ad, featuring Mia Hamm and Michael Jordan competing in various sports, ending with Hamm throwing Jordan over her shoulder.

Longtime NFL quarterback Doug Flutie said he watched the World Cup games with his ten-year-old daughter, Alexa. After they saw the Gatorade ad, Alexa had a question for her father.

"Who's the guy in the commercial with Mia?"

David Letterman dubbed the twenty members of the U.S. team "Babe City" and invited them on his show. That term bothered some, but not me. I couldn't wait to write about it during the final week of the World Cup.

"Welcome to Babe City, population 20," I wrote from Southern California in a column two days before the final game.

> Good-looking people, be they Mia Hamm or Michael Jordan, interest us more than ugly people. That's not sexism. That's reality. And that's not new.
>
> But what is new is the way this team is redefining our image of beauty and body size.
>
> For decades, we've glorified rail-thin models or pixie gymnasts, never wasting much time worrying about their potential eating disorders or the general issues of a woman's self-esteem.
>
> Today, we find ourselves enamored of a group of women who are neither petite nor disarmingly thin: among them goalkeeper Briana Scurry, 5–8, 145; Brandi Chastain, 5–7, 135; Julie Foudy, 5–6, 130; and Michelle Akers, 5–10, 150.
>
> Pardon my language, but a 5–10, 150-pound "babe"?
> Now that's progress.

There was a personal element to my glee. I didn't say it in the column, but of course I'm nearly six feet tall and weigh 160 pounds. Never in my wildest dreams did I believe anyone would view a woman my size as being a "babe." I chuckled with Mom and Dad a few times over the phone about that.

In the game that beautiful day in the Rose Bowl, the United States and China played to a 0–0 tie. That meant overtime, and when there still was no score, penalty kicks. When U.S. goalie Briana Scurry made a lunging save on one Chinese attempt, the United States had a chance to win the game. Moments later, up stepped Brandi Chastain. She sent the ball flying into the upper-right corner of the net. Her kick won the game and the World Cup. She ripped off her shirt and whipped it over her head, revealing what would instantly become the most famous bra in sports history. As she dropped to her knees, her fists clenched, her jersey in her hand, she became the poster child for the modern female athlete: uninhibited, confident, ecstatic.

As the confetti fluttered through the air and the Americans danced across the field, I opened my purse in the press box and reached for my cell phone.

"Can you believe this?" I yelled into the phone.

"It's incredible!" came the voice at the other end.

I called someone who I knew had watched every minute of it on television, and knew exactly what it meant to both of us.

Of course I called Dad.

The story of this team that so captured the attention of people like me, and parents like Mom and Dad, had been building for several weeks. It began during the U.S. team's opening game, when a crowd of 78,972 filled Giants Stadium in New Jersey for the first U.S. victory. There was something significant about that crowd. It was larger than what the New York Jets had drawn for an NFL play-off game in the same place five months earlier. Watching on TV, I heard that and couldn't believe it. More people showed up for women's soccer than attended an NFL play-off game? How could that be? Only the pope, it was announced, had drawn a bigger crowd in the history of Giants Stadium.

Over the next few weeks, the superlatives didn't stop. The United States kept winning and drawing big crowds in huge stadiums. And, even more important, most big newspapers were covering the story, giving it strong play on the front page of the sports section. This was late June and early July, a relatively quiet time in sports, when little else was going on other than baseball and Wimbledon. The timing was perfect.

One night, unable to catch the U.S.–North Korea game on TV, I called Dad to get updates. We laughed. "Dad, do you realize this is the first time we've ever cared about soccer?"

"It's not the soccer," he replied. "It's this team."

In the quarterfinals, the Americans had to face highly regarded Germany at Jack Kent Cooke Stadium in Landover, Maryland. I went to the U.S. practice and wrote my first column on the team. I joked that I was so clueless about soccer, I didn't know the difference between a yellow card, a red card, or a green card.

But I did know this: the players were some of the most unspoiled athletes I had ever met. After every interview that day at practice, they thanked me for coming. It turned out they were thanking every reporter for coming. That was such a rare occurrence, a few of us marveled about it later in the press box.

In the game the next day, the United States came from behind to win, 3–2. There was a message on my answering machine that night: "Tremendous! These girls sure know how to play."

It was the exuberant voice of my father.

Mom chimed in the next day, exclaiming, "My goodness, those girls sure do run!"

They loved it, Mom and Dad did, and I knew why. It was the same reason I loved it. Here was a team of U.S. women, all college graduates or about to be, all of them girls-next-door, none of them petite, coming along ten to fifteen years after I did, doing what my generation of girls never had the chance to do. They were smart enough to understand what they symbolized, what they meant to older observers like my parents and me. They also knew how important they were to children, especially girls. Unlike some of their more famous male counterparts, they completely embraced their status as role models. They were latter-day Johnny Appleseeds, sowing the seeds of women's sports, and they knew it.

"This is history in the making," said Mia Hamm, the reluctant superstar who realized even she had to speak out.

"It transcends soccer," said unofficial team spokeswoman Julie Foudy. "There's a bigger message out there: When people tell you no, you just smile and tell them, 'Yes, I can.'"

These women had captured the attention of the nation almost overnight. This was a minivan revolution; moms and dads and their daughters were filling the great stadiums of this country, the arenas usually reserved for men and their football, to watch women play soccer. How could those who came before—parents like mine, who had driven to games and walked into empty gyms to watch their daughters play, and girl athletes like me, who came along too early for anything like this—not be thrilled to see it? How could we look at these women in their soccer uniforms and tall socks and not see ourselves?

I flew to California for the July 4 semifinal game between the U.S. and Brazil at Stanford Stadium. The U.S. won, 2–0. Then a funny thing happened: the crowd filed out, almost all of it, leaving a nearly empty stadium for the second game of a soccer doubleheader, which was a men's professional Major League Soccer game. A few of us women in the press box couldn't believe our eyes. They come for the women, then leave for the men? It was astonishing.

It wasn't only fans who came. The national media was out in force in the week that led to the U.S.-China final. NBC's Tom Brokaw arrived, so did ABC's Robin Roberts. I was interviewed by both of them.

"This team is the personification of Title IX," I said. "The timing is perfect: twenty-seven years later, the nation is realizing that we have fallen in love with what the law has created."

And what, exactly, was that? For starters, those playing fields full of girls that I never could have imagined growing up. The numbers told the story: in 1971, the year before Richard Nixon signed Title IX, one in twenty-seven girls was playing high school sports. By 1999, the number was one in three, on its way to being one in two and a half by 2005, according to the Women's Sports Foundation. Girls were not only being told they could play sports, they were being strongly encouraged to do so. A lot had changed in a generation. Girls proudly wore baseball caps on their heads. They wore their jerseys to the mall. They all had a complete athletic wardrobe—and no one hid any of it in the closet.

My nieces Leslie and Jennie
in their softball uniforms in 2004.

Girls and women reveled in sports. At the 1996 Olympics in Atlanta, I asked six-foot-tall swimmer Amy Van Dyken if she could put it all into perspective.

"These days," she said, "it's cool for a woman to be able to bench-press her husband."

The law opened the floodgates for waves of strong, confident women competing in basketball, softball, soccer, golf. It created tens of thousands of college scholarships—and a climate that allowed a teen golf sensation named Michelle Wie to sign endorsement contracts worth $10 million a year before she turned sixteen in the fall of 2005.

The law also was having a profound effect on boys. They were growing up with a healthy respect for girls on the playing field and presumably off it as well. Some boys actually wore Mia Hamm jerseys to U.S. soccer games. Others trooped off to WNBA and women's college basketball games with their parents and sisters.

Their appreciation could be summed up in the use of one little adjective: "men's." As in the men's soccer team, or the men's basketball team, to distinguish them from the women's.

When my nephew Brad was twelve, he heard someone talking about "the Final Four."

He didn't miss a beat.

"Which one?" he asked.

After they won the World Cup, the U.S. players appeared on the covers of *Time, Newsweek, Sports Illustrated,* and *People* in the same week. No other story had hit for the cycle like that. The team reappeared on the cover of *SI* at the end of the year as the Sportswomen of the Year. (There was no Sportsman of the Year. Just them.) They stayed together, played in the 2000 Olympics, and settled for the silver medal in an overtime loss to Norway. The next year, their new league, the Women's United Soccer Association, began. In 2003, it folded. It simply could not survive on the crowded U.S. sports landscape.

Disappointment would have settled in for the team and those who followed it were it not for the fact that another Olympics awaited. The 2004 Games in Athens would be the last international tournament for Hamm and Foudy, among other veterans.

Fittingly, they went out as winners, defeating Brazil, 2–1, in the gold-medal game. The U.S. print media came out once again to cover the team; some of us even flew to Crete to report on the Americans' semifinal game. But there was an embarrassing lack of interest in women's soccer among the fans at those Olympics, many of them Europeans who presumably are fans of the men's game only. About eighty thousand fewer people attended the 2004 gold-medal game than were at the Rose Bowl in 1999. But it was standing room only in the press box.

The legacy of the most visible women's sports team of all time is debated to this day. A few months after the 2004 Olympics, a Los Angeles–based sportswriter told me I was "ludicrous" for writing about how important the 1999 World Cup team was to girls in America. I thought he was kidding, but then he mentioned "ludicrous" again. I heard him out.

He believed the women should be judged by the same standards as the men, and with the demise of their professional league, that meant they were a failure. I suggested there was more than one way to measure the success of this team. And I've believed that since July 9, 1999, the day before the U.S.–China final, the day I wrote this column:

> PASADENA, Calif.—Thirty years from now, a woman running for president of the United States will be asked about the defining moment of her childhood. And she will answer, without missing a beat, "The 1999 Women's World Cup soccer tournament."
>
> If it's not a female presidential candidate, it will be a female CEO of one of the nation's most successful Fortune 500 companies. Or the top-ranking woman in the military. Or the female chancellor of one of the great universities.
>
> It's going to happen. In 2029, an important woman will talk about the fact that, for the first time in a non-Olympic year, she watched and cheered for women who looked like she did when she grew up. She will say the World Cup showed her that sports could be as inviting to her as they had been to her brother. She will look back and say that after the summer of 1999, she never felt silly or unpopular or out of place playing sports.
>
> "We're at the epicenter of a big rock being thrown into a huge pond," said Michelle Akers, the 33-year-old heart and soul of the wildly popular U.S. team. "We don't know what the ripple effect will be. . . . "

* * *

There are those in the mainstream sports media, some of them my friends, who wonder why I write so much about women's sports. In both 2004 and 2005, I went from the men's NCAA basketball final game to the women's NCAA final the next evening. Several other writers did this in 2005, when it was a drive from St. Louis to Indianapolis, but as best as I could tell, I was on my own going from San Antonio to New Orleans in 2004. When I told my colleagues in the pressroom at that men's Final Four what I was doing, most looked at me as if I had said I was heading to Iceland; it was fine if I wanted to go, but they certainly didn't want to go with me.

It makes no sense to me why so many reporters won't cover women's sports. Newspapers are losing readers by the hundreds of thousands. Wouldn't it be logical to try to attract new readers through the sports section, which has always been an entry point to the newspaper? And aren't new sports section readers by definition likely to be women and girls?

When I was growing up loving sports, I read about male athletes almost exclusively and never thought to wonder why there was so little coverage of the few women's sports that existed back then. Today, however, girls have dozens of female sports role models, yet the sports media aren't doing a very good job reporting on them. The stories on women's sports can be few and far between, and buried deep in the sports section. This in turn doesn't entice those girls to read the sports section. And then we in the newspaper business scratch our heads and wonder how we're ever going to attract new readers.

Even if these stories didn't bring in one new reader, I'd still be fascinated by them. One hundred years from now, I don't think people will care about who won this year's Super Bowl or NBA championship. But I do believe students will be looking at the social change in America that included the emergence of women in sports in the late twentieth and early twenty-first centuries. This isn't just a sports story. It's a cultural story.

So, when my male columnist friends wonder aloud why I write so much about women's sports, I give them my standard reply:

"I know you won't, but I'm happy to."

I have never minded standing out, not when I was the only girl playing with the boys in Old Orchard, not as an awkward high school girl sports fan. If writing about women's sports makes me an oddball now, so be it.

In the early 1990s, for two years in a row, the *Washington Post* wasn't planning to send a reporter to cover the U.S. Women's Open golf tournament. The *Post* sent its golf writer to the men's Open (the official name of which is simply the U.S. Open, without that pesky adjective). For the women's, the paper was going to hire a freelancer.

"If we cover the men's, shouldn't we cover the women's?" I asked George Solomon, and as soon as the words had left my mouth, he had a reply: "Why don't you cover it?"

Both times, I did. But it wasn't the same as sending the golf writer. By sending me, it made it seem like an afterthought, which, of course, it was.

Then again, the *Post* at least was sending someone. Many newspapers didn't cover the Women's Open in the 1990s.

At the men's Open in 1999 at Pinehurst, North Carolina, I asked a male golf writer from one of the nation's biggest papers why he hadn't covered the Women's Open two weeks earlier at Old Waverly in Mississippi.

"I don't do Mississippi," he said flippantly.

"No," I replied, "you don't do women's golf."

He laughed and walked away.

Still, the vast majority of stories I have written in my career have been about men and male sports: well over 90 percent. For years, I never wrote a word about women in sports. Not that I didn't care about those issues, but my job was to cover college football or the Redskins. Even now as a columnist, I write mostly about men. In 2004, an Olympic year in which coverage of women's sports rose dramatically, I wrote seventy-two columns for *USA Today* and only eighteen dealt exclusively with women athletes or women's issues.

And when I'm writing about women athletes, it's not always positive. How can it be with Tonya Harding still running around throwing jabs and hubcaps? Of those eighteen columns on women in 2004, four were very critical of sprinter Marion Jones and her involvement in the BALCO performance-enhancing-drug scandal heading into the Olympic Games.

So, in a year when topics about women in sports abounded, I devoted just 25 percent of my columns to women exclusively. I'm guessing that's higher than any other general sports columnist at a major daily, which says everything we need to know about the coverage of women's sports in the twenty-first century.

Well before I wrote my first column on women's sports, I was speaking out on behalf of women sports journalists as the first president of the fledgling Association for Women in Sports Media. There were only forty women at the inaugural convention in Oakland that elected me in 1988, but that didn't matter. This was exactly what I had been preparing myself for since I went to Northwestern in 1976 with no certainty that women could become sports journalists.

Controversies abounded, and I found myself diving into them even if I barely knew the people I was defending. In 1990, three New England Patriots sexually harassed *Boston Herald* sportswriter Lisa Olson, whom I had met just once, as she was interviewing players in the locker room.

The story became a very big deal, and while I couldn't believe the locker room was in the news again—none of us in AWSM's leadership could—we all pitched in to calmly return the calls of dozens of frenzied reporters and announcers at TV and radio stations.

AWSM was founded as a kind of "Old Girls Network," the first organized opportunity we all had to help one another. I was proud of what we accomplished during that controversy. But I was puzzled by the fact that to this day, it's called "the Lisa Olson incident." Why do we name news events after the victim?

Speaking out has taken other forms. I've visited dozens of journalism classes over the years from Miami to Lincoln, Nebraska, from Boston to Evanston, Illinois. High school, college; it really doesn't matter. I love talking to students. I feel so fortunate to have turned my passion into my life's work that I want to encourage them to try to do it too. In fact, I find myself getting so wrapped up in wanting to help these students, to urge them to take chances in life as my parents had encouraged me, that, all of a sudden, I hear the words come tumbling out of my mouth:

"This ain't no dress rehearsal."

No matter if it's a young man or woman who wants to talk about getting into the business, I'm happy to encourage them. But because women still make up only 11 percent of the full-time staff of newspaper sports departments, I give a greater nudge to girls and young women.

In 1990, my last year as AWSM president, I started a scholarship/internship program that now honors six to eight students annually. My sister Kate gave me the idea when she reminded me she won a $500 scholarship from Junior Achievement her senior year of high school. "A scholarship doesn't have to be a lot of money to be a big honor," she said.

That was good because we didn't have much money in our bank account. But I came up with an idea. Lesley Visser and I appeared on a sports cable talk show in Washington and donated our payment from the show, $250 each, to start a scholarship fund. Then I asked George Solomon if he and a few sports editors might match our contribution so we could give out $1,000 for our first scholarship. They did, so we did.

The next year, I offered the scholarship to a Princeton electrical engineering student whom I helped convince to become a sportswriter. Five years later, that student, Amy Shipley, replaced me as the *Post*'s Olympics writer.

For all the good that women's sports creates, for all the opportunities, for all the role models, every few years, a strange ritual occurs in the sports media. A female athlete or broadcaster decides to take off all or most of her clothes for a magazine photographer, then CBS's Lesley Visser calls to alert me and commiserate, then radio and TV shows start calling. Lesley used to tease me that I was so intent on finding something positive in any terrible story that it was as if I had "swallowed a lightbulb." But even I couldn't find much good in some of this nonsense.

Call me old-fashioned, I just wish women didn't feel the need to play to the frat house by appearing scantily clad in magazine photo shoots. I wish female athletes would have enough confidence in themselves and what they mean as role models to young girls not to succumb to the lowest common denominator of the male-dominated sports media and disrobe. Even if it might get one or two of them more endorsements (Exhibit A: tennis's Anna Kournikova, who has made millions while never winning a tournament), the vast majority are left playing to the oldest stereotype in the book, sadly emphasizing their sexuality over their athletic talent.

(By the way, tearing off your sweaty soccer shirt after winning the World Cup doesn't count as disrobing. Brandi Chastain's celebration wasn't a photo shoot. Soccer players often pull off their shirts when they score the winning goal. Usually, though, it's the men.)

Occasionally, I'm left shaking my head at the decisions some women make. I was on ESPN's *Outside the Lines* in September 2004 opposite a young track and field athlete who said she posed in provocative photos to become better known in the Olympic world. I didn't have the heart to say on the air that I had never heard of her.

I'm not against looking great, or wearing stylish clothes, or being feminine, or wearing makeup. Not at all. And the reality is most women in sports handle themselves with class and dignity. But every now and then, something bizarre happens.

In August 2000, Olympic swimmer Jenny Thompson, a shy twenty-seven-year-old New Englander who had always been the model of Yankee decorum, decided to become another kind of model in front of the lens of *Sports Illustrated*'s Heinz Kluetmeier. She showed up in a full-page photo in *SI* wearing stylish red boots, the bottom part of her U.S. flag bathing suit, and nothing above her waist. She was, however, clenching two strategically placed fists.

I was covering the U.S. Olympic swimming trials in Indianapolis when I saw the picture and realized I had a column.

> If undressing were a medal sport at the upcoming Sydney Olympic Games, the Americans would be favored to win the gold. . . . We'd have a dozen U.S. track and field athletes who posed in various stages of undress for a calendar of their own. . . . And we'd have our swimmers. Not only Thompson in *SI,* but Dara Torres, Amy Van Dyken, Angel Martino and Thompson, all together in the altogether in *Women's Sports and Fitness* magazine. The four veteran sprint stars are standing in the shower area . . . apparently wearing nothing, seductively draped in one big American-flag towel.

I went on to discuss how Thompson's appearance was already drawing criticism from parents and young swimmers at the Olympic trials.

"It damages her image," a seventeen-year-old competitor told me. "It demeans yourself to do that," said a swimming mother.

> "Why do that?" asked Donna de Varona, a swimming legend and women's sports advocate. "I guess I'm old-fashioned. I want them to keep their clothes on."
>
> So do I. What's troubling about this trend is that there seems to be a warped attitude among some female athletes that it's not only proper to take off your clothes for a picture, it's actually liberating. To them it has become a kind of hyper-feminist act: Now that they've made it, they can take it all off.
>
> "I'm proud of my body and the work that I've done to get it where it is," Thompson said.
>
> Great. Then put on a tank top and strike a pose to show off those biceps. Wear a bathing suit while bench-pressing your boyfriend. Turn around and display your industrial-strength back as you did in an acclaimed print ad a couple of years ago.

By posing topless with her hands covering her breasts, Thompson doesn't send girls a message of empowerment. She instead sends them the insecure message that an old stereotype still lives and thrives.

If you doubt this, look at the picture and notice where your eye goes first.

Not to those amazing legs or arms.

Not to Thompson's all-American face.

Not to her chiseled stomach.

No, right to her chest.

You don't write these things in a national newspaper without thinking of the consequences for the person you're criticizing. After sending in the column, I called Thompson's agent as a courtesy, just to let her know what to expect in the next day's paper. I knew how important the Olympic trials were to Thompson, already a decorated Olympian from 1992 and 1996, and I knew she would be swimming the next morning. I also was pretty sure USA Today would be outside her hotel room door as she got ready to go to the pool. I don't know if she ever read the column, but I do know she swam well and made the Olympic team.

I thought I was finished with this story until I received a phone message from SI's Rick Reilly the next week. Rick and I broke into the business at the same time in the early 1980s and have been friends ever since. Rick said in his message that he was sorry in advance for being critical of me in SI. I didn't know what he was talking about. I had not yet seen the magazine, but it arrived a few days later.

In a column criticizing my criticism of Jenny Thompson, Rick wrote: "Why did USA Today columnist Christine Brennan go all Aunt Bea?"

All Aunt Bea?

I laughed. What a great line.

But what I couldn't have imagined is how that line from Rick's September 4, 2000, column would stick to me, even to this day. Tony Kornheiser picked up the nickname and used it on his nationwide radio show the next time he critiqued one of my columns. Others took it from there. Aunt Bea became my nickname with more than a few friends and foes, even if most had no idea how it started or what it meant.

While Rick still apologizes whenever I see him, I've learned to live with it. At Tony Kornheiser's and Mike Wilbon's charity golf outing in 2003, those of us who were there were asked to sign life-size cutouts of Tony and Mike.

For Mike, my Northwestern classmate, I wrote, "Go Wildcats."

For Tony, I signed, "Aunt Bea Was Here"—across his high forehead.

On January 27, 2003, well past 11 P.M., I was sitting on the blue carpet in my old bedroom in the suburbs of Toledo. It was a cold night and the old house was drafty, especially upstairs, so I was sitting beside a heater, trying to stay warm, with my laptop literally in my lap, starting that week's column.

> Dear Mr. President:
>
> I know you're a busy man with many more important things to do than worry about sports. But, you see, that's exactly what worries me. At this crucial time in our history, you and your administration have decided to pick a fight with the millions of girls and women who play sports in America (and the millions of parents and husbands and families who support them). You have chosen to mess around with one of the most significant laws in our culture over the past 30 years. You appear hell-bent on weakening Title IX, the law that has made it possible for those millions of female athletes to have the opportunity to play sports in this country.
>
> Why you have chosen to pick this battle, I do not know. Have you seen the latest numbers? Your approval rating is 60 percent, which is quite good. But a USA Today/CNN/Gallup Poll found that 70 percent of adults who are familiar with Title IX think the law should either be left as it is or strengthened. And a Wall Street

Journal/NBC poll reported that 66 percent are in favor
of equality for women in sports, even if it means cutting
men's programs.

Sir, Title IX is more popular than you are.

Dad had asked me that afternoon if I might want to recon-
sider writing such a column. We had a conversation as we drove
to my niece's fifth-grade basketball game.

"You really want to take on the president of the United States
in *USA Today*?"

I told him I did.

"You're sure?"

Yes, I said. "In fact, a very wise man has always told me to go
for it, to take chances. I think the direct quote was, 'This ain't no
dress rehearsal.'"

Dad smiled. "A lot of people could be angry with you after
you write this."

"I know. But that's okay. I can take it. You made sure of that."

The previous summer, the Bush administration appointed a
commission to assess Title IX. The commission was actually
formed to weaken Title IX, although the administration never
admitted it. Bush decried what he called the law's "system of
quotas" during the 2000 election, and had been gunning for it
ever since. Why? He seemed to be trying to appease the right-
wing, especially House Speaker Dennis Hastert, a former
wrestling coach. Wrestlers have been very vocal in blaming Title
IX for the unfortunate cuts that have occurred in men's minor
sports programs in colleges around the country.

These critics have a legitimate complaint, but they should
blame athletic directors and other administrators who failed to
act with any sense of urgency after the passage of Title IX, not
the legislation itself. For years, these leaders treated Title IX as a
recommendation rather than the law, failing to confront their
football coaches about the great excesses in their bloated programs. The truth is that big-time college football brings in quite
a bit of money to a university, but also spends so much that
there often isn't any left over.

Then, when the inevitable occurred—when girls and women rightfully complained about inferior conditions, and sometimes even filed lawsuits—these athletic directors were forced to adopt a slash-and-burn strategy of cutting men's minor sports to try to quickly get into compliance with the law.

The prevailing mind-set on those campuses could best be illustrated by Bo Schembechler, the coach of our family's beloved Michigan Wolverines. He actually declared that female athletes at Michigan didn't deserve the same size M letter as football players did. With thinking like that, is it any wonder Title IX became necessary?

Yet even with the changes in the sports landscape over the past thirty years, even with all the opportunities for women, male athletes are still getting more chances than female athletes to play sports, and male sports are still getting more funding than female sports.

One example of the inequity still faced by female athletes was a case that went to the Supreme Court about a Birmingham, Alabama, high school girls' basketball coach. His team was forced to play in an inferior gym, one that was too small, with bent rims on the baskets. When the coach complained in 2001, he was fired.

President Bush wanted to weaken this law? I had another idea: How about strengthening it?

As the commission began its hearings in late August 2002, looking for a column idea, I thought about the president's two daughters. I wondered: What sports did they play?

I called the White House and was directed to a man who was deputy press secretary at the time. It was Scott McClellan. I introduced myself as a sports columnist for *USA Today.* He couldn't have been nicer. When I asked about the president's daughters' sports, he suggested I call the First Lady's press office, which I did later. (No one ever got back to me, and I didn't pursue it.)

I then asked McClellan why the administration set up the commission. He told me the president was supportive of Title IX but wanted to look into it.

"If he's for Title IX, why is he looking into it?" I asked.

"What should he do?"

"He should enforce it."

McClellan started sounding agitated as I pressed him on the issue about why one would appoint a commission if one supported the law.

"You've got a preconceived notion about this," McClellan shot back. "You've got a strong opinion on this."

"Well, you're right. I'm a columnist."

We went back and forth a few more times before McClellan got angry.

"What's your editor's name?"

Monte Lorell, I said. *"L-O-R-E-L-L."*

Before he could ask for Monte's phone number, I gave it to him. I had been through this kind of escalating, knock-down, drag-out conversation a few times in my two decades as a professional journalist, but never with a future presidential press secretary.

"I'm going to call him and tell him what you're doing," McClellan said. He sounded like a whiny eight-year-old.

"Great," I said. (It turned out he did call Monte to complain about me. Monte told him that I was a columnist and my opinion was my opinion.)

McClellan and I went around and around for another minute or so before he had had enough and hung up. Although he had said almost nothing useful or quotable, all my suspicions about the commission were confirmed in that phone call.

I wrote a column on the commission in the August 29, 2002, newspaper. In it, I quoted Dad.

> My father was Ohio vice chairman of President George H. W. Bush's 1988 campaign. He is a fan of the Bushes, father and son. But he also is the father of three sports-playing daughters and the grandfather of two sports-fanatic granddaughters.
>
> He knows sports. He also knows politics. So, the other day, I conducted the Brennan Poll, a survey as

unscientific as the Gallup Poll is scientific, to put my
finger on the pulse of my father on this issue. "It's po-
litically absurd to even discuss Title IX," my Dad said.
"It's political suicide. This guarantees further alien-
ation of soccer moms from the Republican Party."

Dad was a supporter of the president on most issues, but obviously not on this one. Dad was a moderate Republican who always said, "The truth lies somewhere in the middle." He was
the one who stared at the right-wingers twenty years earlier, as
chair of the GOP in Toledo, and told them to quiet down if they
started making a fuss in a meeting. Now they were running the
party. This was frustrating to us all. A good party man like Dad
had two choices: He could swallow hard and keep his mouth
shut. Or he could rock the boat. It was no surprise that in this
case, with his daughters and granddaughters in mind, Dad chose
the latter.

As the commission hearings dragged on over the next six
months, costing taxpayers $700,000 (who said Democrats were
the ones who threw money at an issue?), the witness list was
stacked against Title IX, and it looked as if the fifteen-member
commission was too. Only women's sports advocates Julie
Foudy and Donna de Varona were securely on the side of
strengthening Title IX. But the Bush administration had underes-
timated the nation's support for this law. E-mails poured into the
commission, into Congress, into the White House. Hundreds of
thousands of e-mails from red states, from swing voters, from
fathers supporting their daughters.

Sure enough, in mid-July 2003, with an election year looming,
the administration issued a brief statement saying that it was
reaffirming Title IX in its totality.

Unfortunately, that was not the end of the attack on Title IX
by the Bush administration. In March 2005, the education department quietly put on its Web site a new Title IX clarification
that would allow schools to use online surveys to gauge
women's interest in certain sports, and perhaps opt not to offer a
sport if enough women didn't express a desire to play. "I can

hear it now," Foudy said. "'We lost a women's team because the e-mail survey got stuck in my spam folder for six months.'"

Interest surveys are notoriously unreliable, but that didn't seem to bother the administration. Never before had men been forced to prove their interest in sports. But, with this administration, the rules clearly were going to be different for women.

No matter how much trouble the Bush administration was causing, there was no doubt that most of the nation was smitten with the law that forever changed every neighborhood playing field. I saw this firsthand when I flew to Fort Worth, Texas, in May 2003 to write columns about Annika Sorenstam's groundbreaking appearance in the PGA Tour's Colonial tournament.

There were huge crowds waiting at Colonial for Sorenstam, who said she was coming to the event simply to "test" herself against the best golfers in the world. But she was not warmly welcomed by all of the male professionals. Vijay Singh, one of the world's top players, defiantly told the Associated Press he hoped she missed the cut. Defending champion Nick Price said in the weeks leading to the event that her appearance "reeks of publicity." At his pretournament press conference, Price appeared so hurt that no one was paying attention to him that even he, one of the true gentlemen on the tour, repeatedly refused to say anything kind about Sorenstam's effort to try her luck against the men.

I was sitting in his press conference, not intending to ask a question, when I grew so disgusted that my hand shot up.

"You are a representative of your game just as Annika is a representative of the same game," I said when I was called upon. "She was in here and spoke admirably and wonderfully about challenges and respect for you and for the men on this tour. Do you not find that admirable or honorable at all that she would say that?"

"Sure," Price replied halfheartedly. "Absolutely."

"Could you speak about that, please?"

"Absolutely," he said. "Golf's a game where we all prove ourselves. And there's no doubt she's proven herself. She's a great gal, she's got a great game. And I wish her the very best of luck this week. I really do."

Aside from a few grouchy PGA multimillionaires, Sorenstam was beloved in Fort Worth. The Bible Belt opened its arms to the thirty-two-year-old Swede, who was herself a product of Title IX, having gone to the University of Arizona on a golf scholarship. Waving to children in the swelling gallery, smiling at every turn, Sorenstam played fairly well but still missed the cut. Veteran golf writers who covered Arnold Palmer and Jack Nicklaus in their day, and now cover Tiger Woods, said they had never seen a gallery as big as the one watching Sorenstam tee off on the first hole in the second round. CNBC posted her score on the screen as if it were the Dow Jones Industrial Average.

I was among the large contingent of media members following Sorenstam shot by shot. Walking from the first green to the second tee the first day, I spotted a father with his hands on his daughter's shoulders standing by the retaining rope. The girl had freckles and must have been about six, the age I was when Dad took me to some of those early Toledo Rockets football games.

"Here she comes," the father said excitedly. "Here she comes!"

The girl's eyes grew wide as Sorenstam strode by, smiling as she caught the girl's eye, just for a split second, before she hurriedly moved along. I turned back to look. The girl was looking up at her father; he was beaming back at her.

I think we were on to something, Dad and I.

11

HOOTIE, MARTHA ... AND ME?

It's rare that after eighteen years of reporting on sports, a writer gets asked to cover something new. But that's exactly what happened when my editors at *USA Today* asked if I wanted to go to the 1999 Masters. I said yes. At the *Post*, I never went, never asked, never thought to. The *Post*'s excellent golf writers had that assignment locked up the way I had the Olympics in my back pocket. But now *USA Today* was asking, and I was going.

As soon as I arrived in the media center and told a few friends I had never before been to Augusta National Golf Club, Mike Mayo of the South Florida *Sun-Sentinel* whisked me out of the pressroom and said he had someplace to show me. We were heading right to Amen Corner. The convergence of the eleventh, twelfth, and thirteenth holes was even more beautiful in person than it appeared on TV; I felt as if I had walked onto a movie set.

As we continued to walk the grounds, I couldn't help but notice that almost all of the fans were white and almost all of the people leaning down to pick up trash were black. The contrast was the starkest I had seen at any U.S. sports venue. That got me thinking. I knew Augusta had a black member or two, but how many? And how many women, if any? The occasional story had been written saying there were just a few black members and no women members, or so people thought. Augusta was so secretive, no one could be entirely sure.

I attended my first press conference that day and was surprised by another Augusta National tradition: the manner in which green-jacketed officials running the news conference called on reporters. For the men, it was simple: "Yes, sir." But when they called on one of the few women reporters in the room, they would say "The little lady over there . . ." or "The little lady down front . . ."

What was this? I raised my eyebrows at my good friend Len Shapiro of the *Washington Post,* who was sitting next to me. As soon as the press conference was over, I turned to Len. "Do they do this at every press conference?" If this was Southern hospitality in 1999, send me to Alaska.

Len was on the board of the Golf Writers Association of America. He told me he was going to speak to someone about this immediately. And he did. The next news conference, and every single one I've attended since, the Augusta National member running it has called on reporters by saying "sir" or "ma'am."

The day before the tournament began, I attended new Augusta National chairman Hootie Johnson's press conference, figuring I would ask about the number of black and female members if I got the chance but wouldn't make a huge deal out of it. I knew my colleagues had many golf-related questions to ask, so I would wait and see if there was an opening.

More than halfway through the press conference, Ed Sherman of the *Chicago Tribune* raised his hand and asked "the traditional television question," about the possibility of expanded TV coverage of the tournament.

I saw my opening. After a few more questions on related topics, I raised my hand. "To follow up on the traditional TV question, I'll ask the traditional membership question. We were talking yesterday and trying to get the numbers straight. If you wouldn't mind telling us how many African Americans there are at Augusta National and how many women members, and if there are no women members, why aren't there?"

"Well, that's a club matter, ma'am, and all club matters are private," Johnson replied.

"Are there women members?" I followed up.

"That's a club matter and all club matters are private, ma'am."

The next question concerned the latest renovations to the golf course, and the press conference soon broke up.

"Troublemaker," a few of my sportswriting buddies said, punching me in the arm and smiling. I smiled with them. I didn't mind the teasing.

"You've been at the Masters one day and you're already causing problems," Sherman said with a laugh.

I smiled again, but in the back of my mind, I was wondering: Was that really such a unique question to be asking in 1999? Wasn't this a legitimate issue worthy of conversation? It had been nine years since the issue of golf's discrimination against African Americans reached its boiling point in the summer of 1990. That was the year the PGA Championship was being played at Shoal Creek Golf Club in Birmingham, Alabama. The club's founder, Hall Thompson, also a member of Augusta National, told the *Birmingham Post-Herald,* "The country club is our home and we pick and choose who we want. . . . I think we've said that we don't discriminate in every other area except the blacks."

There ensued such a furor over that comment, obviously, that Shoal Creek named its first African-American member nine days before the PGA Championship began. Augusta soon followed in lockstep. By September 1990, Ron Townsend, then president of Gannett Media Group's television division, had become Augusta's first black member.

I didn't know Townsend, but since he had been at Gannett, which owns *USA Today,* I thought it might be helpful to meet him as I tried to get to the bottom of the membership issue at Augusta. I happened to bump into Townsend on the grounds that week. I introduced myself and shook his hand. I asked my question. He turned and walked away from me without a word.

My first column on Augusta National's membership came out April 8, 1999. It wasn't my first column of the week, however. I wrote about Tiger Woods when I first arrived. But my second column gained much more attention:

"AUGUSTA, Ga.—I made a right turn off the main drag in Augusta the other day and ended up in 1975. Or perhaps it was 1940. It was hard to tell."

The column praised Augusta's lack of corporate logos and its inexpensive prices at the concession stands and the wonderful sense of permanence of the place: "The Masters is a delightful throwback in today's throwaway society."

But, near the end of the column, I segued into the membership issue and quoted my exchange with Johnson from the previous day's news conference.

"Some might say this is nobody's business but Augusta National's, that it's a private club and it can do what it wants. I would agree—if the Masters didn't exist. But it does, and it's held in the luscious backyard of the white men of Augusta National. That means that the discriminatory policies of the host of this 'national treasure,' as Johnson aptly called it, become the nation's business, at least for one week every year."

The next day, Glenn Greenspan, the tournament's director of communications, walked into the pressroom with none other than Hootie Johnson. As they started to climb the stairs in the theater-style work area, I realized they were coming toward me.

I stood up as they approached. Greenspan introduced me to Johnson. This was the kind of happy introduction reserved for cocktail parties, not antagonistic news relationships. I felt completely at ease when I asked Johnson, "So why don't you have a woman member?"

His smile did not disappear. In a kind, quiet voice, he said, "We will, in due time."

"Why not do it now, or sometime soon," I asked, "if only to quiet down people like me who will keep bringing it up?"

Johnson smiled a reassuring smile.

"We will," he repeated. "Just give us time."

We chatted for a few more moments, then said our good-byes. He thanked me for coming to cover the event. I thanked him for having me.

I went back to write about the Masters in 2000 and 2001, mentioning the membership issue in print just once each year. In advance of the 2001 tournament, I had a little fun: "No club this visible is doing more to promote the advancement of poor, beleaguered white men in golf than this one."

As the 2002 Masters rolled around, my editors and I decided I would pass up a trip to Augusta. I had a very busy schedule coming off the 2002 Winter Olympics, so I was content to miss the Masters for the first time in four years. I would still, however, be writing my Thursday column that week. When my editor, Reid Cherner, asked me the week before if I was planning to write on the Masters, I said no. I wasn't going to be there, so I thought I'd write on something else, although I didn't yet have a topic.

On Monday night of Masters week, as I was going through a stack of magazines before placing them in recycling at my Washington home, something caught my eye in the *Golf for Women* May/June 2002 issue. I began leafing through a piece titled "Ladies Need Not Apply" by Marcia Chambers, a highly regarded golf journalist and author who had written far more about discrimination against women in golf than I ever had, or likely ever will.

Buried deep inside her long piece were the names of Augusta National's three African-American members other than Townsend. One name jumped off the page: Lloyd Ward, the new CEO of the U.S. Olympic Committee.

I was surprised to see Ward's name in the article as a member of this discriminatory club. I knew Ward, and in every conversation about the USOC, he preached nothing but inclusion. He was the man in charge of what arguably is the world's most proactive sports organization for women. How could he, of all people, be a member of a club that discriminated against women?

The next day, I was traveling to give a speech but called USOC chief communications officer Mike Moran and asked him what he thought about Ward's membership at Augusta. He said he was as surprised to hear about this as I was. Moran's reaction confirmed my thoughts.

"I'll get him to call you," he said, "but my sense is he's going to have to either resign from Augusta or resign from the USOC. He can't do both."

The following day I was on deadline back in Washington when Ward called. It was clear as we started talking that he never had thought of the connection between his membership at Augusta and his position within the USOC until Moran asked him to call me.

I also quickly realized that he wasn't going to resign from either organization. Ward, who said he had played Augusta National only one time in the two years he had been a member but who clearly enjoyed the prestige of having Augusta on his resume, had a different strategy.

"I want to have influence from the inside," he told me. "I want to talk to members of Augusta and say, quite frankly, that's simply not enough [admitting African Americans]. You've got to have a broader membership, and that includes women."

Once our twenty-minute conversation ended, I immediately called a top editor in the sports department at USA Today. To show what a nonissue this had been in the sports media, just the day before, this editor had told me he had no interest in the story. Now, when he heard what Ward was saying, he was interested. Very interested.

I told him I obviously couldn't write the breaking news story and then write a column off the news. To do both would be a journalistic no-no. He agreed and said he would find a reporter to work on the story. A few minutes later, assistant golf editor

Debbie Becker called and I dictated Ward's quotes to her. She then wrote the news story, which was stripped across the top of the sports section on April 11, 2002, under the headline: AU-GUSTA FACES PUSH FOR WOMEN.

My column appeared inside the section, on page 3:

> In golf, there are two kinds of discrimination: There is acceptable discrimination and then there is unacceptable discrimination.
>
> It took me three visits to Augusta National to fig-ure this out. In the Age of Tiger, it's obviously no longer acceptable to discriminate against African-Americans on the golf course. That's a no-brainer.
>
> It's entirely fine, however, to discriminate against women.

I went on to credit Chambers's story and mention my at-tempts in previous years to write about the issue—"beating my head against a brick wall . . . becoming a wolf-crying cliché among some of my colleagues . . ." I also quoted Ward as want-ing to work within the system to help women become members of Augusta.

> I had been thinking of ending this column with a call for Ward to resign his membership publicly, using his clout to draw attention to the way the gods of golf treat women. My other option was to encour-age him to stick around and work hard to bring Augusta National into the twentieth century before too much more of the twenty-first century goes by.
>
> After talking to him, I'm picking the latter. Now he can beat his head against that brick wall for a while.

And that, I thought, was that. Just another column on Au-gusta. Been there, done that. Some of my golf-writer friends at Augusta called to tell me that Hootie Johnson wasn't at all pleased to have the membership issue being discussed out in the open. Some newspapers followed our story the next day by writing about Ward's comments. But that was it. I didn't write another word about it. As far as I was concerned, the column had no impact and the issue was over for at least another year. Or, perhaps, forever.

Three months later, I was at home in Toledo, checking e-mail, when an online wire story caught my attention: "In a defiant statement about the privacy of Augusta National, chairman Hootie Johnson lashed out at a national women's group for urging the club to have female members before next year's Masters."

The story went on to describe Johnson's "surprisingly long and angry statement," which included his soon-to-be-infamous line: "There may well come a day when women will be invited to join our membership, but that timetable will be ours, and not at the point of a bayonet."

I laughed out loud. *The point of a bayonet?*

The story mentioned a woman whose name I had never heard, Martha Burk, chair of the National Council of Women's Organizations. She had written a letter to Johnson that triggered his tirade.

Several weeks later, I called her for an interview and learned, much to my surprise, that on April 11, she had picked up a copy of *USA Today* at Washington National Airport on her way to visit her adult children in Texas and happened to read my column on Lloyd Ward. That column, she told me, had inspired her to write to Johnson.

I shook my head. You write dozens of columns in a national publication read daily by millions, and out of the blue, you hear from someone who read one of those columns and took some action because of it. I learned many years earlier that as a journalist, you write your story and you let the chips fall where they may. Sometimes people cared. Other times, your work might be met by deafening silence. But when the chips fell like this, it certainly was interesting.

As the news broke that July week, I realized I had another

golf column to write, with a theme already developing. Just a few days earlier during the U.S. Women's Open on NBC, analyst Johnny Miller was in the midst of praising the winning performance of forty-two-year-old mother of two Juli Inkster when he said, "It's big stuff when you win at forty-two. You're supposed to be home cooking meals at forty-two, you'd think, for most women."

I heard the comment live and couldn't believe that Miller didn't immediately follow it up with a correction or an apology. The next day, I called NBC and was given a number for Miller. The good news was, he couldn't believe he said it either. "That was a stupid comment," he said during an extremely cordial conversation. "It was uncalled for. I feel bad I said it."

If only Augusta National had a similar sense of knowing when to say it was wrong, I wrote in my column of July 11, 2002:

"My guess is that Johnson has now guaranteed that if he doesn't have a female member at his club by next April, there will be picketing in front of the club, all sorts of national reporters milling outside the gates and a national boycott of Coke (one of the Masters' sponsors).

"It's the boys vs. the girls all over again. Pull up a lawn chair, ladies and gentlemen. This is going to get good."

I had no idea how good.

Two things in particular surprised me about the Augusta story in its three-year incubation period. One was how little interest there was from the mainstream media until the day Johnson made Burk's letter public. The other was why Johnson decided to go public in the first place with what was a private letter from a woman he didn't know. Why didn't he invite Burk down to the club for some lemonade, shower her with kindness, and thank her for her interest? Or wad up her letter, throw it into a wastebasket, and ignore her entirely? In an interview, Burk told me that she wouldn't have said a word for at least a year if that had happened.

But Johnson didn't ignore her, and now that the media could clearly see they were reporting on the oldest rivalry on earth—

the boys versus the girls—they pounced. I wasn't at the British Open that year but was pleasantly surprised to read that Tiger Woods was being asked about the issue of discrimination at private golf clubs—by Len Shapiro, I later found out.

"They're entitled to set up their own rules the way they want them," Woods said uncomfortably, according to those who were there. "It would be nice to see everyone have an equal chance to participate if they wanted to, but there is nothing you can do about it."

When asked if he would feel the same way if that applied to "African Americans, Asians, whatever," Woods replied, "Yes. It's unfortunate that it is that way, but it's just the way it is."

Woods wasn't always so ambivalent on the subject. Six years earlier, he burst onto the scene in a Nike TV ad that said, "There are still golf courses in the United States that I cannot play because of the color of my skin." He also declared he wanted "to make golf look like America." Meanwhile, his father was comparing Tiger to Gandhi and Nelson Mandela, although that might have been a bit unfair because neither man was ever known to break 80.

This became a watershed moment for Woods, the turning point in the sports world's understanding of exactly where Woods wanted to stand on social issues: right next to Michael Jordan, as far away from controversy as possible.

Not surprisingly, Woods was vilified in the national media.

"Hypocrite!" screamed the *New York Post*.

"Now we can't even believe in Tiger anymore," *Newsweek* said.

Columnists, pundits, talk shows—they all came down on Tiger, so much so that he had to post a statement on his Web site a few weeks later saying that he would like to see female members at Augusta. "Yes, that would be great," he wrote, "but I'm only one voice."

Over the following months, the story grew to stunning proportions. Johnson dropped all three of the Masters' corporate sponsors—Coca-Cola, IBM, and Citigroup—and put on the telecast without commercials (speculation was that they might have wanted to get out anyway); two members quit, including Treasury Secretary nominee John Snow; the *New York Times* editorialized that Woods should skip the Masters to protest its policy toward women; and Lloyd Ward, the man who started it all, resigned as CEO of the USOC in the midst of an ethics controversy. The story had taken on a life of its own. Everyone had an opinion on Hootie and Martha.

Some even had one on me. In its end-of-the-year issue in 2002, *Sports Illustrated*'s Golf Plus named me one of the twelve heroes of the year. But the compliment was entirely backhanded: "The shrill *USA Today* columnist's endless preaching about Augusta National finally got someone's attention—Martha Burk's."

Shrill? That was a first for me. I asked Dad what he thought of this.

"Did they spell your name right?"

"Yes."

"Then, congratulations. You've really gotten under their skin."

A few times during that bizarre year, I marveled at what had happened. Radio interviewers would ask why this topic was so important to me. Aren't there more vital issues to discuss? Yes, of course, I said, but within the realm of sports and the world of golf, the discussion of the advancement of women in a sport (and because this was golf, in the corridors of power in corporate America) was a valid conversation to be having in the twenty-first century. That always was my point—the dialogue was the thing. Maybe some people didn't care about this, and I respected that, but to me, symbols are important. Tokens do matter. And a woman at Augusta National would be a powerful symbol not just in sports, but in our culture. She would be breaking the grass ceiling, so to speak.

I also wondered, whimsically and privately, what if I hadn't picked up Marcia Chambers's article that night back in April? I almost tossed the magazine onto the recycling pile without cracking it open. At least one man in a green jacket probably wished I had.

Dad and I laughed about that a few times. "Good ol' Hootie," Dad called Johnson derisively. He thought Hootie was being ridiculous, so out of touch with the times. Dad knew of what he spoke. More than thirty years earlier, he briefly had been a part of that country-club culture, with a membership at the suburban Toledo club where I took golf lessons. But that seemed like another lifetime ago as the Augusta controversy developed.

Dad told me he occasionally had discussions with his poker buddies about my views—and his—on discrimination at country clubs. Some of his pals were members of clubs that had restrictive membership policies. I have no doubt that Dad got their attention with his defense of me.

I had seen him in action on the topic with a male friend only once. Several years before the Augusta controversy began, Dad and I were at a Washington dinner with a friend who was a corporate executive in Toledo. The man announced proudly that he had played golf that day at all-male Burning Tree in Bethesda, Maryland, a club far more discriminatory than Augusta— women aren't allowed inside the gates except to buy gifts in the pro shop before Christmas—but one that does not host any public events with corporate sponsors, which is of course what makes Augusta so visible and unique. I had known this man for a long time—he had been my Sunday school teacher one year— so I was really surprised.

"You actually played at Burning Tree?" I asked. "You'd go to a place your wife and daughters cannot set foot?"

Our friend started to defend himself when Dad chimed in: "It's hard to believe places like that still exist. It's not good for men to participate in clubs like that."

The conversation was over.

By the time the 2003 Masters rolled around, the membership issue had mushroomed into one of the biggest sports stories of the year. Reporters were everywhere, inside and outside the gates. Protests were planned. And I found myself in the center of it all, part of the story in a way I had never been before. I wasn't entirely comfortable being in that situation, but, realistically, there I was. Radio stations were calling my cell phone constantly, as many as ten stations a day. I try to return all my phone calls, but I couldn't keep up with this.

In the pressroom, I would be in the middle of writing a paragraph of one of the four columns I wrote that week—two on the controversy, two on the golf—when another writer or a TV reporter would tap me on the shoulder and ask if I had a minute or two. Of course, I said. I always made time for my colleagues. How could I, a journalist who constantly asks people to talk to me, not talk to them?

One Atlanta TV sportscaster asked if I planned to join Martha Burk's protest.

"What?"

I hope I looked as startled as I felt.

"I'm a journalist," I said curtly. "I write about these things. I don't protest."

Things were getting a little strange in Augusta that week.

There was quite a buildup to Hootie Johnson's Wednesday press conference. I was dragged into that too:

"Are you going to ask a question?" someone wondered.

"What are you going to ask?" said another.

Writers and TV people were actually coming up to me to ask if I thought Hootie would shun me.

"What will you do then?"

I hadn't thought of any of this until they asked. I figured I would just sit in the room and see if anything Johnson said led me to ask a question, which is the way I go into most press conferences. But with all this interest in what I would do, I changed my mind and decided to quiet the speculation by raising my hand and asking a question early on. I was thinking of asking specifically why there still were no women members at the club, hardly a novel question, but the right one, I thought.

Johnson came into the packed room and began by reading a statement saying that he would have "nothing further to add about our membership or related issues." He wanted to preempt the membership questions and talk only about golf.

Billy Payne, the chairman of the Masters media committee and the man who had been in charge of the 1996 Atlanta

Olympics, was sitting beside Johnson. Once Johnson finished reading the statement, Payne asked for questions.

Sitting in the middle of the room, I raised my hand.

Payne and I had developed a cordial relationship over the eight years I covered him when he ran the Atlanta Olympics. But I knew he was in a different place now. What he was doing at a male-only club, I had no idea, but I couldn't keep bothering everyone about these things. As Dad cautioned, "Sometimes you just have to say to yourself, 'Enough already.'"

Sitting there, I saw no hands raised in front of me, but I had no idea if other reporters were raising their hands behind me. I guessed they were.

As it turned out, they weren't. Payne later came up to me, wrapped his green-jacketed arm around my shoulders, and told me that no one else had raised a hand.

"That's the kind of respect the other writers have for you," Payne said, sounding like a proud big brother in one of the more bizarre twists of a very bizarre week. "They wanted you to have the first question."

When Payne called on me, I made a split-second decision. Normally when a news figure says he or she doesn't want to talk about an issue in a press conference, a journalist will blow right through that request like a base runner missing the sign to hold up at third. But in this case, considering the scrutiny I was under, I figured it wouldn't be right for me to come out swinging. So I improvised.

"Mr. Johnson, with all due respect to your comment, I'm curious if you're comfortable with this environment for your tournament; i.e., all of the attention, all of the questions, all of the controversy that's surrounding it. Does that make you comfortable that your tournament is being treated in the way that you would hope it would be treated? Thank you."

"I think we'll present a great tournament, Christine," Johnson replied. "And I don't think that this issue is going to be a major issue. It's not a major issue. We have been talking about it for ten months and I've made my statement."

It was a softball question and a softball answer. But I looked like Woodward and Bernstein compared to the next questioner:

"Is there any consideration to lift, clean, and place for the tournament?"

The room erupted in laughter. It was a golf junkie's question about a possible rule change due to the week's wet weather that would allow golfers to pick up their ball and clean it before putting it back down.

But enough of that. The *Chicago Tribune*'s Ed Sherman followed right up wondering why Johnson wouldn't take any questions on the membership issue, which, after a pointed exchange, opened the door to Johnson's taking questions about the membership issue. Lots of questions. I thanked Ed later. He did what I felt I couldn't do in that setting that week of all weeks—really take on Johnson.

Four years after giving me the business for asking my membership question back in 1999, Ed laid the groundwork for the most journalistically sound press conference in the history of Augusta National. Twenty-eight of the thirty-eight questions asked of Johnson that day concerned the membership issue. What a change this was from four years earlier, when there was only my one question and a follow-up.

People have asked me what it was I wanted from Augusta, and that was it: a healthy conversation about the discrimination at the club.

As the week and the story wore on, some golf writers viewed me increasingly as the enemy. A reporter I had known for nearly two decades turned on his heel and stormed out of the press center when I tapped him on the shoulder to say hello. I was criticized more in print that week than I had ever been. But I wasn't criticized by everyone. Sally Jenkins, a columnist at the *Washington Post* and a good friend, strongly disagreed with me on the membership issue. But when she heard a radio talk show host railing against me as "worthless and troublesome" as well as a "militant feminist" and "agent provocateur," she came to my defense in print.

"[Brennan] is no firebreather; she's a conservative Republican from Toledo, and so wholesome and affable that an act of headlong excess for her is to leave the butter out overnight," Sally wrote. "Even in her most heated moments, she struggles to be argumentative. A few years ago, when she was covering the Washington Redskins, she got into a dispute with team owner Jack Kent Cooke about her work. Brennan, in defending herself, rose to her full height, and shot back, 'Nuts to you, mister.'"

I don't remember ever saying "Nuts to you, mister," and I'm a liberal Republican, not a conservative, but who's complaining?

Things calmed down in the months that followed, although conspiracy theorists insinuated that Martha Burk and I must have been in cahoots leading up to the 2003 Masters. That would have been impossible because I didn't meet Burk until the week of that tournament, a year to the day after I wrote the column that caught her attention.

Facts like that weren't going to deter everyone. The author of a book on the controversy wrote that when Burk and I met, we "hugged like long-lost sorority sisters."

The truth is we shook hands like two people meeting each other for the first time.

12

FULL CIRCLE

As I entered my forties, Dad started calling me the "Gee Whiz Kid." It came out of the blue one day. He said he liked the way I still got a kick out of what I was doing, relishing my assignments as a columnist even more, it seemed to him, than I did covering beats at the *Miami Herald* and at the *Washington Post*.

My delight also came from my ability to dip back into the past, into my childhood, to find my heroes—or simply bump into them by coincidence. I found myself in some of the old places, looking for the old names that had been such a part of my life. I have always loved the concept of the chance encounter with someone from the past, of reliving moments in time, the kind of scenes that play out in the most magical of movies, such as *Back to the Future* and *Field of Dreams*. I didn't go looking for my past in my travels, but what about the past coming forward and finding me?

Things just started to fall together, one story at a time.

* * *

Covering the Olympics for more than twenty years, I often think of the eleven Israeli athletes and coaches killed at the 1972 Munich Olympics. I've even asked International Olympic Committee officials why they don't have a moment of silence at each Olympic opening ceremonies to remember the tragedy, and have never received a satisfactory answer. The best that IOC Director General François Carrard came up with in an interview two months before the 2002 Salt Lake City Olympics was that there had been too many Olympics-related tragedies over the years to decide which to commemorate, although he did agree Munich stood apart.

Twice, I visited the Munich Olympic village. In 1981, on vacation, my sister Kate and I went to the Olympic sites for an afternoon, poking our heads into the main stadium, the swimming hall, the gymnastics venue. We walked down many streets in the maze of white Olympic dormitories in our quest to find the right spot, but never found the Israelis' living quarters at 31 Connollystrasse.

I was satisfied, though, that we at least had seen those hauntingly familiar dwellings, long since converted into apartments—that we had been there, or almost there.

A dozen years later, I searched again. After covering the 1993 World Track and Field Championships in Stuttgart, *Los Angeles Times* Olympics writer Randy Harvey, Reuters track and field correspondent Gene Cherry, and I hired a car to take us to Munich for the day. When we reached the village, Randy, Gene, and I asked several people, in English, if they knew where the Israelis had been killed. We were met by blank stares until one man pointed down a particular street. We soon were standing in front of a plaque marking the door to what had been the Israelis' rooms. At our feet were two bouquets of flowers and five white candles. We were not the only people to have come to this place.

I wondered, aloud, if we should knock. My friends said no. Of course they were right, even though I had imagined it for so long I wanted to see what one of those rooms looked like. But there was no need to disturb the people who lived in those apartments, as if they didn't already feel like they lived in a memorial, with that plaque outside their door and people like us coming by.

We did snap some pictures, taking turns standing by the plaque. I smiled when they took mine. It was a reflex action, but the moment I did it, it bothered me.

"That was a stupid thing to do," I said. "How could I smile in this spot, of all places?" My friends told me to forget about it.

The picture we took at
31 Connollystrasse in Munich.

I'll never forget the weather that late-summer day we found the Israelis' dormitory, nearly twenty-one years after they had been taken hostage and killed. It was raining, an unceasing veil of rain falling from grim, gray skies. It was perfect.

—

Olympic swimming gold medalist John Naber was a hero to me. I followed his Olympics—the 1976 Summer Games from Montreal—as closely as any, and watched every swimming race that ABC showed. The U.S. women swimmers, many of whom were about my age, had a difficult time against the East Germans that summer, winning only one gold medal in those Games, in the freestyle relay. Shirley Babashoff was supposed to be a female Mark Spitz; instead, she finished behind the East Germans time and again, calling attention to their bulging muscles and deep voices and earning a lovely nickname from the naive media: "Surly Shirley." When the Berlin Wall fell and the truth came out about East Germany's systemic doping of its Olympic athletes, the world found out Babashoff had been right. I always felt she was treated unfairly, and several times have written just that in the pages of USA Today. When I ask myself why I care so much about reporting on steroids today, my answer comes from way back in 1976, when, at eighteen, I sat in our family room and watched athletes like Babashoff be cheated out of their gold medals.

Naber's story was far more uplifting. A backstroker, he won four golds in Montreal, but I remembered him most for escorting the U.S. flag into the closing ceremonies. I loved the haunting, melancholy music from those ceremonies. It fit my mood as the Games ended. I was so sad that they were over. As a high school graduation present, Kate gave me the record album that included that music, the work of the late Canadian composer André Mathieu. It was the music Naber marched to that day.

I met Naber at an Olympic dinner in the 1980s, then kept running into him over the years at other Olympic functions. One night, we were talking in the lobby bar at the Mayflower Hotel in Washington when I told him how fond I was of those closing ceremonies, and his appearance with the U.S. flag, and that music.

"The music!" John said. "You know, I never heard it again."

I was surprised he didn't have the tape, or an album.

"No," he said. "We didn't get those things back then. It's just a distant memory. I try to remember it, but it's hard."

The next time I was in Toledo, I found my album where it always was, by the old record player that Mom and Dad rarely used anymore. I brought the album back with me to Washington and had a music studio make two CDs, one for me, one for the man who escorted the flag.

I e-mailed Naber to get his address. I didn't say why. I

overnighted the CD to his home in California. The next day, I received an exuberant phone call, then this e-mail:

"How can I begin to tell you how wonderful it was to pop the CD into the player and mentally go back in time to the wonderful hand-holding and dancing around the Montreal Olympic closing ceremony," John wrote. "The processional music put me right back on the awards podium. Your disc arrived in great shape and a smile beamed across my face when I recalled our conversation. Thank you, Christine. Thank you so very much!"

As for me, I play my Montreal CD every time I'm packing to go to another Olympics. It always takes me back to the summer of 1976, when I was still a teenager and would have been thrilled to have had the chance to go to just one Olympic Games, much less twelve in a row.

—

As I was growing up, another memorable Olympic moment always seemed to be right around the corner. In 1980, I leaped for joy when I heard the news of the U.S. hockey team's victory over the Soviet Union. It was the greatest sports upset ever, coming at a time when U.S. morale was low, with American hostages being held in Iran and Soviet troops invading Afghanistan.

If the game was thrilling for me back in my sorority house, it was life-altering for U.S. captain Mike Eruzione. He has spent the past twenty-five years giving motivational speeches and teeing off in celebrity golf tournaments, all because, as he jovially once told me, the puck came off the boards to the right spot on his stick at the right time for him to score the winning goal.

"Three more inches to the left and I'd be painting bridges," he said. "But it was right where it was supposed to be."

I met Eruzione in Miami during my summer internship in 1980, and I've bumped into him at least a dozen times since, usually at the Olympics. As the 2002 Salt Lake City Games approached, I called him to talk about a column I was writing saying the entire U.S. "Miracle on Ice" team should light the cauldron at the opening ceremonies.

Eruzione told me then that not once in the almost twenty-two years since the 1980 Olympics had the entire team been together.

There had been weddings and reunions, with "eight here, ten there," Eruzione said, "but never all twenty together."

I had the ending for my column:

> What those 20 now-middle-age men did for a nation, and for the Olympics, should never be forgotten. Who knew sports could lift us so quickly and completely out of our doldrums? But this was not just patriotism run rampant. This was the ultimate triumph of youth and optimism and freshness, a stirring victory of what's right about sports over what's wrong with the world.
>
> I think it's time we saw these guys again.

I seriously doubt the column had anything to do with it—my guess is the decision had already been made—but on a cold Friday night in February in Salt Lake City, with the whole world watching, those twenty men were finally reunited at the top of the Olympic stadium to light the cauldron.

—

I had never met Bo Schembechler in person, never even talked to him, but I thought I'd try to reach the old Michigan coach on the phone for a column previewing the Michigan–Ohio State game in 2002. When I called his office, I was told Bo wouldn't be returning calls that week, but then, around dinner hour, right on my deadline, he returned mine.

Before we talked about the game, Bo gave me grief for writing so much about figure skating. For just a moment, I was a teenage girl again. Bo Schembechler had actually read my work, even if he was teasing me about it? That made me smile.

We didn't talk about figure skating for very long. I told him I had cried when his team lost to Ohio State in 1975, but that I had gotten over it.

"I know, I know," he said sympathetically.

We both agreed we still hadn't completely recovered from the Big Ten athletics directors' vote in 1973 sending Ohio State to the Rose Bowl. "I'll never get over that," Bo said.

We talked for a few minutes about the upcoming game and I got the quotes I needed, then I thanked him for giving us such a wonderful team to root for each Saturday. When I hung up with Bo, I immediately called Dad to fill him in on every word from the man whose teams we cheered starting with that glorious November day in 1969. My deadline definitely could wait for a few minutes.

—

Nearing her fifty-second birthday, Miss O retired from Ottawa Hills High School in May 1998. We held a party for her in a new gym in the elementary school next door, a gym in which fourth-grade girls now play in travel basketball leagues. It was a much grander facility than the little multipurpose gym we often played in at the high school.

We hardly could have known when we helped Miss O mow and line the field before our field hockey games back in the 1970s that she was laying the foundation with us for what eventually would become a prep dynasty. Long after she had stopped coaching, tiny Ottawa Hills won three Ohio state championships in field hockey in the 1990s. By the early years of the twenty-first century, thirty-eight OHHS graduates had gone off to play collegiate field hockey, with twenty-five receiving Division I scholarships at places like Michigan, Ohio State, and Northwestern.

Not bad for the old "Green Beans."

On that day in 1998, Miss O's players and students came back from Seattle, from Chicago, from Detroit. If they couldn't make it, their parents showed up to represent them. Mom, Dad, Kate, and Amy joined me in honoring our coach. I was emcee for the party. Dad gave a short speech, thanking Miss O on behalf of all the parents.

She is no longer Miss O, but Sandy to us now in our adulthood. She marvels as we do at what has happened to girls' and women's sports. "Look at what these girls have now," she said. "I wonder what we could have been with that same opportunity, being able to strive for scholarships. But you know, we did have fun."

"When Miss O started coaching, it was a different time for girls and women in sports," I said that day. "Title IX had not yet been signed by Richard Nixon. Billie Jean King had not yet beaten Bobby Riggs. We had no buses for our games, no cheerleaders, and only one jersey that our mothers had to wash every night so we could wear it the next day.

"Because it was a simpler time in girls' sports, there was no specialization, so we could play several sports. Many of us ran between the field hockey game and the tennis courts for a match, or between volleyball and basketball games, or softball games and track meets. And the best thing was, Miss O was right there, running with us."

In February 2005, at a ceremony during a Title IX celebration at Bowling Green State University, Sandy Osterman and many of her teammates received the varsity letters they deserved but never were given when they were in school. It was purely a coincidence, but I was the keynote speaker at one of the celebratory events at Bowling Green that week.

———

In 1999, the Detroit Tigers played their last season in beautiful Tiger Stadium. The ballpark was a cherished relic. It had opened in 1912, five days after the *Titanic* sank.

On an early August evening eighty-seven years later, I took Dad and Jim to the stadium to pay one last visit. It had been years since we had gone together, the three of us. Dad now was seventy-three, a bear of a man still; Jim was thirty-seven, I was forty-one. We purchased box seats for the Tigers–White Sox game, but because I planned to write about our visit, the public relations man suggested we also come onto the field before the game.

I chronicled what happened next in my *USA Today* column that week:

> As Dad and I stood near home plate, Jim wandered over to the third-base coaching box and then stepped, very briefly, with both feet, onto third base. He had his reasons. He explained that, just once, he wanted to stand in fair territory in Tiger Stadium,

and when he got there, he wanted to see what the ballplayers saw.

From atop third base, Jim quickly glanced into the seats, and sure enough, he realized a player could pick out his wife or a fan, and see their faces, and see them smile or frown. All those years he had imagined it, and now he knew it was true.

We went up to the press box, took in the view from there, then decided to find some of the spots where we had sat in the 1970s and sit in them for an inning or so. I had stuffed a couple of my old diaries in my purse before leaving home. In them, I had written the section where we sat, and sometimes even the row number. Dad smiled as I paged through my 1977 diary to find the day when Chet Lemon's foul ball into the upper deck along the left-field line bounced off my palm and into Jim's cupped hands.

As I read my account of that incident aloud to Dad and Jim, we realized we were within a row or two of where we had been sitting twenty two years earlier.

Finally, we wandered by the radio booth overhanging home plate to see if we could find Ernie Harwell, "the gracious announcer who introduced us to the Tigers on WJR Radio long before we ever saw them in person," I wrote in *USA Today*.

"Within a minute, we were chatting with the great voice of the Tigers, who was in the midst of a break in his broadcast. He acted like we were old friends. Jim even began quoting him, accurately, from 1968. Jim was six then."

Harwell told us that from his perch right behind home plate, if the crowd was quiet enough, the outfielders could hear his every word. That's the kind of story that made you want to tell the Tigers never to leave this glorious old ballpark. What new stadium could provide such an anecdote?

We left after the seventh inning, turning back to look at the gorgeous green field one more time before disappearing down a ramp. I finished my column this way:

"On the ride home, we turned on the radio. The Tigers were still playing; Ernie Harwell was still talking. As we drove into the night, the tremendous light towers atop the ballpark's big, broad-shouldered roof were still blazing in the distance, shining down on a place that, for us, could never grow dark."

—

Two years later, the Mud Hens played their final season at the Lucas County Recreation Center before moving to a downtown, state-of-the-art ballpark. In mid-August 2001, we decided to go to one final game. Dad and I hopped in one car, while Kate, Tom, and their children, Brad, Jennie, and Leslie, came in another.

Our first stop was the place where we had collected autographs thirty years earlier, in that walkway between the stadium and the clubhouse. The kids had been there before with Kate and Tom, but never with me. I hadn't been back for a Mud Hens game in years. I told the kids we were coming back after the game, and we did, and it was exactly the same. Players with their spikes clicking on the concrete; children swirling around, grabbing as many signatures as they could; the adults standing

Dad and I at our last Toledo Mud Hens
game in the old ballpark in 2001.

back, watching. The only difference was Kate and I now were the adults, standing with Dad.

During the game, we sat close to where our box seats once were, on the first-base side, near the dugout and the bag. I looked up and spotted the tiny press box above home plate. That reminded me of something.

Actually, it reminded me of someone.

I asked Dad about good old Frank Gilhooley, the radio announcer I listened to every night when I was a girl, the man who read my Mud Hens' all-time team on the radio, the one without my name on it.

"Whatever happened to him?" I asked. "Is he dead?"

"Frank Gilhooley?" Dad said, his face brightening, his arm beginning to reach, his finger starting to point.

"Frank Gilhooley . . . is right up there."

Dad pointed to the press box.

"He's still doing the radio broadcasts."

I had no idea. "You're kidding. Let's see if we can get up there and meet him."

We shot up, all seven of us, and when I flashed my press pass to a kindly security guard, we all ended up in the press box. During a commercial, the seventy-seven-year-old Gilhooley got up slowly from his seat, smiled warmly, and said hello to us. He and Dad knew each other fairly well, but I had never met him.

"Chris listened to you for years," Dad said with a smile. Gilhooley nodded, but there was little time for small talk. He had to get back to work, so we said our good-byes. On our way out of the press box, Dad told us that Frank Gilhooley's father had played in the major leagues. A few minutes later, we passed a series of framed historic photographs hanging in a special display, including one of Babe Ruth holding the small son of a former teammate.

The little boy was Frank Gilhooley.

—

A few days before Christmas of 2001, I was flying in a puddle-jumper from Pittsburgh to Toledo. There were two seats on one side of the aisle, two on the other. I sat at the window on the right, and next to me happened to be a young man flying in to work a Bowling Green men's basketball game for ESPN. He and I struck up a conversation, and when he mentioned his assignment, I, of course, launched into my stories of my favorite Mid-American Conference basketball player ever, Steve Mix of the Toledo Rockets.

After the plane landed, I happened to look to my left across the aisle. The man sitting in the next seat was extremely tall, and he was leaning over to put away a *Sports Illustrated*. Another sports nut, I thought.

When he sat back up, I saw his face. I did a double-take. It was Steve Mix. It had to be. Although I had never met him, I knew what he looked like.

I nudged the ESPN guy. "You will not believe this."

"Excuse me, sir," I said across the aisle, "you're Steve Mix, right?"

And indeed he was. "The Mixmaster," as Dad had deemed him more than thirty years earlier. I introduced myself and we chatted all the way to the terminal, where Dad was standing where he always stood, so straight, shoulders back, awaiting my arrival.

I couldn't contain my smile as I presented our first real sports hero.

"Dad, this is Steve Mix."

Dad broke into a big smile. "Well, how about this . . ."

Mix played in the NBA for thirteen seasons, nine of them with the Philadelphia 76ers. He has been a commentator on the 76ers television broadcasts for nearly two decades, but still lives in Toledo. Like me, he was coming home for Christmas. In Toledo, he owns the Steve Mix Basketball Academy, where hundreds of kids play in leagues five months of the year on four side-by-side, hardwood-floor courts. Kate's daughters, Jennie and Leslie, are two of those kids.

—

Then there was Chuck Ealey. Jim and I shook his hand and said hello at a charity golf outing for the University of Toledo in the late 1990s, but I never heard another thing about him until I was watching the Fiesta Bowl on television at a party in Arlington, Virginia, in early January 2003.

Ohio State and Miami were playing a national championship game that would come to be seen as one of the best ever, a game that reminded me of Miami's 1984 Orange Bowl triumph. Near the end, a graphic came onto the screen detailing the greatest winning streaks by starting quarterbacks in NCAA football history. Miami's Ken Dorsey was second on the list, with thirty-four consecutive games. He was trying for number thirty-five that night.

At the top of the list, with the magical thirty-five, was the name Chuck Ealey.

"Who's that?" asked one of the men at the party.

I have never been more ready to answer a question in my life.

"He was the great quarterback of my childhood in Toledo," I said. "He never lost a game with the University of Toledo Rockets from 1969 to 1971. They were thirty-five and oh and finished fourteenth in the final AP poll in 1971."

My friend looked genuinely confused. "Why haven't I heard of him?"

"Because he wasn't drafted by the NFL."

"Why not?"

"Because he was a black quarterback and it was 1971."

Ohio State won the game in overtime, so Ealey's record remained intact. A few days later, looking for a column idea, I thought of Ealey. Why not try to find him?

I called the University of Toledo sports information department and obtained a work number for him in the Toronto suburbs. I called it—and there he was.

Ealey said he had been watching the game, so I asked what he thought when his name popped onto the screen.

"I missed it," he said. "It was the beginning of the fourth quarter and I was taking out the garbage. When I came back in, my daughter said, 'Hey, Dad, your name was just on.'"

He didn't mind that he missed it. "It's all right. I don't need to see it. I remember."

I launched into my story of growing up in Toledo and cheering for him and his team and feeling so rewarded by their victories that I eventually found myself in a career in sports journalism.

He sounded surprised. "You really think you became a sportswriter because of watching us?" he asked.

Chuck filled me in on what he had been doing all these years, staying in Canada, getting married, having three children, now running a financial-planning office. The day we spoke was his fifty-third birthday.

Chuck sounded as I expected him to: he was soft-spoken, calm, modest. When I asked him if he ever grew bitter about not being drafted, he said no, never.

"I never felt good about this, but I was prepared for it," he said. "In my mind, I never thought all those NFL teams could be racist. You just got sensitized to it, the fact they were looking for a six-three, 230-pound, in-the-pocket quarterback, and then I started rationalizing that that was okay. I couldn't do anything about it anyway. I just moved on."

After my column ran, Mark Standriff, the morning radio host on WSPD in Toledo, interviewed both of us on the phone. WSPD was the station that broadcast all of Ealey's games, the station I called to answer that baseball trivia question in 1969.

I made sure on the air to thank Chuck for what he and his teammates meant to me, and to our entire family, during their glorious winning streak.

Dad was listening back home in Toledo. I called as soon as I got off the air.

"Can you believe it, Dad?"

My voice was cracking. Dad's too.

"Honey, it's great. You and Chuck Ealey, together on the radio. Amazing."

Chuck and I soon would be linked in another way. A Toledo charity called Connecting Point, a children's services agency, asked us to cochair an annual fund-raising golf tournament, where we enjoy telling our unusual story of the quarterback who won every game on the field and the girl who cheered him on from the stands. The charity first got in touch with us because of my 2003 column.

When we talk at the tournament, I tell my part of the story, and Chuck says he's about to cry whenever he hears it.

Chuck Ealey and I at our charity
golf tournament in 2004.

—

USA Today asked me to go to the Rose Bowl on January 1, 2000. I knew Dad had never been, and even though the Big Ten representative was Wisconsin, not Michigan, I asked him to go with me. I bought a ticket from the Big Ten office and gave it to him for Christmas. It was time I returned the favor from Christmas Day 1971, when a Tangerine Bowl ticket was waiting under the tree for me.

I flew home to Toledo to spend December 31, 1999, with Mom, Dad, Kate, Tom, and the kids. I hadn't been home for a New Year's Eve in years, but if I was going to be there for any, I figured this was the one. Date freak that I had become (I wonder why), I wanted to see Mom and Dad, born in the 1920s, hit the new century. They both said they never thought they would see it. "The year two thousand," Mom said, "was like something out of a science-fiction comic book."

That day, we put together a time-capsule-style diary in which we all contributed a page or two of thoughts and pasted in a few newspaper articles, then I suggested to Kate's kids that they hold on to it for a long time, pass it along to their kids, and see if someone could open it on December 31, 2099. They said they would try, but we all agreed it probably would be misplaced in 2065 or so. Still, it was worth a shot.

A mood of trepidation enveloped many around the world due to fears about the Y2K bug. Not Dad and me. After getting two hours of sleep, we awoke before dawn January 1, 2000, to fly out of Detroit to Los Angeles. We arrived at the Rose Bowl in plenty of time for the game.

On vacation with Dad, showing his true colors for his
two favorite football teams, Toledo and Michigan.

Unfortunately, Pasadena's usual chamber of commerce weather had been replaced by low gray clouds and a chill wind. Dad sat bundled among the Wisconsin faithful near the field; I was comfortably indoors in the press box. After Wisconsin defeated Stanford, 17–9, I had to dash to the locker room to get quotes for my column. As a favor, I asked my friend Marty Aronoff, who had finished his work as the statistician for ESPN Radio's broadcast team, if he would walk down to Dad's seat and bring him to the press box to wait for me.

When they met up in the stands, Marty told Dad to make sure to tell him if he needed to stop as they climbed the steep stairs to the top of the Rose Bowl.

"Are you kidding?" Dad bellowed. "How about you, old man?"

Off Dad charged, beating Marty to the press box.

At dinner that night at our hotel in Century City, we put Marty's miniature TV set on the table to watch the Orange Bowl. We had our reasons: Michigan was playing. And when the Wolverines were in a bowl game, no matter where we were, Dad and I didn't miss it.

13

ANOTHER KICKOFF

On May 17, 2001, Dad's seventy-fifth birthday, the day my "Happy Birthday" column appeared in *USA Today*, I flew to Toledo. Before I boarded my flight, I called home from National Airport.

Mom answered. "What you did for your father today in your column . . ." Her voice trailed off. "My goodness."

As he always did, Dad met me at Toledo Express Airport. He was shaking his head slowly as I came toward him.

"Thank you, honey," he said, wrapping me in an incredibly strong embrace.

He told me he picked the newspapers off the driveway as usual before his 5 A.M. walk and, because it was Thursday, my column day, he opened *USA Today* first. As he started to read the column, he said he wanted to jump ahead and see how it ended, but resisted.

When he got to the end, he dabbed his eyes and then went out the door for his four-mile walk. Friends brought him copies of the column all weekend, especially at his birthday party that Saturday night.

I was home for Mom's birthday on July 17 as well, her seventy-third. It was no big deal, she said, but her birthday never was a big deal for her. Occasionally, we didn't listen to Mom. On her sixtieth, we surprised her by renting a limo and taking her and a few good friends to all her haunts, including the dry cleaner. This birthday, Mom's knees were killing her and she was on steroids for a problem with the blood vessels near her eyes, so we stayed around the house. She still swam her laps all summer long and climbed onto her stationary bicycle, but we could see that our hard-charging mom was slowing down.

I saw Mom and Dad again in August when I came in to co-host the grand reopening of the Toledo–Lucas County Public Library with *M*A*S*H* star Jamie Farr. Mom and Dad attended the event. Corporal Klinger wore a suit.

Mom, Dad, and I were back together again on Labor Day weekend of 2001 in New York City. I was in the city to cover the U.S. Open tennis tournament. Mom and Dad flew in to take care of Amy and Derrick's infant son, Peter. I picked up my parents in a cab at LaGuardia and we spent a day and a half together before they began their baby-sitting duties.

Dad and I walked along First Avenue as Mom put up her feet in the hotel. The city always becomes a ghost town on Labor Day weekend, but that weekend seemed quieter—perhaps only in hindsight.

On Saturday night, September 1, 2001, the three of us walked up First Avenue to find a place for dinner. I ran ahead to peek inside an Italian restaurant and look at the menu before dashing back to tell Mom and Dad it looked fine for us.

They stood on the street corner a block away from me, Dad in khakis, so athletic and proud; Mom in her favorite summer pink top and capri pants, leaning on Dad's arm, smiling as I jogged back toward them.

Who knew I was taking a mental snapshot that would be with me forever, the two of them in that city at that moment, ten days before September 11, and less than two years before they both would be gone?

* * *

On my forty-fourth birthday in May 2002, after joining Dad to sing "Happy Birthday" into my answering machine, Mom went into the hospital. Feeling terrible, she had been having tests for several months, but doctors kept telling her they could find nothing wrong. Finally, they found something. Kate, who had been with Mom and Dad all day, called Jim, and he called me late in the afternoon to tell me Mom had a huge mass in her liver. I flew home the next day.

In a column two months later, I described what I had witnessed a few days after I arrived:

> The doctor had told us the terrible news in the hallway moments earlier, and now he was walking into my mother's room in Toledo Hospital to tell her. We gathered around her as he sat on the side of her bed. If she was afraid, she didn't show it. She smiled at the doctor and said hello. He looked her square in the eye. She looked right back at him.
>
> The doctor started talking, telling my mother the most awful personal news I imagine she had ever heard: that she had terminal cancer—a huge, fast-growing tumor in her liver. The prognosis was so bad that even trying to say something positive proved futile. He said they could discuss options for treatment, except for the sad fact that there were no options.
>
> My mother took a deep breath. "Wow," she said. "I wasn't expecting this."
>
> The sound of her voice surprised me. It wasn't sad. It sounded more like the voice of a wondering child.
>
> The doctor kept talking; my mom kept listening. As for me, I couldn't stop looking at her eyes. They were steady, bright, inquisitive. But what I didn't see surprised me most. There were no tears. I knew my mom was strong, but this was remarkable.
>
> "So I guess what you're saying," my mother said, "is, 'Don't quit, but almost.'"

She smiled. It was a soft, gentle, melancholy smile, the kind of smile that breaks your heart. The doctor smiled back. "Yes," he said. "That's what I'm saying: 'Don't quit, but almost.'"

Within a few minutes, the doctor had finished. Then my mother did something that I'll never forget. She lifted her right hand off the sheet on her bed, took the doctor's hand, firmly shook it and said, "Well, thank you, Doctor."

Talk about your great sports upsets. There was my mother, warmly thanking the doctor who had just told her she was dying. I had never seen anything like it.

Dad and I spent the next three nights in the hospital with Mom. One of those nights, I slept in a chair as Dad snored on the foldout bed. I didn't sleep much that night. I really didn't feel like sleeping. I was helping Mom take sips of water when she wanted them, so I often looked over to check on her.

Mom was awake much of the night as well.

"What are you looking at?" Mom asked in a strong voice in the middle of the night.

"I'm looking at you."

"Go to sleep," she urged.

I said all right and turned my head the other way.

A few moments later, I looked back at Mom. She was staring at me.

"What are *you* looking at?" I said, grinning.

"I'm looking at you."

We took Mom home to live her last days under hospice care in her favorite room of the house, the family room, with a beautiful view of the backyard and garden she loved. We didn't know how long she would live; we were prepared for it to be a week or two, maybe a little longer.

But Mom, who had been staring into our faces for days as we desperately tried to smile through our sorrow, had other ideas. Always watching out for us, even to the end, she went into a deep sleep the night she came home and died the very next night,

May 24, 2002, the forty-ninth anniversary of the day she and Dad met. Dad, Amy, and I were at her bedside; I was holding her left hand, telling her how much we loved her, when she took her last breath.

At Mom's memorial service, her three daughters spoke and her grandchildren lit a candle, read a Psalm, and sang of angels, but none of us cried openly. Not because our hearts weren't broken, but because we knew how much Mom hated blubbering. There was no crying in baseball, and there would be no crying at her memorial service, at least from us.

When it was my turn to speak, I played the tape of Mom and Dad's Happy Birthday message, their singing, their back-and-forth chatter, Mom's hope that "there will be a time to make a birthday cake" when I came home next. That message was only fifteen days old. How could all of this have happened in fifteen days?

I made copies of the tape and gave one to Dad. For many nights, I could hear him playing it in their room before he went to sleep.

All of us tried to live as normally as possible in the months after we lost Mom, but it was hard. There were times I actually reached for the phone to call her, only to pull my hand back, wondering what I was thinking. We encouraged Dad to take a few big trips—one to Alaska, another to Italy—and he did and said he enjoyed them. I went home even more than usual to be with Dad when he was in Toledo. We were doing okay, I thought.

But then came March 17, 2003.

Dad and I got in the car in the predawn darkness to go to a place we had been dozens of times before. We were going to Ann Arbor, to the University of Michigan.

As we went down the driveway, I couldn't help myself.

"Dad, do you have the tickets?"

"Ah," Dad answered, sounding far away, "the tickets."

Kate and Jim were in their cars, following behind us on a foggy, eerie morning. We were going to the University of

Michigan medical center—alas, not the football stadium. Dad was going to have a lobe of his left lung removed. He had lung cancer.

We were still dealing with Mom's death when Dad told us his news. That morning, I was the last one with Dad before he was wheeled into surgery. *What if I never see him again? What do I say?*

I thought of Mom and something popped into my head.

"Dad, you're in a win-win situation. You either wake up and see us or you wake up and see Mom."

"You're right," Dad said, lying there, smiling. He looked vulnerable to me for the first time in his life. I couldn't stand seeing him that way.

I pumped my fist at him as they wheeled him away. He pumped his back.

He woke up and saw us.

Dad was walking the hospital hallways that night and two days later, he strode to the parking garage to go home, refusing a wheelchair. His recovery continued at breakneck speed for a month until, one day, Dad couldn't move his right foot. The cancer had moved to his brain.

He underwent radiation, testing himself by watching *Jeopardy* every night to see if he was slipping. He happily reported that he knew almost all of the answers, as usual.

I came home for his seventy-seventh birthday and, just after midnight on May 17, stuck all his pink flamingos and yard ornaments and signs in the front yard in his honor. That night at dinner, he said it was the best birthday he had ever had. Two days later, when I went off to cover Annika Sorenstam's appearance on the PGA Tour in Texas, Dad said he hoped she would make the cut "and show all those men how good she is."

Dad had a personal goal: he wanted to take a trip to Norway with friends in June. He made the trip. But when he returned, he could barely walk, and he ended up in the hospital in early July.

I had been at Wimbledon, and when Dad went into the hospital, I went right to Toledo. I brought some pictures from London.

"Look at you, standing up so straight, shoulders back," Dad said, holding a photo.

As the days turned into several weeks, I spent hours in Dad's hospital room. We all did.

I asked Dad for advice. "What would you like me to do with the rest of my life?"

"Just keep doing what you're doing. It's been working pretty well so far."

I apologized for the arguments we sometimes had. He told me not to give it a second thought. I thanked him for everything he had done for me, for all of us kids. I told him I had never met a smarter, more impressive person, ever. I said that in private, but I also was proud to say it in front of nearly two hundred of our friends as we honored Mom with the dedication of two rooms in her memory at the Sunset House retirement community on July 17, what would have been her seventy-fifth birthday. Dad came to the ceremony in a wheelchair.

As bad as things were, Dad never lost his sense of humor. Even near the end, when a nurse asked him if he was allergic to anything, Dad answered the same as he always did: "Liberal Democrats." The last time he said it was three days before he died, faintly, but we heard it just fine, and so did the nurse.

On Sunday, August 10, we four kids were all in his hospital room, lying on the floor, propped up on pillows, telling stories, most of them about something funny Dad had once done, as he snored loudly in his bed. We all giggled about the bets we made months earlier on the gender and date of birth of Jim and Angela's third child. Dad had been one day off. Amy's two-year-old son, Peter, had the exact date. (I'm pretty sure his parents picked it for him.) Dad always ran the family betting pools, so that day, as soon as he realized what had happened, he stomped around the house in mock anger, muttering, "I lost to a two-year-old!"

It was just past midnight when Kate left Dad's hospital room to go home to her family. Amy, seven months pregnant with her second child, had gone home earlier. Jim and I remained. We talked until we fell asleep. But I dozed for only ten minutes when something woke me up. It was a sound that was no longer there. Dad's snoring had stopped.

I dashed to his bed. Dad was still breathing, barely. I called to

Jim and he scrambled over. I dialed Kate on my cell phone. We knew she couldn't make it back in time, so I put my phone to Dad's ear so she could tell him she loved him one last time.

Dad and I had been together for forty-five years, two months, twenty-seven days, and five hours, give or take a couple of minutes, when he took his last breath at 1 A.M. on Monday, August 11, 2003. I was holding his right hand, telling him how much we loved him, when he died.

How many times had I held that right hand as I was growing up, crossing the street, walking to a stadium for a game, standing in line to go through the turnstile? There was always such anticipation in holding that hand. Always, it seemed, another kickoff awaited us.

Like Mom, Dad was cremated. His memorial service occurred the day after the big electrical blackout along the eastern United States. In my remarks, I said the blackout must have been Dad's first prank from heaven: "He wanted to just dim the lights at his wake, but things got a little out of hand."

Much was written and said about Dad's remarkable life. U.S. Senator Mike DeWine of Ohio flew in to give a eulogy. I was asked to write a tribute on behalf of our family on the op-ed page of the *Blade*.

Passing through town from Canada, Chuck Ealey stopped in Toledo to visit friends and happened to pick up a paper. Dad's death was mentioned on the front page, with a photo. The full obituary ran inside.

When Chuck came back through town heading home, he bought the *Blade* again. That was the day my op-ed piece appeared.

"I read every word," Chuck told me in an e-mail. How honored Dad would have been: Chuck Ealey, reading about him.

Dad had asked that his ashes be spread over his beloved Gettysburg, but, by the end of the year, we hadn't been able to get there as a family. In a wonderful coincidence, Michigan was representing the Big Ten in the 2004 Rose Bowl, and I was on my way to write a column on the game.

I had come up with an idea, and Kate, Jim, and Amy gave me their permission to pursue it. I didn't know if my credential would allow me on the field at the Rose Bowl before the game, but that's where I needed to be, so I thought I'd give it a try.

I walked down the stairs that Dad had climbed four years earlier and stepped onto the sideline. No one stopped me, so I kept going. As Michigan's players were fielding punts and stretching an hour and a half before kickoff, I walked into the Michigan end zone and opened a small plastic bag I had carried from Toledo, a bag containing a few tablespoons of Dad's ashes.

In the bright sunshine on the first day of the new year, I stepped onto the M in "MICHIGAN"—the beautiful maize and blue lettering in that glorious end zone—and let Dad's ashes slip slowly through my fingers.

Soon, the Michigan Wolverines and USC Trojans were lining up on the field and the game was about to begin. I smiled as I looked down from the press box. One more time for Dad and me, there would be another kickoff.

A tribute to Dad in the Rose Bowl end zone in 2004.

ACKNOWLEDGMENTS

Writing about my father and our family was a labor of love, but hardly a singular effort. I had quite a team to help me tell this story.

My dear friends Laurie Hansen Saxton, David Hansen, Douglas Hansen, Cliff Siegel, and Karen Howard were generous with their time and most helpful in recalling our childhood days in Old Orchard.

There are many friends from Ottawa Hills to thank: Sandy Osterman, Shelley Wolson, Richard Sanzenbacher, Jim Casper, Bob O'Connell, Alice Lora, Ron Stewart, Carol White Loper, Kim Young Fioretto, Lauren Shaffer Fox, Julie Anderson, Deborah Klein, Cathy Collins Fitzpatrick, Jo Cooley, Sharon Simmons, Ron Coffman, and Marc Thompson. Sadly, Laurie Lay Gladieux passed away in September 2005. She was a loyal friend and teammate.

At the University of Toledo, the athletic media relations department kindly opened its doors to me to go through photo files and check various facts. Thanks to Paul Helgren, Steve Easton, and Brian DeBenedictis. Max Gerber brought to life a few great memories of the 1969–71 Rockets, and Andrew Langenderfer, Matthew Choma, and James and Cynthia Nowak assisted with details about the campus. Thanks especially to Chuck Ealey and Steve Mix, my heroes, now my friends.

At the University of Michigan, David Ablauf and Bruce Madej from the sports information office and athletic department archivist Greg Kinney were extremely helpful.

From the Toledo Mud Hens, Jason Griffin answered every one of my e-mails, and Frank Gilhooley, the man who taught me the language of sports, answered every question on every phone call. When I spoke to him, it was 1969 all over again. I almost didn't want to hang up.

Thanks to my friends at the *Toledo Blade* for the opportunities they gave me as a young reporter and for the articles they wrote to inspire me then and remind me now of the Rockets' 35–0 streak. I particularly want to acknowledge Tom Walton, Bill and Liz Day, Dave Hackenberg, John Bergener, and Dave Woolford.

From the days at the *Miami Herald,* thanks to Paul Anger, Ed Storin, Dave Wilson, Gary Long, and Larry Dorman. Thank you to my friends at the *Washington Post* for their assistance: George Solomon, Len Shapiro, Michael Wilbon, Tony Kornheiser, Jill Grisco, and Russell James. Some of the stories and events described in this book first appeared in my stories in the *Herald* and the *Post.*

At *USA Today,* thanks to Monte Lorell, Ken Paulson, Reid Cherner, Mel Antonen, Gary Kicinski, Kelly Whiteside, Vicki Michaelis, Jim Welch, Julie Ward, Leslie Spalding, Deborah Yovanovich, and Lisa Washington.

Friends, colleagues, and in some cases, people I never met offered a vital piece of information, looked up a statistic, remembered an old conversation, offered advice. Thanks to Donna Lopiano, Nancy Hogshead-Makar, Harvey Schiller, Mike Moran, Joe Browne, Greg Aiello, Susan and Bill O'Brian, Jeannie Hylant, Sara Just, Helene Elliott, Rick Wamre, Dean Murphy, Nery

Ynclán, Alan Abrahamson, Nancy Jackson, Jeff Siegel, Brian Sumers, Sarah Rothschild, Kristin Huckshorn, Bruce Schoenfeld, Meredith and Barry Geisler, Matt Winkler, Mark Henderson, Mike Barrowman, Jere Longman, Philip Hersh, Jo-Ann Barnas, Michael Janofsky, Steve Woodward, Randy Harvey, Gene Cherry, Gene Wojciechowski, Ed Sherman, Mike Mayo, Peter Finney Jr., Kerri Alexander, Tracy Dodds, Joanne Gerstner, Lisa Olson, Suzyn Waldman, Ann Killion, Amy Shipley, Mike Littwin, Lori Nichol, Joe Inman, Lynn Plage, Patricia Davies, James McCusker, Jocelyn Serranilla, Clay Luraschi, Brian Britten, Lindsay McHolm, Jim Young, Linda Costell, Craig Fenech, Becky Timmons, Keith Olbermann, Liam Bowen, Genny Ekstrom, John Naber, Susan Polakoff, Leslie King, Tracy Kerdyk, Dan Riley, Marty Parkes, Bob and Helen Sommers, Joe Starita, Tom Timmermann (the pitcher), Tom Timmermann (the sportswriter), Steve Chapman, Sherry Krieger, Roger Holliday, Claudia Fischer, John Humenik, Artis Twyman, Jeff Sibel, Jerry Foster, D. C. Koehl, Michael Lipman, Jason Romano, Joan Backoff, Joe Horrigan, Peg Lewis, Ted Eagle, Joe Horvath, Brenda Murray, Bill Hancock, Glenn Greenspan, Marianne Chappuis, Jeff Orleans, and LeslieAnne Wade.

A special thanks to Kim McLendon Strother for her help with this book. She is the widow of Shelby Strother. Shelby died of liver cancer March 3, 1991. He was forty-four. The press box has never been the same without him, but whenever I sit over my keyboard, searching for a lead, I know somewhere out there, a cricket is chirping.

A group of talented friends-turned-editors came through for me in ways I never could have imagined. Victoria Churchville skillfully read and edited this book, not once but twice. Sandy Evans and Steve Hoffman were an editing tag team, providing guidance for months. Kevin Modesti called in from his cell phone in Los Angeles with advice and support. Jill Lieber checked in on her phone and via e-mail with numerous ideas from a bit farther south in San Diego. Jeffrey Marx was meticulous in his attention to the smallest detail. Marty Aronoff read all the words—and checked all the statistics. Rem Rieder made editing house calls. Jill Schuker provided great advice. Kay Coyte gave the book a strong final read. Lesley Visser was an astute adviser, as she has been for twenty years.

Christine Spolar performed world-class double duty, e-mailing ideas and suggestions while covering events in the Gaza Strip as a foreign correspondent for the *Chicago Tribune*. She took all my calls too, and every time we hung up, the book was better.

In this Murderers' Row editing lineup, Tony Reid batted cleanup. The *Washington Post* foreign-desk copy chief was my personal copy chief as well. He read this book several times, spent days at my desk with me, and amazingly, is still speaking to me. (I think.) I will never forget the night he cut and pasted a draft of my first few chapters on my living room floor. Now, that's an editor.

Chris Calhoun, my agent and friend, took care of business with his usual aplomb. As always, he was jumping through the phone line with enthusiasm and energy. A better advocate I could not have.

More than a decade ago, renowned editor Lisa Drew took a chance on publishing my figure-skating book. That book changed my life, allowing me the freedom to be my own boss, to become independent, and to eventually write more books for Lisa. That freedom in turn allowed me to spend tremendous amounts of time in Toledo with my parents, especially near the end.

Lisa, there are dozens of reasons for me to thank you, but that's number one on my list.

I also want to express my gratitude to Samantha Martin, Lisa's assistant, who was always there with a reassuring voice and a steady hand.

And then there is my family. With Mom and Dad gone, I turned to my aunts and uncles—my parents' wonderful sisters and brothers—to help with stories and facts about their lives, and they came through in gracious and kind ways. I want to acknowledge Dad's sister, Peggy Brewer, and brother, Bob Brennan, as well as Mom's sister, Ruth Lochow, and her brothers, Irv and Bill Anderson.

Tom Backoff, Angela Brennan, and Derrick Swaak were very supportive and patient as their spouses—my siblings—helped me with this book.

The eight grandchildren of Jim and Betty Brennan are my favorite people on earth: Brad, Jennie, and Leslie Backoff; Henry, Kathryn, and Ralph Brennan; and Peter and Helena Swaak. Just remember, kids, this ain't no dress rehearsal.

Thanks especially to the older kids, the Backoffs, for offering advice, checking facts, and finding some of the photos for this book.

I have dedicated this book to my siblings, Kate Brennan Backoff, Jim Brennan Jr., and Amy Brennan Swaak. They read and edited the manuscript. They offered advice. They encouraged me. They were tough and strong and demanding and challenging.

As I spoke with them, I also heard another voice in my head. I'm pretty sure I know whose it was.

ABOUT THE AUTHOR

CHRISTINE BRENNAN, author of the best-selling *Inside Edge,* is an award-winning sports columnist for *USA Today.* She also is a commentator for ABC News, ESPN, and NPR's *Morning Edition.* Brennan previously worked at the *Miami Herald* and the *Washington Post.* She lives in Washington, D.C.